√ SOC

D0482231

LIBRARY IN A BOOK

DRUG ABUSE

Harry Henderson

Facts On File, Inc.

DRUG ABUSE

Facts On File, Inc.
132 West 31st Street
New York NY 10001

Library of Congress Cataloging-in-Publication Data
Library of Congress Cataloging-in-Publication Data
Henderson, Harry, 1951–
    Drug abuse / Harry Henderson.
        p.cm.—(Library in a book)
    Includes bibliographical references and index.
    ISBN 0-8160-4858-4
    1. Drug abuse—United States—History. 2. Drug abuse—Government policy—United States. I. Title. II. Series.
    HV5825.H435 2005
    362.29′0973—dc22
            2004001068

Facts On File books are available at special discounts when purchased in bulk quantities for businesses, associations, institutions or sales promotions. Please call our Special Sales Department in New York at (212) 967-8800 or (800) 322-8755.

You can find Facts On File on the World Wide Web at http://www.factsonfile.com.

Text design by Ron Monteleone
Maps and graphs by Dale Williams

Printed in the United States of America

MP Hermitage 10 9 8 7 6 5 4 3 2 1

This book is printed on acid-free paper.

To everyone who has had to make difficult choices about drugs.

CONTENTS

PART III
APPENDICES

PART I

OVERVIEW OF THE TOPIC

CHAPTER 1

INTRODUCTION TO DRUG ABUSE TREATMENT AND POLICY

About 30 years before the war on terrorism became an urgent national preoccupation, another war was declared against an equally elusive and problematic enemy that was said to threaten the very fabric of our society. Like the war on terrorism, the war on drugs has raised many questions about the nature of the threat, the best ways to respond, and even whether the chosen tactics might be doing more harm than good.

There are some major differences between the two wars, however. Terrorists, for all the devastating damage they can cause, are relatively few in number, as are their victims. This is not true about the use of illegal drugs or the abuse of legal ones. According to the 2002 National Survey of Drug Abuse and Health, about 19.5 million Americans have used illicit drugs. Of these, about 14.6 million have used marijuana, 2 million indulged in powdered cocaine, 567,000 are users of crack cocaine, and 1.2 million have used hallucinogens (including 676,000 users of ecstasy). There are also about 166,000 heroin users. About 6.2 million people have illicitly used drugs normally available only by prescription, such as pain relievers, tranquilizers, sedatives, and stimulants. About 1.9 million reported abusing just one such drug, the pain reliever OxyContin, at least once. All together users spend at least $70 billion a year on illegal drugs in the United States.

By 2003 the total annual federal budget for drug control efforts exceeded $19 billion, with many hundreds of millions of dollars more spent by state and local governments. An estimated 3.5 million Americans received some sort of treatment for drug abuse during the year preceding the 2002 survey. Of these, about 2.2 million received treatment for alcohol, about 974,000 for marijuana, 796,000 for cocaine, 360,000 for abuse of pain relievers, and 277,000 for heroin.

3

Drug Abuse

The direct costs of drug control and treatment are only part of the story. Indeed, they are dwarfed by the impact of drug abuse on health and the economy:

- At least 375,000 infants are estimated to be born each year with some exposure or effects from their mother's drug use.
- More than 60,000 infants suffer from fetal alcohol syndrome (FAS), a condition that is largely irreversible and whose effects include serious developmental and learning problems.
- About $13 billion in health care costs can be attributed to the effects of drug abuse, and drug problems account for one in every five dollars spent by Medicaid for hospital expenses.
- The loss of workplace productivity due to alcohol and drug abuse is estimated at about $160 billion a year; 500 million workdays a year are lost to alcohol use alone.

Contrary to popular belief, about 70 percent of abusers of illegal drugs are employed, which makes drug use in the workplace a major concern. However, drug abuse has a particularly devastating effect at the margins of society—especially poor inner city minority neighborhoods, where drug trafficking and the associated crime often create an atmosphere of terror and despair.

The seemingly intractable problem of homelessness in many cities is also closely related to drug abuse. For example, at least 70 percent of San Francisco's estimated 8,000–15,000 homeless people are drug or alcohol abusers, 30 to 40 percent are mentally ill. Among the 3,000–5,000 "hard core" homeless in San Francisco who live full-time on the streets and seldom use shelters or other services, these percentages are doubtlessly higher. The city spends about $200 million a year on food distribution, medical clinics, housing, and rehabilitation programs for the homeless, but experts say that the hard-core homeless seldom use services other than the emergency rooms.

When drug abusers are not on the street, they are often in jail. A survey of federal prison inmates found that 41 percent were involved in drug production, importation, or trafficking. What has been called the "incarceration industry," where the United States imprisons a higher proportion of its citizens than any other developed democracy, is thus considerably fueled by drugs.

There is, however, another side to the war on drugs that makes it still more complicated. By law, drugs have been classified as over-the-counter, legal by prescription, or illegal. But there are many paradoxes. The most commonly used drug by far is alcohol, which is legal for adults, apparently harmless to many users, but subject to widespread abuse and addiction. The most dangerous drug in terms of deaths caused is tobacco, which is highly addictive yet legal for adults.

The most widely used illegal drug, marijuana, is felt by many people to be an acceptable social drug that is at worst no more dangerous than alcohol. Acceptance of marijuana is so widespread that in 2003, three of the candidates running in the Democratic primary for president, Senators John Kerry and John Edwards and former Vermont governor Howard Dean, all admitted that they had, along with millions of people, tried marijuana in the 1960s and 1970s. Indeed, notes Joseph Califano, former U.S. health secretary and current chairman of the National Center on Addiction and Substance Abuse, "If we disqualified guys that had used drugs in those years we'd probably eliminate half the potential candidates or more."[1]

One common response to the demand that people "just say no" to drugs and the reality that millions say yes is to consider alternatives to the war on drugs. While some advocates argue that all drugs should be legalized, others believe in a more nuanced approach that emphasizes treatment over incarceration and suggests that marijuana be treated more like alcohol (legal but taxed, regulated, and age-restricted) than like heroin and other "hard narcotics."

In order to further explore how different drugs and their abusers should be treated, it is necessary to have a basic understanding of the different types of drugs, how they are used, how they work, and why they can be addictive.

DRUGS OF ABUSE:
A SURVEY

Part of the problem in considering what to do about drugs is that people tend to think of drugs as exotic substances that are separate from those encountered in ordinary life. This is not true. A drug is simply a substance that has particular effects on the human body beyond simple nutrition.

Nature is full of drugs. Even animals use and abuse drugs. For example, birds eat certain kinds of berries that ferment on the tree, literally getting drunk on them until they can barely stagger, let alone fly. Elephants have been known to seek out piles of grain fermenting in the fields and even learn to break into enclosures where such grain is stored. Made rowdy by the effects of the alcohol, the elephants can be a serious or even deadly nuisance.

Early human societies (and many tribal societies today) have used various psychotropic (consciousness altering) plant drugs such as peyote in ceremonies designed to unlock spiritual knowledge, for healing, or to initiate young people into adulthood. However, such drug use is not primarily recreational and generally does not involve addiction.

ALCOHOL

The development of permanent settlements and agriculture made it possible to produce alcohol in quantities that allowed it to be an everyday social drug. Egyptian papyri dating back to about 3500 B.C. describe the brewing of beer, a process that had probably already been going on ever since early agriculturalists discovered that grain or fruit naturally ferments and that the resulting product had interesting effects. The beer, which was likely very weak and drunk like water, would continue to be a staple (with some nutritional value) through the Middle Ages. Wine, a more expensive and potent spirit, was prized and enjoyed by those who could afford it.

The problem of drunkenness was well known in ancient and early Christian times, and many religious and other leaders condemned the use of alcohol. At the same time, though, wine was celebrated in Greek religion as the gift of Dionysus (or Bacchus), and in the New Testament and subsequent Christian tradition it became the blood of Christ. Alcohol had a less prominent role in Jewish culture. The Muslims, however, banned its use. Attitudes toward alcohol and other intoxicating beverages vary widely in other world cultures.

By the 18th century in Europe, distilled spirits such as gin had become a devastating new problem, particularly among the poor in cities such as London. Gin was cheap, produced a quick "high," and proved highly addictive to people seeking to escape the misery of poverty. Gin houses advertised that one could get drunk for a penny and "dead drunk" for two pence. The problem was made worse by employers who paid their employees in gin instead of cash. The British government tried to control the gin "epidemic" with laws such as the Gin Act of 1736. One could say that gin was the crack cocaine of its time.

Around that same time, the growing problem of alcohol abuse began to be confronted by the pioneers of modern medicine. In the United States, Benjamin Rush published an "Inquiry into the Effects of Ardent Spirits on the Human Body and Mind." He referred to the intemperate use of distilled spirits as a disease, not a moral failing. He also estimated that at least 4,000 people a year were dying due to alcohol abuse—this at a time when the nation's population was only about 6 million.

During the 19th century, public drunkenness was probably even more common a sight than it is today. Alcohol was blamed for breaking up many families and driving others into poverty as male breadwinners succumbed to the drug, which also exacerbated domestic abuse.

If the 19th century was a time of deep-rooted social conflicts, it was also a time for activism. A number of women, including Susan B. Anthony and other veterans of the abolitionist and early women's rights movements, formed the Women's Christian Temperance Union (WCTU) in 1874. This

6

and other organizations fought to end what they saw as a scourge of drunkenness that was particularly victimizing women whose husbands drank to excess. The group worked to pass laws to ban the sale of alcoholic beverages, and many states did so. The movement reached its high (or some would say low) point with the passage of the Eighteenth Amendment to the U.S. Constitution in 1919. Only 14 years later, however, Prohibition, America's first "war on drugs," had been repealed. Alcohol consumption had indeed declined somewhat, but those who wanted to keep drinking had found a network of gangsters willing to provide for them.

Alcohol is a complicated drug. Although actually a depressant rather than a stimulant, alcohol removes inhibitions so that people under its influence are often quick to express anger and to fight, as well as being more likely to engage in possibly unsafe sex. The impairment of judgment and reflexes also increases the chances of involvement in traffic accidents.

Heavy alcohol use can lead to dependency as well as damage to the liver and other organs. With heavy users, alcohol withdrawal is quite dangerous, sometimes involving convulsions and hallucinations (delirium tremens).

In the 1970s doctors learned that even moderate drinking by pregnant mothers exposes their future child to the risk of fetal alcohol syndrome, with accompanying physical and developmental problems. Government-mandated warnings on alcoholic beverage containers now urge women not to drink at all while pregnant. On the other hand recent studies suggest that moderate drinking of red wine (a glass or two a day) seems to reduce the risk of heart disease and the clogging of arteries. (This is apparently related to antioxidants from the grapes, not the alcohol.) Clearly the decision of whether to drink, and how much, is a complicated one that is likely to vary with individual circumstances.

Alcohol is by far the most widely used social drug in most countries, which also makes it the most abused drug. According to the 2002 National Survey on Drug Use and Health, approximately 120 million persons in the United States age 12 years or older drink alcoholic beverages in some form. About 22 percent, or more than 54 million, have had at least one drinking "binge" in the month surveyed, and about 15 million can be classified as chronic heavy drinkers. Among persons aged 12 to 20, there were 10.7 million drinkers, among which 7.2 million were binge drinkers and 2.3 million were heavy drinkers.

The social impact of alcohol use is major. For example, about one in seven Americans reported they had driven under the influence of alcohol at least once in the year prior to the survey. A large proportion of fatal vehicular accidents involve drunken driving.

Alcohol is also a major problem for teenagers and young adults. The federally funded Task Force on College Drinking estimates that about 1,400 college students are killed in alcohol-related accidents each year (including overdoses and traffic accidents). Alcohol is also believed to be involved in more than 500,000 injuries, including 70,000 cases of sexual assault or date rape.

TOBACCO

Tobacco, the other leading legal social drug, was native to the Americas and smoked by some Indian tribes for ceremonial purposes. It was introduced to European society in the mid-16th century; in 1613 English settlers in Virginia exported their first shipment of tobacco. In a scenario that is common with many newly discovered drugs, tobacco was touted by some enthusiasts as having great medical value. However, in 1604 King James I of England expressed his royal disapproval of the drug in his *Counterblast to Tobacco*, and he even taxed the drug to discourage its use.

Up through the 19th century smoking tobacco in pipes was popular, but in the 20th century inexpensive, handy cigarettes made the drug "democratic." Smoking literally permeated American culture until the late 20th century. Cigarette companies touted their products as symbols of women's emancipation, gave millions of packs to soldiers in World War II, and then used figures such as cowboys and glamorous partygoers in television commercials.

Although many doctors (and others) had their suspicions about "smoker's cough" and the other apparent effects of a lifetime of tobacco use, it was not until the 1960s when definitive studies led the surgeon general of the United States to begin issuing a series of warnings about the health effects of smoking. By then the incidence of lung cancer—once a rare disease—was becoming alarming. Today it is known that smoking brings a greatly elevated risk of lung cancer, emphysema, and heart disease.

About 71.5 million persons surveyed in the United States reported they were regular tobacco users. The difficulty in quitting smoking despite the dire health warnings comes, of course, from the fact that nicotine is addictive. The addiction process with tobacco is more subtle than with many other drugs, however. First-time smokers often find the drug's effects to be actually unpleasant, but if they persist (perhaps because of social pressure or the enticing images from advertising), they come to like the relatively mild "high" delivered by the nicotine entering the lungs and crossing directly into the bloodstream. Then, as they continue to smoke, users often find that the association of these little "bursts" of pleasure with the mechanics of smoking (lighting, holding, and puffing on the cigarette) further reinforces the habit.

The good news is that restrictions on tobacco advertising and smoking in public (because of the danger of secondhand smoke) seem to be gradually reducing the prevalence of tobacco use in the United States, with a reduction in new smokers of about one-third.

Introduction

Since smoking is hard to quit and the risks increase with continued use, it makes sense to focus on preventing young people from taking up the habit in the first place. There, too, gradual progress is being made. As Lori Fersina, a spokesperson for the American Cancer Society of Massachusetts has observed, by creating an environment in which smoking is more marginalized and less acceptable, "You are changing the world you raise kids in, not just telling them it's bad for them."[2]

OPIUM AND OPIATES

Opium is one of the oldest widely used drugs. Records from Mesopotamian civilizations more than 4,000 years old refer to the opium poppy. Early healers valued the extract of this plant (often a dark, chunky powder) for its ability to relieve pain and soothe distress. At a time when there was little specific knowledge of disease, opium at least provided a way to make people feel better until, perhaps, natural healing could occur. Opium and its derivatives, called opiates, belong to the class of drugs known as narcotics. (The term *narcotic* is often inaccurately used to refer to all illegal drugs regardless of their chemical structure.)

By the 16th century, laudanum, a more potent and consistent opium extract, had begun to be widely used in Western medicine. One writer, Thomas Syndenham, observed that "Among the remedies which it has pleased the Almighty God to give to man to relieve his sufferings, none is so universal and efficacious as opium."[3]

As late as the 19th century, dilute laudanum was a popular preparation for soothing babies suffering from teething pain. Meanwhile, "opium eating" had become a popular pastime for the literary and artistic set. Poet Samuel Taylor Coleridge credited the drug with inspiring much of his exotic and elaborate imagery. Thomas DeQuincey's *Confessions of an Opium Eater* (1820) includes one of the earliest detailed accounts of how dependence on a drug can gradually take over one's life.

Doctors tended to be enthusiastic about the powers of opium and to minimize its negative effects. In 1868, George Wood, a noted medical professor at the University of Pennsylvania and the president of the American Philosophical Society, described opium's pharmacological effects as follows:

A sensation of fullness is felt in the head, soon to be followed by a universal feeling of delicious ease and comfort, with an elevation and expansion of the whole moral and intellectual nature, which is, I think, the most characteristic of its effects. . . . It seems to make the individual, for the time, a better and greater man. . . . The hallucinations, the delirious imaginations of alcoholic intoxication, are, in general, quite wanting. Along with this emotional and

9

intellectual elevation, there is also increased muscular energy; and the capacity to act, and to bear fatigue, is greatly augmented.[4]

In China, however, opium was a widespread social problem. Habitual opium smoking made people listless and unproductive. When the government tried to control the drug by taxes and tariffs, enterprising criminals set up black markets. In 1729, the Manchu dynasty went so far as to enact a law specifying that anyone who sold opium was to be strangled.

However, supplying opium to millions of Chinese addicts was a profitable business, and it was under the control of British companies. In 1839, when China tried to ban the opium trade, Britain sent its navy and marines to force open the ports. In 1842, the "Opium wars" ended with China forced again to allow the drug to be sold.

Meanwhile, opium had been joined by other narcotics. Back in 1805 a German pharmacist's assistant had discovered how to isolate its main ingredient, morphine. A preparation of morphine is about 10 times as potent as raw opium. In 1832, another morphine derivative called codeine was isolated. By the 1850s, a more effective way to administer these powerful narcotics was developed—the hypodermic needle. During the American Civil War, battlefield surgeons had one effective way to relieve the pain of a shattered limb or punctured lung—an injection of morphine. Soldiers who survived their wounds after this treatment often became addicted to the drug. Morphine addiction was thus sometimes referred to as the "soldier's disease."

Codeine, which could be derived either directly from opium or (more usually) from morphine, came to be preferred by many as a pain killer. Compared to morphine, codeine was less powerful as a painkiller but also produced less sedation and potentially dangerous respiratory suppression. Codeine is sometimes combined with aspirin or other drugs to provide moderate pain relief. However, steady users can become addicted to the drug.

By the end of the 19th century, chemists (particularly in Germany) had begun to learn to create new drugs. The Bayer Company had already made a fortune from aspirin, a marvelously effective pain reliever and fever reducer. In 1898, the company introduced a much more powerful pain killer that was also an effective cough remedy. The drug, which had actually been synthesized back in 1874, was given a name befitting its "heroic" ability to fight pain. It was called heroin.

In 1900, James R. L. Daly, writing in the *Boston Medical and Surgical Journal*, declared that, "It [heroin] possesses many advantages over morphine. . . . It is not hypnotic; and there is no danger of acquiring the habit."[5]

As with many other powerful drugs, people were slow in realizing heroin's addictive potential. However, the drug was withdrawn from over-the-counter use and was regulated by the Harrison Narcotics Act of 1914.

Introduction

When under the influence of heroin, users generally feel euphoric but sleepy ("nodding"). Failure to secure regular doses leads to withdrawal symptoms such as sweating, chills, nausea, cramps, and a racing of the pulse. The severity of withdrawal, or "cold turkey," has been reported by users as ranging from being comparable to a bad case of flu to sheer agony.

Although many in the 1960s counterculture who had embraced marijuana and LSD had shunned heroin and other hard drugs, heroin had become fashionable among some groups "living on the edge" in the 1980s. One writer describes the heroin scene in New York in the 1980s as follows:

> *There were many people who found heroin addiction glamorous. The idea of being beautiful and damned was a perennial youthful myth in the downtown area. People went on smack when they had money and stayed on smack after all the money got used up, and then started ripping off their friends and families and usually became incredibly sick and horrible-looking and got those strange diseases like lupus or hepatitis B and now . . . half the addicts in New York have HIV infection through needle-sharing, and of course the terrible thing is, the addict knows all this but he can't do anything about it because it's the drug that makes the decisions.*[6]

As a street drug heroin is usually sold in small bags as a white powder in which the drug is usually mixed with sugar, powdered milk, or other substances. The drug is usually dissolved in water and then injected into the bloodstream or subcutaneously ("skin popping"), although it can be smoked or snorted (inhaled through the nose). The latter methods of administration became more popular starting in the 1980s, when the danger of getting HIV/AIDS from contaminated needles became widely recognized. Also during the 1990s the purity of street heroin rose dramatically, sometimes leading to fatal overdoses. Lower prices and higher purity have led to a resurgence in heroin's popularity.

A variety of other synthetic opiates are abused. These include hydromorphone (Dilaudid), which is powerful and highly addictive. Hydrocodone, now available under the name OxyContin, was intended to be a time-release long-acting painkiller. However, users found they could remove the contents of a capsule and swallow or inject it for an intense "high." In 2003, the drug received more publicity when talk-radio host Rush Limbaugh admitted that he had become addicted to OxyContin after taking it for chronic back pain.

There are also synthetic narcotics that are not related to opium. They include the painkiller Meperidine (best known as Demerol), which is frequently given during childbirth or after surgery. Patients can become dependent on these drugs depending on the dose, length of time taken, and individual chemistry.

The drug methadone, although not chemically related to heroin, mimics many of its effects. It has been widely used to treat heroin addicts because it prevents craving for the latter drug as well as the symptoms of heroin withdrawal. However, methadone can also be abused and has become part of the illegal drug market in some areas.

BARBITURATES

Named for their derivation from barbituric acid, barbiturates produce a sedative or soporific effect after a brief period of stimulation. By the 1930s barbiturates were widely used as sedatives or sleep aids, but by the 1950s barbiturate addiction had become rampant. At a time when Americans seemed enamored about modern conveniences, the idea that science could provide pills for managing the emotional roller coaster of daily life also seemed appealing. As one observer noted, "Today you can take a pill to put you to sleep, wake you up, put on weight, take it off, pep you up, calm you down, boost your confidence, deaden pain."[7] In the 1960s, the Rolling Stones song "Mother's Little Helper" satirized what many in the younger generation saw as their parents' hypocrisy in "popping pills" while condemning the use of marijuana and LSD.

Depending on the drug, barbiturates can induce anesthesia rapidly (as with pentathol), or produce a more gradual sedation or sleep (Nembutal, Seconal, and Amytal). The latter drugs are abused by persons craving a feeling of well-being or just oblivion. Another barbiturate, methaqualone (marketed as Quaalude and other names), was originally thought to be safer and less addictive but proved to be neither.

The depressant effect of barbiturates is often sought by persons who are self-medicating for anxiety-related problems or insomnia. Drugs of the benzodiazepine family (Librium, Valium, and Xanax) are also legitimately prescribed for the treatment of anxiety as well as muscle spasms or convulsions. However, doctors and patients must be careful because prolonged or excessive use can lead to dependence. Illegal use often involves forged prescriptions or the cooperation of illicit doctors.

Some abusers mix barbiturates with alcohol or marijuana in order to create a better "high." A different kind of abuse occurs when rapists mix another drug, Rohypnol (flunitrazepam), into a woman's drink in order to render her incapable of resisting a sexual assault. The capacity for criminal abuse has led to higher penalties for its possession or use.

COCAINE

Just as the opium poppy literally grew up with civilization in the Old World, the coca leaf was used in the ancient civilizations of Central and South America. Unlike the soporific effect of narcotics such as opium, chewing coca leaves produced a renewed feeling of energy and mild euphoria. (Technically, cocaine is an example of a stimulant.) When the Spanish conquerors set up plantations, they began to grow coca systematically and give it as wages to workers. The active ingredient, cocaine, also seemed to ease the effects of altitude sickness.

By the mid-19th century the medicinal value of coca began to be more widely recognized in Europe and the United States. Coca extract began to appear in teas, chewing gum, and coca wine, as well as being featured as an ingredient in patent medicines.

A recurring theme in the history of drugs is the touting of a new drug as a treatment for older addictions. In the 1880s, as the temperance movement grew, some people suggested coca as an alternative to alcohol. John Pemberton, a pharmacist in Atlanta, Georgia, concocted a syrup that contained coca extract along with kola nut extract. He called his product Coca-Cola, marketing it as a "temperance drink."

Meanwhile, some medical researchers, including Sigmund Freud, began for a time to tout the advantages of medicinal cocaine as a stimulant for depressed or lethargic patients and even as a cure for morphine addiction. In 1884, Freud, treating his own bout of depression with cocaine, reported feeling

exhilaration and lasting euphoria, which in no way differs from the normal euphoria of the healthy person. . . . You perceive an increase in self-control and possess more vitality and capacity for work. . . . In other words, you are simply more normal, and it is soon hard to believe that you are under the influence of a drug.[8]

Cocaine did have genuine medical value as a topical (local) anesthetic, but it would be replaced later with similar chemicals (such as novocaine and lidocaine) that did not affect the brain.

By the end of the 19th century, however, it had already become clear that cocaine was quite addictive. (In later experiments, monkeys allowed to self-administer cocaine will do so to the exclusion of all other activities, including eating.) Cocaine addiction began to be featured as a social problem—it was often associated with ugly racial stereotypes in the assertion that it made "Negroes crazy" and prone to robbery and rape.

When "snorted" (inhaled through the nose), cocaine enters the bloodstream rather quickly, producing both an intensely pleasurable "high" and an enhancement of other sensations. (Many users also believe it enhances sexual pleasure.) Users tend to feel mentally sharp, clever, and active.

Starting in the late 1970s, cocaine was adopted as fashionable by some "yuppies" (young urban professionals), who sometimes referred to it as "the champagne of drugs." One such person later ruefully observed that:

The problem with cocaine . . . is that it feels great in the beginning. The problem is, that by the time you realize it's a problem, it's a problem. . . . Everyone is telling you there is nothing wrong with it. And someone would think, "Hell, I'm a bright guy making two million bucks a year. I can control this."[9]

By the mid-1980s a new, more potent form of cocaine appeared. "Cooking" cocaine with baking soda turned it into a rocklike substance that could be smoked. Besides packing a lot of punch for its relatively low price, "crack" cocaine enticed users who were afraid of needles and the infections (such as HIV/AIDS) they could bring. Crack affected the body differently than powder cocaine:

Even though pharmacologically it is not different, the method of ingestion, by smoking, means that more of the drug hits the brain faster. . . . With [powder] cocaine the high usually onsets in three to six minutes, depending on the person. Crack's high onsets in about ten to twenty seconds. It's also a far more intense high.[10]

Psychologically, crack tends to produce both feelings of powerfulness and invulnerability and paranoid ideas that enemies are all around. This particularly bad combination of feelings promotes outbursts of violence from users.

Crack spread mainly through inner city neighborhoods, but its effects in increased crime could spread in widening circles. What became known as the "crack epidemic"

literally changed the entire face of the city. I know of no other drug, except maybe LSD in its heyday, that caused such a social change. . . . Street violence had grown. Child abuse had grown hugely. Spousal abuse.[11]

Use of crack declined in the 1990s due to crackdowns on street traffickers, the outrage of ordinary people in affected communities, and perhaps also because even confirmed drug users began to stay away from a drug known to be a particularly fast route to self-destruction.

AMPHETAMINES

As with cocaine, amphetamines are stimulants. Amphetamines began to be marketed in the 1930s as Benzedrine. The drug produces a feeling of energy and alertness (albeit a brittle sort of alertness). During World War II, Benzedrine was given to pilots to help them stay awake on long missions. Later they found their way into so-called diet pills. Although amphetamines originally had legitimate medical uses (such as for treating narcolepsy and other sleep disorders), they were gradually replaced by safer drugs, only to appear increasingly on the black market in the 1960s.

A related but stronger family of drugs are methamphetamines. Like amphetamines, "meth" was originally marketed in the 1930s as a treatment for conditions such as narcolepsy and what is now called attention deficit disorder (ADD), an inability to concentrate. During the 1960s users began to take the drug under the street name of "speed." Although the drug was somewhat displaced by cocaine in the 1970s, use grew in the 1980s and 1990s. The drug is produced in clandestine "meth labs" using chemicals that are toxic and highly flammable. Large-scale production is controlled mainly by Mexican traffickers. A smokable form called crystal meth became popular (particularly in western and rural areas) because it avoided the risks of injection.

Many users prefer meth to cocaine because, while its effects are similar, they are longer lasting and can be maintained for days at a time. However, after prolonged use, users often suffer from paranoia, hallucinations, and weird repetitive behavior.

MARIJUANA (CANNABIS)

As with the opium poppy, the hemp plant *(cannabis sativa)* was also known in ancient times. It probably was first grown in Central Asia and China but soon spread to India and the Middle East. Ancient healers found that the plant could reduce pain, promote relaxation, and stimulate the appetite—all ways of helping a sick person recover.

Hemp was grown in Colonial and Revolutionary America. Indeed, farmers were sometimes required to grow hemp because it was used to make ropes for the sailing ships that were the lifeblood of international commerce and military power.

Widely used in India and the Middle East, marijuana was viewed as an innocuous social drug by many British and other foreign observers. In 1894, the Indian Hemp Commission issued a voluminous report that concluded:

> *There is no evidence of any weight regarding the mental and moral injuries from the moderate use of these drugs. . . . Moderation does not lead to excess in hemp any more than it does in alcohol. Regular, moderate use of ganja or bhang [forms of marijuana] produces the same effects as moderate and regular doses of whiskey.*[12]

However, in the United States exotic-appearing drugs often became associated with marginal groups—in this case, Mexican immigrants. Harry J.

Anslinger, who led the fight to regulate narcotics in the 1930s, claimed that marijuana was actually a very dangerous drug: "How many murders, suicides, robberies, criminal assaults, hold-ups, burglaries, and deeds of maniacal insanity it [marijuana] causes each year, especially among the young, can only be conjectured."[13] Although there was little evidence for such claims, marijuana was effectively banned by the federal Marijuana Tax Act of 1937.

Marijuana is by far the most commonly used illegal drug in the United States. Indeed, during the 1960s and 1970s, especially among young people, the drug was nearly as widely used as alcohol. About a third of the adult population reports having tried marijuana at least once.

Marijuana is usually prepared from the leaves and flowers of the cannabis plant and cut and smoked like tobacco. The potency of marijuana (also called "pot" or "weed," among other names) varies with the concentration of its active ingredient, THC (delta-9-tetrahydrocannabinol). Generally the more potent strains come from Mexico, Colombia, or Jamaica. The most potent form, sinsemilla (Spanish for "without seed"), can contain more than 15 percent THC. (Hashish, the resinous extract of the marijuana plant, was potent and popular among some users in the 1960s and 1970s, but the greater potency of regular marijuana has now made "hash" less popular.)

Marijuana tends to produce moderate euphoria together with mild hallucinations. Short-term memory loss is common. Users are unable to concentrate well. After use there is often a craving for food ("the munchies").

Much controversy surrounds the effects and potential dangers of marijuana use. The drug is not physically addictive, although users may acquire a psychological dependence. It is not known whether prolonged heavy use might result in permanent cognitive impairment or affect other areas of the body such as the reproductive system. The process of smoking and deeply inhaling the drug is likely over time to cause lung damage and cancer risk similar to that found with tobacco use.

Marijuana has also been promoted as a medicine, however. Claims that the drug relieved glaucoma (excessive pressure in the eye) seem to have been overrated. However, the drug does seem effective in relieving nausea in cancer patients undergoing chemotherapy and it can improve the appetite of patients who are wasting from the effects of AIDS and other conditions. As described later, the issue of whether patients have a right to use marijuana despite its illegality continues to be litigated in the courts.

HALLUCINOGENS

While a number of drugs, including marijuana, have psychoactive effects (such as altering mood, perception, or judgment), certain drugs are sought after especially for their ability to induce hallucinations—imaginary visual or auditory images.

LSD (lysergic acid diethylamide) was first synthesized by Dr. Albert Hoffman in 1938. In 1943, he accidentally ingested some of the substance and experienced a succession of surreal, vivid hallucinations. Through the 1950s some researchers used LSD experiments in an attempt to understand more about the hallucinations experienced by mental patients. By the 1960s the medical establishment had repudiated such experiments, but author Ken Kesey and rogue psychologist Timothy Leary continued to experiment with the drug and popularized it among young people who were seeking to break free of what they saw as a stultifying "establishment."

LSD continues to be used today by a relatively small number of users. The drug is not physically addictive, although tolerance develops, requiring increasing doses to achieve the desired effects. The physical effects of the drug itself usually do not cause much problem, but the psychotic-like behavior it can induce can lead to self-destructive behavior, such as jumping out a window or into traffic. Users can also experience recurrent hallucinations ("flash backs") even after discontinuing use.

A variety of other hallucinogenic drugs are known. The crown of the peyote cactus and its active ingredient mescaline have been used in Native American religious ceremonies for hundreds of years. The drug produces hallucinations that could be interpreted in traditional contexts (such as a spirit journey). However, starting in the 1960s peyote and mescaline were also used by non–Native Americans seeking psychedelic experience. During the 1990s the illegality of the drug was upheld despite objections based on religious freedom, although some states allow bona fide religious use.

"DESIGNER DRUGS"

Designer drugs is a catchall term for drugs that have been synthesized by researchers or adopted by illicit chemists with a view to producing substances that can deliver the same effects sought by drug abusers at a lower cost, or to take advantage of loopholes in drug control laws.

Probably the best known designer drug today is MDMA, commonly known as ecstasy, which emerged in the mid-1980s and became popular at many all-night dance parties, or "raves." Users have described several phases of an ecstasy experience. About an hour after the drug is taken in pill form, the drug is said to "come up." Users have a "rushing" feeling often accompanied by dizziness and mild nausea. Then, in what is called the "plateau," lasting for several hours, users feel their senses enhanced. Ecstasy apparently breaks down social inhibitions and creates a sense of emotional connection or communion with others, as well as promoting sexual feelings. Finally, during the "comedown" period, the drug gradually wears off over a number of hours, without producing the wrenching "crash" feeling caused by many narcotics.

There has been considerable controversy over the dangerousness of ecstasy. Some researchers, based on animal studies or positron emission tomography (PET) scans of users' brains, believe the drug causes a destruction of the brain cells responsible for producing serotonin, an important neurotransmitter. However, it is unclear how lasting or dangerous these effects are in humans. Ecstasy can also cause severe dehydration and unpredictable cardiovascular effects.

PERFORMANCE-ENHANCING DRUGS

Another class of drugs are abused not in search of pleasure or oblivion but in quest of a winning edge in athletic performance. Some drugs, such as amphetamines, cocaine, and even caffeine, provide a short-term stimulant "boost" that can increase performance. These drugs can be easily detected in the routine testing required by many athletic programs and competitions. However, other drugs, such as anabolic steroids and human growth hormone (HGH), are subtler and harder to detect. They increase the mass and strength of muscles, which improves upon the natural effects of rigorous training. As a result, a runner artificially boosted by such drugs might easily be a fraction of a second faster or a batter may hit a ball a few feet farther—and at the highest levels of competition, that can make all the difference.

Steroids are not physically addictive, but they can be psychologically addictive as the athlete depends on the real or perceived "edge" they give. Being already young and supremely self-confident, many athletes who use these drugs have a hard time believing in the medical warnings that drugs that enhance performance today might lead to such problems as sterility, heart failure, or even cancer sometime later in life.

The problem of abuse of performance-enhancing drugs was publicized in 1988 when Canadian track star Ben Johnson was deprived of an Olympic gold medal when his steroid use was detected. Meanwhile some major league baseball stars have reported "off the record" that steroid use was prevalent in their sport. In 2003 a federal investigation of a San Francisco Bay Area laboratory again highlighted concerns that new "designer steroids" that were particularly difficult to detect were now in circulation and may have been provided to athletes such as baseball superstar Barry Bonds. In response, the major sports leagues, which have been relatively slow to tighten testing and sanctions against steroids, have begun to increase their penalties. With the exception of the National Hockey League (NHL), the major sports subject athletes to random testing. The National College Athletic Association (NCAA) tests all participants in major competitions.

THE BEGINNINGS
OF DRUG REGULATION

By the late 19th century a variety of medicines containing powerful opiates or cocaine were readily available in the United States over-the-counter without a prescription. While conscientious pharmacists might warn customers about the potential dangers of such drugs, there was essentially no regulation of their use.

By the first decade of the 20th century, however, there was growing evidence that the untrammeled use of over-the-counter medicines was creating serious social consequences. Besides the dangers of ineffective or contaminated patent medicines, drugs such as opium, morphine, and heroin were very addictive.

The first federal law to regulate drug use was the Pure Food and Drug Act of 1906. In addition to dealing with contaminated food (a very serious health problem that had been highlighted by reformers such as writer Upton Sinclair), the new law also required that patent medicines bear labels accurately describing their ingredients, including narcotics. The label could not make unwarranted health claims, and it did have to note the danger of addiction where applicable.

Narcotics abuse was not, of course, confined to the United States. In 1909 the International Opium Commission had its first meeting. Two years later an international treaty banned the distribution of narcotics except under medical supervision.

The next major advance in regulation was the Harrison Narcotics Act, passed in 1914. The law required that anyone manufacturing, selling, or dispensing drugs be registered with the federal government. The law also further restricted the use of opium and coca derivatives, requiring a doctor's prescription.

The Harrison Narcotics Act had only a limited effect on the growing traffic in illegal drugs. Many antidrug crusaders began to draw closer links between drugs and what was perceived in the 1920s as a growing urban crime wave.

Since the late 19th century many people had begun to associate drug use (and abuse) with crime, particularly among immigrants and other "outsider" groups. One popular racist stereotype was that of the Chinese opium user who spent hours in a smoky den under the control of shadowy ganglords. Another stereotype said that blacks were becoming addicted to inexpensive cocaine, which allegedly caused them to go on crime sprees and rape white women. Another drug, marijuana, was particularly associated in the popular mind with Mexican immigrants and loose-living jazz aficionados.

Drug Abuse

One prominent anti-narcotics crusader, Richmond P. Hobson (who had also worked for alcohol prohibition), broadcast a radio call during the second annual Narcotic Education Week in 1928:

> *Suppose it were announced that there were more than a million lepers among our people. Think what a shock the announcement would produce! Yet drug addiction is far more incurable than leprosy, far more tragic to its victims, and is spreading like a moral and physical scourge. . . . Most of the daylight robberies, daring holdups, cruel murders and similar crimes of violence are now known to be committed chiefly by drug addicts, who constitute the primary cause of our alarming crime wave. Drug addiction is more communicable and less curable that leprosy. . . . Upon the issue hangs the perpetuation of civilization, the destiny of the world, and the future of the human race.[14]*

The Marijuana Tax Act of 1937 brought that drug under federal control, although in a rather odd way. It was supposedly a revenue measure, requiring that all batches of marijuana be accompanied by a federal tax stamp. However, since marijuana was already illegal in most states, someone who actually bought a stamp would be opening him- or herself to prosecution. The absence of the stamp, however, allowed federal agents to make an arrest for the tax violation.

The 1938 Food, Drug and Cosmetic Act led to the creation of the Food and Drug Administration (FDA), which has wide powers to control the use of medicinal drugs. The agency was charged with determining which drugs were safe enough to use without a prescription. While narcotics were already banned from over-the-counter use, the FDA soon added amphetamines and barbiturates to the list. Until 1968 the FDA was the main federal agency enforcing laws against drug abuse, cracking down on pharmacists and doctors who violated the prescription laws.

THE "WAR ON DRUGS"

The 1960s (or more accurately, the period from about 1963 to the early 1970s) was marked by profound social, political, and cultural upheaval. In addition to social and political reforms (such as the Civil Rights movement), racial unrest and the war in Vietnam, the decade was also marked by a cultural revolution. As the admittedly simplistic phrase would have it, the 1960s was the era of "sex, drugs, and rock n'roll."

Drug use was no longer to be associated just with the poor and with marginalized communities. Drugs entered mainstream white culture. Marijuana, previously associated mainly with Hispanic immigrants and bohemians, was widely used by young people and formed a haze over many a rock concert venue. Cultural figures such as Ken Kesey (with his "acid tests") and Timothy Leary (with his slogan "turn on, tune in, and drop out") proclaimed the use of the hallucinogenic drug LSD for expanding consciousness and breaking free of the stultifying perceptions of conventional culture. References to drugs would be found in much of popular music. Use of harder drugs also grew. In particular, GIs in Vietnam who desperately sought escape from the misery and terror of combat found that heroin was available and cheap.

In the 1960s the rhetoric of war began to be applied to the effort to overcome social problems. The first well-known example was the War on Poverty proclaimed by the administration of President Lyndon B. Johnson. And when Richard Nixon ran for president in 1968, he called for a "war on drugs." He had little patience with the complexity of the problem, declaring that, "The country should stop looking for root causes of crime and put its money instead into increasing the number of police. Immediate and decisive force must be the first response."[15]

After his election Nixon created the President's National Commission on Marijuana and Drug Abuse. In 1970, Congress passed the Controlled Substances Act (CSA), the first comprehensive narcotics control law since 1914. The CSA systematically arranged drugs in "schedules" according to an assessment of addictive potential, dangerousness of effects, and pervasiveness of abuse.

In 1973, the Drug Enforcement Agency (DEA) was created to take primary responsibility for enforcement of federal narcotics laws. Finally, in 1974 the National Institute on Drug Abuse (NIDA) was established. Its purpose was to carry out research and pilot programs for drug abuse prevention and treatment.

As with the War on Poverty and Nixon's other domestic war (on cancer), the war on drugs made only limited headway. Drug use continued to grow in the 1970s. As some of the '60s generation grew in affluence, they turned to cocaine. However, powder cocaine was expensive, which somewhat limited its appeal, leading to the popularity of crack in the 1980s. While a single dose of crack was relatively cheap, an addict needs many doses a day, and will do almost anything to get the money needed to buy the drug. Crack thus fueled prostitution, robbery, and other crimes, particularly in the inner cities.

Law enforcement efforts, harsh sentences, and community efforts gradually reduced the use of crack in the 1990s. However, some users turned to heroin, which was now available in inhaled or smoked form. Heroin prices had gone down, and the drug offered a longer-lasting "high."

The Anti-Drug Abuse Act of 1988 created a new Office of National Drug Control Policy (ONDCP), whose head became popularly known as the "drug czar." The efforts under the Reagan and first Bush administrations tended to emphasize enforcement over treatment or prevention. President

Bill Clinton, though, shifted the emphasis somewhat away from enforcement. As implemented today, the struggle against drug abuse and drug trafficking has many levels or aspects. It stretches from the street corner to the courthouse, from the border inspection post to fields of coca in Bolivia or of opium poppies in Afghanistan.

ARREST, PROSECUTION, AND SENTENCING

Many Americans experience the drug war in terms of drug "busts," raids, and other activities they see on the nightly news. Police departments typically have a narcotics bureau that focuses on investigating and arresting drug trafficking organizations, including the many gangs that are heavily involved in the narcotics trade (sometimes there is a separate bureau dedicated to combating organized crime). The use of undercover officers, paid informers, and "stings" is common. At the street level, regular patrol officers frequently have to deal with lower-level drug dealers as well as users.

Because police resources are always limited and must be prioritized, particular crackdowns or "drug sweeps" are often the result of pressure brought by neighborhood activists or groups (such as merchants or parents of school-age children) who have been particularly affected by the dangerous activities of drug traffickers. Public fear and anger about the growth in drug trafficking was soon transmitted to political leaders. As Peter Kerr of Phoenix House (a major private drug treatment program), who was working "in the trenches" with drug abusers noted:

> *When crack hit the newspapers in 1986 and began transforming the inner city and the drug trade, there was a sense of desperation and a whole lot of new laws were written. The drug laws of the 1970s and 1980s are now reaping a toll. We've never had this many people in prison, and there are very few countries with as many as we have.[16]*

One reason for this explosion in the prison population was the growing popularity of mandatory sentencing laws. However, critics argued that it was not only unjust but uneconomical to lock someone up for five years for growing marijuana plants, for example.

TREATMENT ALTERNATIVES

A number of alternatives to incarceration have emerged, however. Diversion, or the assigning of drug offenders to compulsory treatment programs, is now common, especially for mere drug possession or even first-time or low-level trafficking offenses.

Introduction

As the criminal courts became increasingly clogged with drug-related cases, many observers worried that attention and resources were being taken away from serious violent crimes. Regular judges and courts also had little experience in working with or assessing drug abusers.

Increasingly, special "drug courts" were established: Today there are more than 600 of them in the United States. Drug courts emphasize treating offenders and then closely supervising them to try to prevent relapses. Even federal drug czar Barry McCaffrey expressed his approval of the drug court movement, saying:

> *If you're arrested at 2 in the morning and you're dazed, drunk or drugged, you're a male street prostitute or you're breaking into a car when arrested, we would like to get you into the drug court system at the front end. . . . If you go into treatment and get a job, we'll arrange the social services and medical care you need . . .* [17]

There are many obstacles to treatment as a way to reduce drug abuse, however. In 2002 about 3.1 million people received drug or alcohol treatment. Another 100,000 persons reported they had sought drug treatment but were unable to get it—often sufficient resources were simply lacking. Many more drug or alcohol abusers are believed to need treatment but are unwilling to admit to that need.

Simple drug possession is a low law enforcement priority in cities where police budgets are badly stretched. Further, unless someone is actually caught in possession of drugs, he or she cannot be arrested and forced into involuntary treatment. Some "hard-core" homeless drug users express a quite realistic view of their predicament. One, known only as "Tommy," said it this way to a reporter for the *San Francisco Chronicle*:

> *Day clinics? Jail? You think anyone out here on the street, all over this city, can stick with that? Why the hell do you think we are out here? Because we can't get over what's going on with us by ourselves, that's why. We want to get off the street, but I got to tell you true. Unless they take people like us and put us somewhere where we can't f—ing up, we're going to keep f—ing up.* [18]

APPROACHES TO ADDICTION AND TREATMENT

To consider how drug treatment might succeed in reducing drug use, one must first look at what happens when someone becomes addicted to a drug. Starting in the 1950s, experimenters observed that animals that were allowed to control the stimulation of "pleasure centers" in the brain would continue to do so until they collapsed from exhaustion. The pleasure centers are a vital part of our evolutionary heritage: They reward necessary actions (such as eating or mating). Many addictive drugs such as cocaine and heroin create direct chemical connections to the reward centers, producing feelings so intense that after a few repetitions many people feel urgently compelled to repeat their use of the drug.

The chemical connection between brain cells is by means of neurotransmitters—chemicals such as dopamine that convey nerve signals. In normal brain connections a neuron "fires" (discharges electrical potential). This in turn releases a small quantity of the neurotransmitter, which attaches itself to a receptor molecule in an adjacent neuron, causing it to "fire" in turn. Eventually the dopamine is returned to the cells until the next signal comes along.

Addictive drugs work in various ways to amplify this process. The rate of neuron firing or the amount of dopamine released into the synapse can be increased. Others promote the attachment of dopamine to the pleasure centers. Some drugs, such as cocaine, inhibit the "reuptake," or return, of dopamine to the originating cells. Finally, some drugs act as neurotransmitters themselves, mimicking the operation of dopamine. Whatever the mechanism, the result is a sustained increase in the amount of dopamine in circulation, which the brain interprets as an intense feeling of pleasure or contentment. Drugs such as heroin also increase the production of endorphins, naturally occurring morphinelike compounds the body uses to fight pain and stress and help promote survival in emergencies.

The chemical basis of addiction is that the brain's pleasure centers gradually adapt to the drug as physical and chemical changes begin to affect their activity even when the drug is not present. As a result the drug is needed even for "normal" feelings of contentment. At the same time, for many drugs the body begins to respond less to the drug, thus requiring that larger doses be taken in order to achieve the same level of effect. This is called tolerance. Meanwhile, the association between the drug and pleasure (and withdrawal of the drug and pain or distress) creates a conditioned response that is continually reinforced.

Other brain changes following drug addiction also affect the neurotransmitter norepinepherine, which plays an important role in regulating the body's autonomic functions, such as heart rate, respiration, and so on. As a result withdrawal of many addictive drugs produces symptoms such as rapid heartbeat, nausea, and chills as well as mental symptoms roughly the opposite to the drug's effects—symptoms such as anxiety, irritability, and restlessness. The fear of these symptoms serves as a further reinforcement to drug use, albeit a negative one.

Drugs have a variety of other important effects on brain function, and thus on mood, perception, and consciousness. A variety of popular prescription antidepressants (such as Prozac) work by reducing the reuptake of the neurotransmitter serotonin into brain cells. This increases the amount of serotonin in the nerve synapses, which in turn can improve mood, the quality of sleep, and appetite. Some of the hallucinogenic drugs, such as LSD and psilocybin, achieve a similar result because their chemical structure is closely related to that of serotonin.

Drug addiction is much more complex than this simple summary can indicate. This can be seen in the fact that millions of people use alcohol, for example, without becoming addicted to it—but some people can literally drink themselves to death. Even for drugs such as cocaine and heroin that are considered highly addictive, the amount of use needed to induce addiction varies considerably among individuals, and some individuals seem to be able to wean themselves off the drug when desired.

Some of this difference in outcomes can be attributed to differences in metabolism—how the drug is absorbed, distributed in the body, chemically converted, and excreted. Thus two persons with the same body weight can consume the same number of drinks and have different blood alcohol levels two hours later. For more subtle and less known reasons, the effectiveness of the drug in creating its effects and in reinforcing drug-taking behavior also varies.

Although specific genes have not yet been identified, it seems clear that there is a genetic component in disposition to drug use and addiction. Studies have shown that even when children of alcoholic parents are adopted and raised by nonalcoholic caregivers, these children remain at higher risk of becoming addicted to alcohol in later life.

Addiction is also strongly influenced by the social and physical setting in which drugs are taken. Factors include parental, peer, and community pressure or influence; the price and availability of drugs; the chance of being arrested; and the harshness of sentences or other sanctions.

Finally, because drugs are often sought as a way to escape from or ameliorate the effects of psychological conditions such as depression, clearly there is a close relationship between mental illness and drug abuse. Obviously not all drug abusers are mentally ill, and not all mentally ill persons turn to drugs. However, it is estimated that about half of all drug abusers have significant mental problems, and this overlap is considerably greater in populations such as "hard-core" homeless.

Because the reasons people use (and continue to use) drugs are complex and varied, treatment must address a challenging array of issues. Generally the first step after assessing a client's condition and situation is to deal with the physical aspects of the addiction. This can be done through "detox," or a controlled, supervised withdrawal—a process that can be very unpleasant with drugs such as heroin and even dangerous in the case of alcohol. An alternative for heroin users is methadone, a synthetic narcotic that satisfies the craving for heroin while "stabilizing" the user.

The psychological component of drug addiction must then be addressed. People generally seek drugs in the first place either because they are searching for new forms of sensation or pleasure, or because they are seeking to escape from or suppress psychological problems such as depression. In the latter case it is unlikely that the drug use will stop unless the psychological problem is treated or managed. This might be done through cognitive or behavioral therapy, perhaps in combination with appropriate antidepressant or other prescription drugs.

Another psychological aspect of drug treatment focuses on educating the client about the effects and implications of the drug use, and promoting such factors as self-esteem and decision-making capabilities. "Peer" or group settings are also frequently used, allowing recovering drug or alcohol abusers to provide support and emotional validation for one another. (The 12-step programs pioneered by Alcoholics Anonymous combine this with a sort of generically religious commitment to a "higher power," as well as restitution to and reconciliation with persons who have been hurt by the client.)

Perhaps an equally great challenge is to deal with the many other aspects of a client's life that must be addressed if they are to find alternatives to their drug use. Many drug users suffer from serious medical conditions such as HIV/AIDS, hepatitis C, and, especially in injection drug users, virulent infections caused by dirty needles.

Although as noted earlier most drug abusers are employed, many drug abusers whose problems have gotten them into treatment have left the world of work, or they simply do not have enough education or marketable job skills. A recovering drug abuser must then be linked to employment or vocational services. Even something as basic as housing (to get away from the pressures and temptations of the street) and transportation (to get to the available resource providers) can make the difference in whether a client stops using drugs.

REDUCING DEMAND THROUGH EDUCATION

Recognizing the need to try to prevent young people from getting into drugs in the first place, political leaders have emphasized drug education since the 1970s. DARE (Drug Abuse Resistance Education) is the largest and best-known such program. More than 100,000 police officers participate in DARE programs, reaching into the classrooms of about 5,000 children a year. Many thousands of packets of educational materials and other aids are distributed to teachers and parents. In general, the objectives of DARE and other drug education programs include teaching children how to identify drugs and explaining about their effects and dangers. Children are encouraged to resist peer pressure to use drugs and taught how to say no to offers of drugs. Because low self-esteem tends to result in a greater desire to conform to what is considered popular or "cool," there is an attempt to improve students' self-esteem and to identify ways in which they can be successful and creative. Other aspects of school antidrug programs address problems that put students at greater risk of drug involvement, such as academic failure, dropping out, teen pregnancy, and involvement in gangs and petty criminal activity.

There is considerable controversy about whether drug education programs really work, and little hard evidence to back up the assertions that are made by proponents. In February 2001, DARE admitted that there were serious questions about the effectiveness of its program. Aided by a $13.7 million grant from the Robert Wood Johnson Foundation, DARE undertook to revise its curriculum in light of discouraging findings by researchers such as a 1994 study by the Research Triangle Institute in North Carolina. However, having an organization evaluate its own performance is always problematic. Further, pressure from politicians on DARE and other programs such as Life Skills Training (LST) to show encouraging results has, many researchers believed, further compromised the objectivity of the evaluations.

Another drug education effort involves the media, which makes sense given the number of hours teenagers spend watching television. Since 1997 the federal government has funded public service announcements (PSAs) with antidrug themes. Studies suggest that PSAs that tell teenagers to "Just say no" to drugs have little effect. More effective are those messages that realistically convey the consequences of drug use. On the other hand, trying to oversell the dangers of marijuana, a drug widely believed to be not very harmful, could well backfire, as did crude "reefer madness" depictions of the 1930s and 1940s.

A balanced view on drug education suggests that it is not a cure-all for the problem of drug abuse, but that the teaching of "life skills" is probably broadly useful. But good decision-making requires good, quality information. Traditional programs such as DARE emphasize only the negative aspects of drugs and are geared to getting kids to decide to say no to drugs and to abstain completely from their use. Marsha Rosenbaum, director of the San Francisco office of the Lindesmith Center-Drug Policy Foundation, asks, "for the kids who don't say no, where can they go for honest, realistic, information about drugs in a life-or-death situation?"[19]

An alternative approach, dubbed "resiliency education," takes a broader approach. Rather than narrowly focusing on saying no to drugs, it emphasizes developing the ability of young people to cope with the changing challenges in their lives by becoming more skilled decision makers. This approach sees drugs (including drugs such as alcohol and tobacco that become legal with adulthood) as just one such challenge.

REDUCING THE DRUG SUPPLY

Historically the suppression of a particular source of sought-after drugs has resulted in a new source coming into prominence. Thus in response to the explosion of demand for marijuana in the United States in the 1960s, growers in Mexico and Jamaica expanded their plantings. When the U.S. government sponsored a program to eradicate marijuana plants using Paraquat, a powerful (and toxic) herbicide, growers in Colombia began to take up the slack. A thriving industry soon developed, with distributors buying the production of peasants and flying or otherwise getting it across the border into the United States. In turn, however, the United States by the late 1970s was putting intense pressure on the Colombian government, which raided the distributors, destroying planes, boats, and processing equipment. The pressure on the price of marijuana, however, made it profitable for more growers in remote rural regions of the United States to grow marijuana.

Meanwhile, the Colombian drug entrepreneurs, who had developed more sophisticated practices after years of marijuana growing, began to shift to cocaine, a product that was more valuable and also more compact, making it easier to smuggle. Between 1990 and 1995 the production of coca more than doubled and had almost doubled again by 2000. Production was aided by the fact that large portions of Colombia were under the control of guerrilla or paramilitary groups that protected the peasants who planted and tended the coca crop in return for a cut of the proceeds. Production of opium poppies also became significant.

The great value of illegal drug production and the need to protect it from law enforcers or competing producers resulted in the formation of large drug cartels or syndicates. Once grown and harvested by the peasants, the raw materials had to be shipped to laboratories where chemists supervised drug production. The finished drugs had to be smuggled into the United States and other consuming countries. "Soldiers" guarded the valuable product and sometimes fought against competing cartels for control of markets or routes. When drug producers or smugglers were arrested by the authorities, the cartels supplied lawyers, compensation for families, or intimidation to prevent anyone from informing on cartel activities.

The large Colombian cartels became a victim of their size and power, however. Colombian political factions opposed to the hold of drug lords on their society fought back after the assassination of leading presidential candidate Luis Carlos Galán in 1989. Succeeding governments destroyed first the Medellín and then the Cali cartels, which were replaced by smaller, lower-profile operations.

Today a number of antidrug initiatives continue to be pursued by the United States in (sometimes uncertain) cooperation with foreign governments. The "Andean Initiative" (a coordinated effort to reduce drug production) has apparently considerably reduced the amount of land in coca production in South America starting in the late 1990s. These supply-reduction efforts typically involve some combination of destroying illicit crops and giving aid to peasant farmers to encourage them to grow legitimate products such as grain or coffee.

However, most of the benefits of any success in coca eradication have probably been lost because of the new growth in cocaine production in Colombia, where drug production is now controlled mainly by leftist guerrilla groups. On the other side of the world in Afghanistan, the overthrow of the Taliban (which had suppressed heroin production) has resulted in a great increase in production of opium poppies.

The effort to reduce drug supplies has also raised human rights issues. As with the earlier cold war and the war on terrorism today, many of the leaders with whom the United States might want to cooperate have regimes that oppress their people. It has always been tempting to overlook such issues in favor of gaining that cooperation. During the 1980s, for example, the United States first supported and then overthrew Panama's Manuel Noriega. In the 1990s, some U.S. officials supported the Taliban in Afghanistan because it promised to reduce opium and heroin production.

It seems to remain true that as long as there is strong demand for illegal drugs in the United States, efforts to reduce the drug supply or to interdict drugs at the border will have at best limited effects. New supplies spring up to meet the demand, and if one drug becomes scarcer and more costly, many users will switch to something else.

The war on terrorism has had conflicting effects on the war on drugs. For example, when the anti-terrorism efforts following September 11, 2001, led to stricter inspections along the Mexican border, drug smuggling did decline somewhat. But as cocaine became scarcer, the production of methamphetamines in criminal labs inside the United States continued to grow.

Leaders in both the antidrug and anti-terrorism efforts have sought to link the two under the term "narcoterrorism." New public service announcements somewhat hyperbolically suggest that people who buy drugs are helping terrorists obtain the weapons they will use in their next devastating attacks. However, the combining of many federal agencies into the Department of Homeland Security in 2002 and the shifting in emphasis of the FBI, CIA, Customs, and other agencies from stopping drugs to stopping terrorism probably means that antidrug efforts on the ground will suffer.

Finally, the attempt to stem the flow of illegal drugs is facing a new challenge in the form of the Internet. Thousands of illicit or dubious online pharmacies are flooding users' mailboxes with "spam" messages offering drugs such as the painkiller Vicodin, often without requiring a prescription or more than a cursory medical check. The existing regulatory apparatus seems ill-equipped to cope with the problem. As Rep. John Dingell (D-Mich) notes, online illicit drug traffic

> *is growing exponentially because the regulatory agencies charged with enforcement have not applied adequate resources, nor have they approached the issue systematically. DEA, FDA and Customs must find those resources and change their policies, as well as have a nice chat with the various players enabling these illegal transactions—specifically, the consignment carriers and credit card companies who are plastered all over [the trafficker's] Web sites.*[20]

However, both the complexity of the Internet and its strongly libertarian culture make regulation both technically and politically difficult.

DRUG POLICY ISSUES

Any social problem as pervasive, serious, and contentious as drug abuse is bound to have a number of impacts on public policy, including civil liberties, public health, the workplace, and other areas.

CIVIL LIBERTIES ISSUES

The effort to stop drug abuse and trafficking raises a number of important general civil liberties issues, including whether persons are being stopped without probable cause that they have committed a crime, whether racial or ethnic profiles are being used instead of specific evidence involving a particular individual, and whether the use of intrusive search techniques (such as use of aircraft or heat detectors) violates privacy.

Once someone is arrested, the use of asset forfeiture (the seizing of money, cars, or even homes said to be involved with drug trafficking) raises another contentious issue. In many cases the seizing of assets is treated as a civil rather than criminal matter. This means that the authorities do not need to prove guilt beyond a reasonable doubt. Since the proceeds of seized assets are often included in the police budget, there is added incentive to use this tool expansively.

Another major issue brings in the always contentious and painful matter of race. Sentences for possession of crack are much higher proportionally than those for powder cocaine. Crack has been used mainly by blacks and other minorities in the inner cities, while powder cocaine is used more by whites. This leads to the argument that the sentencing amounts to discrimination against minorities, and efforts have been made to at least reduce the disparity.

DRUG TESTING

The use of drug testing is prevalent today in the American workplace. With millions of employed people abusing drugs to some extent, employers are concerned with the effects of drugs on workplace productivity, absenteeism, health care costs, and even legal liability. Most states offer employers incentives for promoting a "drug-free workplace," including lower workers' compensation premiums. Many major companies test job applicants as well as conducting periodic or random testing of existing employees. Proponents of testing believe that statistics showing a decline in workplace drug use demonstrate the value of drug testing.

Civil liberties and privacy advocates, however, oppose workplace drug testing as an invasion of privacy. Critics argue that few companies have conducted cost-benefit analyses that might demonstrate bottom-line benefits to having testing programs.

State laws regulating workplace drug testing vary. Some states ban or limit the use of random tests without individual suspicion. Some states also provide for some form of appeals process or retesting for employees found to test positive.

Drug testing is also prevalent in middle and high schools. Courts have upheld testing for student athletes, based on the increased potential for injury during competition. In 2002, the Supreme Court in *Board of Education v. Earls* extended allowable drug testing to students who participated in nonathletic extracurricular activities. Apparently the remaining distinction is that these activities are voluntary and that students could still obtain an education without them.

The American Civil Liberties Union (ACLU) has spoken strongly against the extension of drug testing to more students, arguing that students prone to drug abuse will be further isolated from the very extracurricular activities that might provide positive alternatives to drug use.

DRUG ABUSE AND PREGNANCY

Historically men have been heavier users of illicit drugs than women. Most heroin addicts, for example, have been male. However, the appearance of crack cocaine starting in the mid-1980s brought many more women into the drug world, including young, pregnant women. Many stories began to appear about "crack babies" born with severe impairments.

Exposure to powerful drugs does have a serious impact on infant mortality, including low birth weight, developmental disabilities, and sudden infant death syndrome (SIDS). Use of crack cocaine has declined somewhat since the 1990s, but a 2001 study by the *Journal of the American Medical Association* concluded that much of the damage previously attributed to cocaine use may in fact be attributable to alcohol or tobacco that was also used by the mothers in question. Even moderate use of alcohol poses a risk to the fetus.

Prosecutors began to charge pregnant mothers of abusing or "assaulting" their fetus through their abuse of drugs. In a 1991 Michigan case *(People v. Hardy)*, however, an appeals court ruled that a mother was not criminally responsible for "delivering" cocaine to her unborn child. In 1992 the Supreme Court of Florida overturned a similar conviction in *Johnson v. State*. In 1997, the Wisconsin Supreme Court ruled that a fetus is not a child entitled to the protection of the state's child welfare laws, so a mother who abuses drugs cannot be incarcerated solely to protect the fetus. Although the South Carolina Supreme Court did uphold a conviction for child neglect because the mother used cocaine during pregnancy, courts in general seem reluctant to hold mothers responsible for infants born impaired by or addicted to drugs, but rather give greater weight to the privacy and other rights of the mother.

In Charleston, South Carolina, a public hospital, in cooperation with local police, began to give pregnant patients drug tests without their consent. In 2001, however, the U.S. Supreme Court ruled that such testing violated the rights of the patients, and that a law enforcement action could not be justified solely on public health grounds. Indeed, many of the justices as well as public health experts believe such a policy might even harm public health by driving pregnant mothers away from prenatal care.

MEDICAL MARIJUANA

In recent years federal authorities have pressured doctors not even to discuss medical marijuana as an option for their patients. They sought to revoke an offending doctor's license to prescribe federally controlled narcotics. Such an action would make it virtually impossible for many doctors to practice medicine in their specialty. However, in October 2002, a federal appeals court in San Francisco ruled that such a sanction violates the constitutional right of doctors and patients to discuss health matters freely. About a year later the Supreme Court let the decision stand. The decision does not affect the illegality of actually prescribing medical marijuana, however.

In the 1990s a number of cities, particularly in California, gave their blessing to "buyers clubs" that would sell marijuana to persons who claimed to have medical recommendations for the drug. Federal authorities shut down many of the clubs in the later 1990s. The attempt of the city of Oakland, California, to declare a "public health emergency" and authorize alternate means of marijuana distribution was given no weight in federal court.

Since 1997 nine states (Alaska, Arizona, California, Colorado, Hawaii, Maine, Nevada, Oregon, and Washington) have approved laws or ballot initiatives allowing medical use of marijuana. The conflict between state and federal laws has led to contentious court battles and public activism. Federal agents have shut down medical "cannabis clubs" despite their being licensed by the state. When the case gets to federal court, the judge has generally followed the standard practice of not allowing the defense to refer to the state law in justifying the defendant's actions, because federal law supersedes state law. Thus Ed Rosenthal, a California medical marijuana activist, was convicted in 2003 by a jury that was not allowed to hear that the defendant had received a local license for his club. When the jury later learned of this, many jurors were angry and said they would have voted to acquit.

However, a number of medical experts doubt that marijuana really has medical value. They cite the risk of lung cancer and other smoking-related diseases as being present in marijuana as well as tobacco. Currently an aerosol version of THC is being developed. Like smoking, it would get the drug into the bloodstream quickly and allow for control of dose, but it would eliminate the "tars" and other dangerous components.

LEGALIZATION AND DECRIMINALIZATION

In recent decades there has been strong advocacy by reformers who question the very basis of the war on drugs—that certain drugs should be illegal to possess and use. Such advocates often begin with an argument based on history:

> *Prohibition didn't work for alcohol in the 1920s, and it's never going to work for drugs. When something doesn't work, you have two choices: Face up to the fact and change course, or refuse to admit you're failing and escalate. And that's what's been happening over the past 20 years.*[21]

Supporters of current policy deny that the drug war is failing. They admit that the struggle is complex and difficult, but cite declines in the use of some drugs during the 1990s.

The argument can also be carried out on a philosophical level. Libertarians point to a fundamental right of persons to decide what they want to do to or with their own body. The pioneer free-market economist Ludwig von Mises, for example, also argued that if the government can control drugs, it can control anything else that it decides is harmful:

Opium and morphine are certainly dangerous, habit-forming drugs. But once the principle is admitted that it is the duty of government to protect the individual against his own foolishness, no serious objections can be advanced against further encroachments. A good case could be made out in favor of the prohibition of alcohol and nicotine. And why limit the government's benevolent providence to the protection of the individual's body only? Is not the harm a man can inflict on his mind and soul even more disastrous than any bodily evils? Why not prevent him from reading bad books and seeing bad plays, from looking at bad paintings and statues and listening to bad music? The mischief done by bad ideologies, surely, is much more pernicious, both for the individual and for the whole society, than that done by narcotic drugs.[22]

Clearly this is a minority view even if it is consistent. Most people believe government should protect people from things that are sufficiently (and directly) dangerous but should not control what people read, see, or think. Many legalization advocates focus instead on the harm they see the drug war doing to both drug users and to society as a whole.

For example, a group of judges and attorneys wrote an antidrug war manifesto in which they

observe that neither drugs nor drug abuse have been eliminated or appreciably reduced, despite massive spending on interdiction and harsh punishments. Attempts at enforcement have clogged the courts, filled the prisons with non-predatory offenders, corrupted officials at home and abroad, bred disrespect for the law in important communities, imperiled the liberties of the people, burdened the taxpayers, impeded public health efforts to stem the spread of HIV and other infectious diseases, and brought the nation no closer to abstinence. As Congress and state legislatures enact more punitive and costly drug control measures, we conclude with alarm that the war on drugs now causes more harm than drug abuse itself.[23]

Critics of drug legalization argue that just as alcohol use increased after Prohibition was repealed, drug use would increase—perhaps drastically—if drugs were legal and there was nothing to deter people from using them. Whether or not this is true, many more moderate legalization advocates prefer that drugs be "decriminalized" rather than simply left uncontrolled. Economist Milton Friedman takes this approach, suggesting that we

Legalize drugs by subjecting them to exactly the same rules that alcohol and cigarettes are subjected to now. . . . Television advertising is forbidden today for alcohol [and] for hard liquor. And I say treat this the same way as you would treat alcohol. So presumably such ads would be forbidden for this.[24]

Critics tend to argue that decriminalization is just legalization in disguise. Nevertheless, support for legalization—at least for marijuana—appears to he slowly growing.

HARM REDUCTION: A COMPROMISE APPROACH

Milton Friedman's approach is closely related to harm reduction, an approach that has also attracted increasing support in recent years. In this approach the focus is not on stopping people from using drugs but on trying to manage the problem in such a way that the least harm is done both to drug users and to society as a whole.

One of the best known (though somewhat contentious) implementations of harm reduction is needle-exchange programs, where drug users are provided with sterile hypodermic syringes in exchange for their used ones. Because dirty needles are one of the main ways in which HIV/AIDS and other deadly infections are spread, it is hoped that needle exchanges will reduce the sharing of dirty (used) needles.

Opponents of needle exchange argue that it will increase drug use (much as opponents of condom distribution argue that it would increase sexual activity). However, in 1998 Donna Shalala, secretary of Health and Human Services, announced that "a meticulous, scientific review had now proven that needle-exchange programs can reduce the transmission of HIV and save lives without losing ground in the battle against illegal drugs."[25] Nevertheless, President Clinton evidently bowed to political pressure and refused to provide federal funding for needle-exchange programs, which continue at the local level.

Needle exchange is not the only example of harm-reduction strategies. Another example is providing a safe area where people can use drugs without exposing themselves to being preyed upon by criminals. However, the most famous example of this approach, the "needle park" in Zurich, Switzerland, was eventually closed due to increases in crime.

Another example of harm reduction is Dance Safe, a program that allows ecstasy users at raves to test their pills for contamination.

Another important harm-reduction strategy attempts to separate marijuana users from those of harder drugs. Marijuana has been called a "gateway drug" in some antidrug literature. In 1994, it was reported by the Center on Addiction and Substance Abuse that 43 percent of students who used marijuana by age 18 later moved on to use cocaine. However, there is a question of cause and effect here: Does marijuana make people want to use other, harder drugs, or does this just mean that people who use marijuana tend to have a personality type that also predisposes them to other illegal drugs? Harm-reduction advocates suggest that whichever is the case, it may

35

make sense to make marijuana legal and regulated—perhaps sold in coffee houses, as in the Netherlands. That way people using marijuana will not be in contact with illicit dealers who have an incentive to offer the harder, more profitable drugs.

THE FUTURE OF DRUG ABUSE

If this survey of drugs, the war on drugs, and drug policy issues does nothing else, it should make it clear that the problem of drug abuse is filled with questions that are hard to answer and over which there is much disagreement. Although perhaps temporarily overshadowed by the war on terror, the war on drugs continues. Strategies will continue to be debated and implemented, depending on the political process. There are signs, however, that a more pragmatic approach may be winning out.

Meanwhile, advances in designer-drug chemistry and the availability of new channels such as the Internet are likely to bring new challenges to the effort to control drug abuse. The growing availability of "enhancement" drugs (not just steroids but also drugs alleged to improve mental functioning, increase energy, or even promote longevity) is widening the scope of the drug debate. Perhaps the most important thing is for people—particularly young people—to obtain the best information they can and to consider it carefully when making decisions that can have such a profound effect on their future.

---

[1] Connie Cass. "Candidates' Past Pot Use No Big Deal: Dems Seeking Presidency Talk Frankly About Inhaling." *San Francisco Chronicle*, November 29, 2003, p. A2.

[2] Quoted in Marianne Lavelle. "Teen Tobacco Wars: An Antismoking Ad Blitz vs. New Cigarette Marketing Ploys." *U.S. News & World Report*, February 7, 2000, pp. 14–16.

[3] Quoted in Louis Goodman and Alfred Gilman, *The Pharmacological Basis of Therapeutics*, First Edition (1941), p. 186.

[4] Dr. George Wood, *Treatise on Therapeutics*, quoted in David F. Musto, *The American Disease: The Origins of Narcotics Control*. New York: Oxford University Press, 1987, pp. 71–72.

[5] Quoted in Henry H. Lennard, et al., "Methadone treatment (letters)," *Science*, vol. 179, March 16, 1973, pp. 1078–1079.

[6] Gary Indiana, *Horse Crazy*. New York: Penguin Books, 1989, pp. 133–134.

[7] Quoted in Anthony Miles, Keith Waterhouse, and Ronald Bedford. "Drugs: Are They a Help or a Menace?" *Daily Mirror*, September 19, 1955, pp. 6.

[8] Quoted in Ernest Jones, *The Life and Work of Sigmund Freud*, New York: Basic Books, 1953–1957, vol. 1, p. 82.

[9] PBS *Frontline:* Drug Wars. "Interview: Robert Stutman." Available online. URL: http://www.pbs.org/wgbh/pages/frontline/shows/drugs/interviews/stutman.html. Updated in 2000.

[10] PBS *Frontline:* Drug Wars. "Interview: Robert Stutman."

[11] PBS *Frontline:* Drug Wars. "Interview: Robert Stutman."

[12] Quoted in Norman Taylor, *The Pleasant Assassin: The Story of Marihuana,* in David Solomon, ed. *The Marijuana Papers.* London: Panther, 1969, p. 41.

[13] Quoted in John Kaplan, *Marijuana: The New Prohibition.* New York: World Pub. Co., 1970, p. 92.

[14] Quoted in David F. Musto, *The American Disease,* p. 191.

[15] Quoted in Dan Baum, *Smoke and Mirrors: The War on Drugs and the Politics of Failure,* 1996, p. 7.

[16] Quoted in Mary H. Cooper, "Drug Policy Debate: The Issues." *CQ Researcher,* July 28, 2000, pp. 595–604.

[17] Quoted in Mary H. Cooper, "Drug Policy Debate: The Issues." pp. 595–604.

[18] Quoted in Kevin Fagan, "Homeless Island." *San Francisco Chronicle,* November 30, 2003, pp. A1, A20–23.

[19] Quoted in Jason Cohn, "Drug Education: The Triumph of Bad Science." *Rolling Stone,* May 24, 2001, pp. 41ff.

[20] Quoted in Gilbert M. Gaul and Mary Pat Flaherty. "Google Just Says No to Unlicensed Pharmacy Advertising." *San Francisco Chronicle,* December 1, 2003, p. A4.

[21] Quoted in Mary H. Cooper, "Drug Policy Debate: The Issues." pp. 595–604.

[22] Ludwig von Mises, *Human Action, A Treatise on Economics.* 4th Rev. Ed. Irvington-on-Hudson, N.Y.: Foundation Education, 1996, pp. 728–729.

[23] Voluntary Committee of Lawyers, Inc. "An Open Letter from Judges and Attorneys." Available online. URL: http://www.vcl.org.

[24] Milton Friedman and Thomas S. Szasz. *On Liberty and Drugs.* Washington, D.C.: Drug Policy Foundation Press, 1992, pp. 76–77.

[25] Quoted in David Murray, "Clean Needles May Be Bad Medicine," *Wall Street Journal,* April 22, 1998, n.p. Also available online. URL: www.mapine.org/drugnews/v98.n301.a12.html.

CHAPTER 2

THE LAW AND DRUG ABUSE

In the United States, federal, state, and local authorities are all able to legislate on issues concerning drug abuse. Federal authorities primarily prosecute when production or distribution of illegal drugs crosses state lines or national borders—which is the case with many drug trafficking organizations. Although states can and do have their own drug laws, as the medical marijuana controversy has shown, making an activity legal under a state's laws does not preclude prosecution under federal law.

FEDERAL NARCOTICS REGULATION

As with most matters pertaining to commerce, there was little federal drug regulation in the 19th century. The Import Drugs Act of 1848 did allow the U.S. Customs Service to inspect shipments of imported drugs and reject those that were contaminated, adulterated, or counterfeit. In 1909, with growing concern about opiate abuse, Congress passed a law banning the importing of opium "for other than medicinal purposes."

PURE FOOD AND DRUG ACT (1906)

The Pure Food and Drug Act was passed mainly in response to widespread public concern about contaminated meat and other food, but patent medicines with dubious contents and misleading labels were also a significant problem. Among its other provisions this law required that any narcotic ingredients in a patent medicine be disclosed, and prohibited unwarranted claims of curative powers.

HARRISON NARCOTICS ACT (1914)

The Harrison Narcotics Act represents the first federal effort to gain control over the burgeoning use of harmful drugs in the United States. Chapter 1 of the law is titled "An Act to provide for the registration of, with collectors of internal revenue, and to impose a special tax on all persons who produce, import, manufacture, compound, deal in, dispense, sell, distribute, or give away opium or coca leaves, their salts, derivatives, or preparations, and for other purposes."

The law required anyone importing, selling, or otherwise dispensing drugs to register with the federal government. Heroin and cocaine could no longer be used in over-the-counter medicines; they had to be dispensed with a physician's prescription—and federal policy and interpretation soon greatly discouraged even prescription use of these drugs. These provisions reflected U.S. compliance with the first international narcotics control treaties.

It should be noted that the Harrison Act was structured as a tax law. Until the Supreme Court expanded the interpretation of Congress's power to regulate interstate commerce, Congress often relied on the better established taxing power.

During the 1920s and early 1930s, drug regulation was expanded and tightened somewhat. The Narcotic Drug Import and Export Act of 1922 tried to ensure that narcotics could be distributed only for legitimate medical uses. The Heroin Act of 1924 outlawed domestic manufacture of the drug. The Uniform Narcotic Act of 1932 improved drug tracking by standardizing prescription and sale forms.

MARIJUANA TAX ACT (1937)

Marijuana had not been included under the Harrison Act. The Marijuana Tax Act brought the plant under federal regulation, also using the form of a tax law. The essential feature was that a tax was imposed on the manufacture and distribution of marijuana. Because a growing number of states had already made possession of marijuana illegal, a dealer or user faced a Catch-22: either pay the tax and thereby furnish evidence of intent to violate the state law, or not pay the tax and be subject to being charged with a federal tax offense.

The criminalization of marijuana proceeded swiftly: By 1939 there were no longer any legal medicines containing marijuana, and in 1941 marijuana was removed from the U.S. Pharmacopeia and the U.S. National Formulary, the two definitive sources for medical legitimacy of drugs.

REGULATORY CHANGES

The 1950s saw a ratcheting up of penalties for federal drug offenses. The Boggs Amendment to the Harrison Act (1951) removed much judicial discretion by imposing mandatory prison sentences. The Narcotics Act of 1956 imposed still harsher penalties. In cases where a person over 18 years of age sells heroin to a minor, the jury could now recommend the death penalty.

The 1960s was a time of both increased drug use and changes in policy toward treatment of drug addicts. The Drug Abuse Control Amendments of 1965 put stricter controls on barbiturates, amphetamines, LSD, and other drugs. A year later, however, the Narcotics Addict Rehabilitation Act of 1966 (NARA) marked a shift from punishment to treatment for "certain persons charged with or convicted of violating Federal criminal laws, who are determined to be addicted to narcotic drugs, and likely to be rehabilitated through treatment." Congress also established procedures for civil commitment of addicts who had not been charged with any criminal offense. Of course the effectiveness of such laws depends largely on the amount of resources actually provided for treatment.

Another nod toward rehabilitation was the Drug Abuse Control Amendments of 1968, which provided that a drug offender who remained "clean" for a year could have the offense removed from the criminal record.

CONTROLLED SUBSTANCES ACT (1970)

Formally known as the Comprehensive Drug Abuse Prevention and Control Act of 1970 (U.S. Code Title 21), this law established the "scheduling" or classifying of all drugs regulated under federal law. It made the legal treatment of drugs more systematic and provided a mechanism for evaluating the dangers and abuse potential of new drugs. The CSA remains the legal framework for regulation of federally controlled drugs.

The CSA defines its scope as covering drugs that have "a potential for abuse." Such drugs or substances are placed in one of five schedules (from strictest to least restrictive) based on a number of factors. These include the current scientific understanding of a drug's effects, how dangerous the effects are to health and safety, and the likelihood that users will become addicted to or dependent on the drug, including the possibility of psychological rather than physical addiction. The extent to which the drug has been abused in the past and is being abused today is also taken into account, as are the social and health costs involved.

Based on these considerations, drugs are placed into one of five categories, or "schedules," with Schedule 1 being the most restrictive and Schedule 5 the most relaxed.

Schedule 1

Schedule 1 includes the most dangerous and most addictive drugs that have no currently accepted medical use (and are not considered safe for medical use, even under close supervision). Drugs in this category include heroin and most of the other opiates that are now considered too dangerous (or no longer necessary) for medical use.

Hallucinogenic drugs such as LSD, mescaline, and peyote are also included. Although not addictive, these drugs are considered too dangerous because of their unpredictable psychological effects. The most controversial Schedule 1 drug is marijuana, a relatively mild hallucinogen that many critics feel should be treated more like alcohol or at least placed in Schedule 3 or 4.

Schedule 2

Schedule 2 is intended for drugs that also have a high potential for abuse and for addiction but do have a currently accepted medical use, albeit often a highly restricted one. These drugs include many opiates that are used medically, as well as certain coca extracts. Examples include fentanyl and methadone (the latter being used medically for maintenance of heroin addicts)

Schedule 3

Schedule 3 involves drugs with a significant abuse potential, but lower than for Schedules 1 and 2. Such drugs may "lead to moderate or low physical dependence or high psychological dependence." Examples include many stimulants such as amphetamines and methamphetamines as well as various barbiturates. Anabolic steroids (used by athletes and bodybuilders) are also included because of their serious health risks.

Schedule 4

Drugs in this category have an accepted medical use and a relatively low potential for abuse compared to Schedule 3. Use may lead to "limited physical dependence or psychological dependence." Many drugs in this category are hypnotic (sleep-inducing) or anesthetic in effect. Phenobarbital, barbital, and chloral hydrate are examples.

Schedule 5

Drugs in this least restrictive category have an accepted medical use and relatively low potential for abuse and dependence compared to the drugs in Schedule 4. Most Schedule 5 drugs are compounds or mixtures that contain narcotics mixed with other active ingredients that also have a medical effect.

Other drugs have been subsequently added to the schedules. For example a 1990 amendment added GHB (gamma hydroxybutyric acid), also known as Rohypnol, to Schedule 4.

Drug Abuse

Penalties and Special Provisions

The CSA also provides a system of penalties for drug possession or trafficking. The basic penalty for possession of a controlled substance is up to one year in prison plus a minimum fine of $1,000. This increases to up to three years and $5,000 for a third offense (counting previous convictions under state law). There are special higher penalties for possession of certain substances such as "a mixture or substance which contains cocaine base," starting at up to three years and a fine of $5,000.

For trafficking, penalties are based on the schedule for the drug in question, the amount of drug, whether it is the person's first or second (or subsequent) offense, and (in some cases) whether another person's death or serious bodily injury is involved. The various permutations make determining the sentence for a given individual fairly complex. To this must be added the possibility of civil penalties and asset forfeiture.

There are also a variety of special offenses and sanctions covered in the following sections:

- endangering human life while illegally manufacturing a controlled substance
- distribution to persons under age 21
- distribution or manufacturing in or near schools and colleges
- employment of persons under 18 years of age
- denial of federal benefits to drug traffickers and possessors
- denial of assistance and benefits for certain drug-related convictions
- sanctioning for testing positive for controlled substances
- drug paraphernalia
- anhydrous ammonia.

ANTI-DRUG ABUSE ACT OF 1986

During the 1980s the emergence of the huge Colombian and Mexican drug cartels and the globalization of the illicit narcotics trade led to a variety of congressional responses. The Anti-Drug Abuse Act of 1986 provided for $1.7 billion in new appropriations for the war on drugs. Mandatory minimum sentences are again specified: possession of at least one kilogram of heroin or five kilograms of cocaine is punishable by at least 10 years in prison. Sale of at least five grams of crack brings a mandatory five-year sentence. Disparity between this sentence and that for cocaine powder became a point of contention when critics charged it had a racially discriminatory effect toward predominately black crack users.

The Law and Drug Abuse

The Anti-Drug Abuse Act of 1986 also changed the federal agency structure on the research and education side. It created the U.S. Office for Substance Abuse Prevention (OSAP), which consolidated alcohol and other drug prevention activities under the Alcohol, Drug Abuse, and Mental Health Administration (ADAMHA). In a 1992 reorganization, OSAP was changed to the Center for Substance Abuse Prevention (CSAP), part of the new SAMHSA (Substance Abuse and Mental Health Services Administration) under the U.S. Department of Health and Human Services. It retained its major program areas, while the National Institute on Alcohol Abuse and Alcoholism (NIAAA) and the National Institute on Drug Abuse (NIDA) were transferred to the National Institutes of Health (NIH). However, the National Research Council has recommended that these two organizations be merged.

OTHER FEDERAL LAWS

In addition to the legislation already discussed, a number of important federal laws that have a relationship to the war on drugs have been passed since the 1970s. These include:

- The Bank Secrecy Act of 1970, despite its name, actually requires that banks keep detailed records of any transaction(s) by an individual or organization totaling more than $10,000 in cash (i.e., does not include checks nor money orders) in a single day in order to make money laundering more evident. A later "anti-structuring" provision also makes it illegal to make smaller cash transactions (such as $9,999) in an attempt to evade the law.

- The Controlled Substance Analogue Enforcement Act of 1986 declares that drugs that have similar effects to banned drugs are also automatically banned despite their having differences in chemical structure. This is an attempt to close a loophole exploited by illicit chemists.

- The Chemical Diversion and Trafficking Act of 1988 defines "precursor chemicals" that can be used in the process of producing illicit drugs. Companies producing or supplying such chemicals must keep certain records and report orders that are suspicious or above a specified size prior to delivery. The Domestic Chemical Diversion Control Act of 1993 further expanded these controls, dealing particularly with the diversion of ephedrine (found in over-the-counter antihistamines) to the production of methamphetamines ("speed").

- The International Narcotics Control Act of 1992 required increased reporting on money laundering and on stockpiles of precursor chemicals. Countries not certified as cooperating could be denied loans or other aid by the United States.

43

- The Comprehensive Methamphetamine Control Act of 1996 attempts to deal with the proliferation of "meth labs" since the 1990s. Chemicals used in producing methamphetamines are more tightly controlled and penalties for illicit production of both precursor chemicals and the drugs themselves are increased.

- The Drug-Induced Rape Prevention and Punishment Act of 1996 deals with the use of flunitrazepan (also called Rohypnol, or "roofies") to facilitate so-called "date rape." The law provided for an additional sentence to be imposed in such rapes.

- The Illicit Drug Anti-Proliferation Act of 2003 (better known as the "Rave Act") makes operators of nightclubs, concerts, and other venues responsible for drug violations by partygoers. The law has raised concerns that it might be used to target political or cultural gatherings that are unpopular with the authorities.

FEDERAL AGENCIES

Since 1973 the principal agency charged with enforcement of federal laws against illicit drug activity is the Drug Enforcement Administration (DEA). The DEA was essentially a consolidation of many existing agencies in response to the growing threat of large-scale cocaine and heroin trafficking. In 2002, the DEA's 4,625 special agents made 27,635 arrests and seized more than 250,000 kilograms of marijuana, cocaine, heroin, and other drugs.

There are a number of other federal agencies that play a supporting role in the antidrug effort. (Note that several of the following agencies such as the Border Patrol and Coast Guard are now part of the Department of Homeland Security.)

- The Federal Bureau of Investigation (FBI) is the principal investigative arm of the Department of Justice. It can become involved in drug cases, especially those involved with its investigation of organized crime activities. The DEA reports to the attorney general through the director of the FBI.

- The U.S. Border Patrol is responsible for about 8,000 miles of borders and intercepting illegal immigrants and smugglers (particularly drug smugglers).

- The U.S. Customs Service inspects passengers, luggage, and shipments passing through ports of entry into the United States. Detecting illegal drugs is a high priority. Agents can be assisted by specially trained dogs and high-tech chemical "sniffing" gear.

- The U.S. Coast Guard plays an important role in intercepting ships and boats used to bring drugs ashore, such as in Florida.
- In addition to the DEA, the Department of Justice has other units fighting organized drug trafficking. These include the Organized Crime Drug Enforcement Task Force, special High Intensity Drug Trafficking Area programs, and the Southwest Border Initiative.
- The U.S. Marshal Service operates posts throughout the United States and much of the world. It helps apprehend drug fugitives and is in charge of managing and selling property confiscated from drug offenders. The Marshal Service also operates the federal Witness Protection Program.
- The Department of the Treasury's Bureau of Alcohol, Tobacco and Firearms (ATF) includes among its duties the enforcement of taxes and other regulations involving the two most popular legal recreational drugs.
- The U.S. Department of Labor has programs to promote "drug-free workplaces," particularly reaching out to small businesses.
- The U.S. Department of State has a Bureau of Narcotics and Law Enforcement Affairs. It seeks to use U.S. diplomatic efforts to persuade foreign nations to cooperate with drug control efforts and to enter into bilateral and multilateral agreements in relevant areas.
- The Food and Drug Administration (FDA) is in charge of regulating legitimate prescription and over-the-counter drugs. It determines whether a new drug is legal to use based on its safety and efficacy.
- Finally, the Office of National Drug Control Policy has as its tasks the coordination of federal, state, and local drug control efforts, as well as the formulation of a comprehensive National Drug Control Strategy, which is outlined in an annual report.

INTERNATIONAL AGREEMENTS

The United States has entered into numerous bilateral or multilateral agreements with particular countries, seeking cooperation in drug eradication and interdiction efforts. Additionally, there are several important international treaties that have been signed by the United States and many other nations.

HAGUE CONVENTION (1912)

By the first decade of the 20th century many of the world's leading industrial and mercantile nations had realized that the curbing of drug abuse required concerted international effort. The Hague Convention not only regulated international commerce in opiates but also required that signatory nations restrict domestic manufacture, distribution, and use. In the United States, these requirements would be implemented by the Harrison Narcotic Act of 1914.

UNITED NATIONS SINGLE CONVENTION ON NARCOTIC DRUGS (1961)

This convention was enacted by a UN conference in 1961, but it was not ratified by the United States until 1967. U.S. narcotics control officials were concerned that the convention was too lax in allowing additional nations to produce opium. However, it was eventually decided that the codification and expansion of existing international provisions outweighed that disadvantage. Standards were given for control of manufacturing, production quantities (intended to be no more than necessary for medical use or for producing other medically needed drugs), and import and export of opium, coca (cocaine), and marijuana. Drugs are classified into schedules according to hazardousness and medical application; there are provisions for adding new drugs to the schedules.

UNITED NATIONS CONVENTION ON PSYCHOTROPIC SUBSTANCES (1974)

This treaty extended international narcotics regulation to substances that have the capacity to produce "A state of dependence, and . . . [c]entral nervous system stimulation or depression, resulting in hallucinations or disturbances in motor function or thinking." These include drugs such as marijuana and LSD. The treaty specifies that signatory parties:

(a) *Prohibit all use except for scientific and very limited medical purposes by duly authorized persons, in medical or scientific establishments that are directly under the control of their governments or specifically approved by them;*

(b) *Require that manufacture, trade, distribution, and possession be under a special licence or prior authorization;*

(c) *Provide for close supervision of the activities and acts mentioned in paragraphs (a) and (b);*

(d) *Restrict the amount supplied to a duly authorized person to the quantity required for his authorized purpose;*

(e) *Require that persons performing medical or scientific functions keep records concerning the acquisition of the substances and the details of their use, such records to be preserved for at least two years after the last use recorded therein; and*

> *(f) Prohibit export and import except when both the exporter and importer are the competent authorities or agencies of the exporting and importing country or region, respectively, or other persons or enterprises that are specifically authorized by the competent authorities of their country or region for the purpose.*

There are also general guidelines for such matters as the issuing of prescriptions, record keeping, labeling of packaging, prohibition on advertising, and control of import and export of these substances.

UNITED NATIONS CONVENTION AGAINST ILLICIT TRAFFIC IN NARCOTIC DRUGS AND PSYCHOTROPIC SUBSTANCES (1988; REVISED IN 1996)

This convention specifies guidelines and mechanisms for international cooperation in fighting narcotics trafficking, including conduct of multinational law enforcement operations. It specifies standards that signatory nations should enact into law regarding such matter as the manufacture, import, export, and transportation of controlled substances.

STATE NARCOTICS LAWS

As early as 1874, Connecticut passed a law providing for treatment of narcotics addicts. New York established civil commitment procedures for narcotics addicts in 1909 but did not provide treatment facilities. Although California authorized a state hospital for narcotics addicts in 1927, states in general were slow to provide facilities even when authorized by law.

As for laws against drug possession or trafficking, by 1930 the majority of states had passed laws against the sale or possession of cocaine or the opiates. However, penalties varied and enforcement was generally lax or given a low priority. At the same time, however, public concern about organized crime and its interstate operations was growing, as highlighted by the activities of the Federal Bureau of Investigation.

At the time there was a general movement in the states to adopt uniform or "model" laws. The Uniform Narcotic Drug Act was drafted over the 1925–32 period. By 1937, 35 states had enacted the Uniform Act, sometimes with supplemental provisions specific to the state.

Today most states offer commitment to a treatment program in lieu of jail for addicts charged with certain criminal offenses. (In 1962 the U.S. Supreme Court ruled that addiction itself could not be made a crime, but states could impose involuntary treatment or confinement for treatment.)

COURT CASES

The following selection of court cases (mainly from the U.S. Supreme Court) deal specifically with drug laws. Note that there are many other cases that deal with related issues of search and seizure, privacy, self-incrimination, and so on.

For convenience in researching particular legal issues, the following summary lists major topics or issues and lists the cases covered for each.

- **Addiction as a Disability:** *Raytheon v. Hernandez*, Docket Number 02-749 (2003)
- **Addiction as an Offense:** *Robinson v. California*, 370 U.S. 660 (1962)
- **Addiction and Pregnancy:** *Ferguson v. City of Charleston*, (No. 99-936, 2001); *Whitner v. South Carolina*, 492 S.E. 2d 777 (S.C. 1997), cert. granted 2003
- **Controlled Substances Act:** *United States v. Oakland Cannabis Buyers Cooperative*, No. 00-151 (2001)
- **Drug Testing:** *Schmerber v. California*, 384 U.S. 757 (1966); *National Treasury Employees Union v. Von Raab*, 489 U.S. 656 (1989); *Veronia School District v. Acton*, 515 U.S. 646 (1995)
- **Harrison Narcotic Act:** *U.S. v. Doremus*, 249 U.S. 86 (1919); *Jin Fuey Moy v. United States*, 254 U.S. 189 (1920)
- **Juveniles:** *New Jersey v. T.L.O*, 469 U.S. 325 (1985); *Veronia School District v. Acton*, 515 U.S. 646 (1995)
- **Marijuana Tax Act:** *United States v. Sanchez*, 340 U.S. 42 (1950); *Leary v. United States*, 395 U.S. 6 (1969)
- **Medical Practice:** *Jin Fuey Moy v. United States*, 254 U.S. 189 (1920)
- **Medical Use of Marijuana:** *United States v. Oakland Cannabis Buyers Cooperative*, No. 00-151, (2001); *U.S. v. Rosenthal*, U.S. District Court, Northern District of California, 2003; *Raich v. Ashcroft*, U.S. Supreme Court, 03-15481 (2003)
- **Religious Use of Drugs:** *Employment Division v. Smith*, 494 U.S. 872 (1990)
- **Search and Seizure:** *New Jersey v. T.L.O*, 469 U.S. 325 (1985); *United States v. Dunn*, 480 U.S. 294 (1987); *United States v. Sokolow*, 490 U.S. 1 (1989); *Wilson v. Arkansas*, 514 U.S. 927 (1995); *Maryland v. Pringle*, Docket No. 02-809 (2003)
- **Self-Incrimination (Fifth Amendment):** *Leary v. United States*, 395 U.S. 6 (1969)

- **Sentencing:** *Neal v. United States*, 516 U.S. 284 (1996)
- **Surveillance:** *California v. Ciraolo*, 476 U.S. 207 (1986); *Kyllo v. United States*, No. 99-8508 (2001)
- **Taxation:** *U.S. v. Doremus*, 249 U.S. 86 (1919); *United States v. Sanchez*, 340 U.S. 42 (1950)

U.S. V. DOREMUS, 249 U.S. 86 (1919)

Background

The defendant, a physician, was indicted for violating section 2 of the Harrison Narcotics Act by selling 500 tablets of heroin to a known addict, such sale not being part of any legitimate medical practice. The Harrison Act required that forms be filed with the government for any such nonmedical distribution of controlled drugs; other provisions required payment of an excise tax.

The District Court held the section unconstitutional "for the reason that it was not a revenue measure, and was an invasion of the police power reserved to the state . . . " The case came to the U.S. Supreme Court on appeal.

Legal Issues

The constitutional issue is whether Congress has stepped beyond its power to levy taxes in making numerous restrictions and requirements applicable to commerce in drugs. (The power of Congress to regulate interstate commerce might also be used to justify regulating drugs, but at the time, this power had not yet been interpreted very expansively by the Court.)

Decision

The opinion of a 5-4 majority written by Justice Rufus Day begins by noting that "this statute purports to be passed under the authority of the Constitution, article 1, 8, which gives the Congress power 'To lay and collect taxes, duties, imposts, and excises to pay the debts and provide for the common defence and general welfare of the United States; but all duties, imposts, and excises shall be uniform throughout the United States.'" The opinion goes on to note that the only requirement for taxes is "uniformity," and that "Subject to such limitation Congress may select the subjects of taxation, and may exercise the power conferred at its discretion.' The only exception would be if Congress legislated in an area that the Constitution reserves exclusively to the states.

Because of this broad taxing power, the only test that needed to be applied to the Harrison Act is whether "the provisions in question have any relationship to the raising of revenue." The Court concluded that the requirements for reporting such drug transactions might well help prevent evasion of the tax, and therefore they did have a relationship to the objective of raising revenue. The decision of the district court was therefore reversed.

The four dissenting justices argued that the district court was correct in its belief that the Harrison Act actually represented an attempt by Congress to exercise a "police power" reserved to the states, in the guise of a tax measure.

Impact

This decision established a firm constitutional basis for federal requirements being imposed on the distribution of drugs and upheld the Harrison Narcotic Act of 1914, which would be the main instrument for federal control of dangerous drugs until the passage of the Controlled Substances Act in 1970. (Congress would also use its taxation power to control drugs in the Marijuana Tax Act of 1937.)

JIN FUEY MOY V. UNITED STATES, 254 U.S. 189 (1920)

Background

The defendant, a physician, was convicted under the Harrison Narcotics Act of unlawfully selling morphine. The law allowed an exception for distribution of narcotic drugs "to a patient" by a registered physician "in the course of his professional practice only." The government charged that Jin Fuey Moy had sold morphine to persons who were not his patients, and thus the prescriptions were not legitimate. The defendant appealed his conviction, and the appeal was heard by the U.S. Supreme Court.

Legal Issues

The defendant on appeal argued that he should not have been charged with unlawful selling of the drug because he had written a proper prescription for it in each case. The act of prescribing a drug is fundamentally different from selling it. The government argued that the language about prescriptions essentially did not affect that about selling.

Decision

The Court ruled by a 7–2 vote to reject the appeal and affirm the defendant's conviction. It disagreed that the language about a prescription was "surplusage" and not relevant to the charge of selling. It agreed that *unless defendant could "sell," in a criminal sense, by issuing a prescription, the indictment is bad. If "selling" must be confined to a parting with one's own property there might be difficulty. But by § 332 of the Criminal Code, "Whoever directly commits any act constituting an offense defined in any law of the United States, or aids, abets, counsels, commands, induces, or procures its commission, is a principal."*

The Court found that the record showed that Dr. Moy was supplying morphine to users not for medical purposes but simply to keep them supplied with the drug. All prescriptions were filled at a single drugstore in Pittsburgh. In turn, "persons inquiring at the drug store for morphine were sent to the defendant for a prescription." This arrangement meant that the prescriptions were essentially a cover for an operation involved in selling morphine to addicts. They were not the result of legitimate medical practice.

Impact

This decision was part of the process of defining and narrowing the acceptable use of medical prescriptions for narcotics. In *Webb et al. v. United States* (1919), the Court had already agreed that a pharmacist (not a physician) was not allowed to write narcotic prescriptions under the Harrison Act and that, at any rate, prescriptions could not be used to justify supplying drugs to allow an addict to "continue his accustomed use." In *United States v. Behrman* (1922), the Court would rule that drugs could not be prescribed to an addict by a physician simply to maintain a patient's addiction. However, in *Linder v. United States* (1925), the Court did uphold the prescribing of a narcotic to a bona fide patient in reasonable amounts to ease withdrawal symptoms. In that decision the Court also differentiated from large drug transactions that were properly the concern of the government in enforcing tax laws such as the Harrison Act and prescriptions that fell within the boundaries of acceptable medical practice. Considerable weight was given to medical judgment.

UNITED STATES V. SANCHEZ, 340 U.S. 42 (1950)

Background

The United States brought an action against defendant Sanchez for recovery of taxes due under the Marijuana Tax Act of 1937. This law imposed a tax ranging from $1 to $24 per ounce on sales or transfers of marijuana. If this tax was not paid and the proper paperwork filed, then an additional levy of $100 per ounce tax came into effect. The district court dismissed the government's claim for the tax. The court of appeals, however, reversed that decision, and Sanchez appealed to the U.S. Supreme Court.

Legal Issues

Sanchez argued that the $100 levy in the Marijuana Tax Act was really a penalty, not a tax. He argued that the law's purpose was not primarily to raise revenue but rather to regulate the sale of marijuana.

Decision

The Court's decision began by noting the expressed legislative intent of Congress: "the development of a plan of taxation which will raise revenue and at the same time render extremely difficult the acquisition of marihuana by persons who desire it for illicit uses and, second, the development of an adequate means of publicizing dealings in marihuana in order to tax and control the traffic effectively."

The Court agreed that imposing such a high levy did have a regulatory effect in discouraging transferring the drug "outside accepted industrial and medical channels." However, the Court stated, "It is beyond serious question that a tax does not cease to be valid merely because it regulates, discourages, or even definitely deters the activities taxed. . . . The principle applies even though the revenue obtained is obviously negligible . . . or the revenue purpose of the tax may be secondary."

Impact

This decision affirmed the use of taxes as a form of regulation and indeed control of commerce in drugs that Congress feels are dangerous and should not be available outside restricted channels. The Court would not try to set a threshold where a tax becomes too punitive or no longer a reasonable source of revenue.

Further, the Court did not really question the law's other intended effect—discouraging sale of marijuana by putting sellers between the rock of a federal tax and the hard place of numerous state laws that criminalized the sale of marijuana. They simply observed that federal tax law did not make the transfer of marijuana a criminal act but did impose a civil penalty.

ROBINSON V. CALIFORNIA, 370 U.S. 660 (1962)

Background

The defendant was charged with violating a California law that made it a misdemeanor punishable by imprisonment for any person "to be addicted to the use of narcotics." The defendant had been arrested because a police officer had observed discolorations and scabs on the arms that in his experience resulted from the use of dirty hypodermic needles. The defendant had denied that he used narcotics and attributed the marks to a previous allergic condition. The judge indicated that the jury could convict if the defendant had the "status" of being a drug addict. The defendant was convicted and sentenced to 90 days in jail. He appealed but the superior court affirmed the conviction. The U.S. Supreme Court then took up the appeal.

Legal Issues

The central issue is whether the mere status of being a drug addict could be criminalized without any specific, current allegation of use of illegal drugs.

Decision

The Court's opinion, delivered by Justice Potter Stewart, began by acknowledging the "broad power of a State to regulate the narcotic drugs traffic within its borders." Citing previous cases the Court noted that "There can be no question of the authority of the State in the exercise of its police power to regulate the administration, sale, prescription and use of dangerous and habit-forming drugs. . . . The right to exercise this power is so manifest in the interest of the public health and welfare, that it is unnecessary to enter upon a discussion of it . . . "

The problem here, the Court found, is that the state court did not construe the law as requiring proof of actual use of narcotics on the part of the defendant. The jury had been instructed that it could convict if it simply found that the "status" of addict applied to the defendant—that he had the "chronic condition" of "being addicted to the use of narcotics." This meant that

> *This statute, therefore, is not one which punishes a person for the use of narcotics, for their purchase, sale or possession, or for antisocial or disorderly behavior resulting from their administration. It is not a law which even purports to provide or require medical treatment. Rather, we deal with a statute which makes the "status" of narcotic addiction a criminal offense, for which the offender may be prosecuted "at any time before he reforms." California has said that a person can be continuously guilty of this offense, whether or not he has ever used or possessed any narcotics within the State, and whether or not he has been guilty of any antisocial behavior there.*

The Court noted that it was unlikely in these relatively enlightened times that any state would attempt to make it a criminal offense for a person to be mentally ill or to be afflicted with a venereal disease.

> *A State might determine that the general health and welfare require that the victims of these and other human afflictions be dealt with by compulsory treatment, involving quarantine, confinement, or sequestration. But, in the*

light of contemporary human knowledge, a law which made a criminal offense of such a disease would doubtless be universally thought to be an infliction of cruel and unusual punishment in violation of the Eighth and Fourteenth Amendments.

The Court found that a law criminalizing the status of being a narcotics addict was likewise unconstitutional, amounting to "cruel and unusual punishment."

In his concurring opinion Justice William O. Douglas further emphasized that drug addiction was a disease, and the addict a sick person. An addict can be confined involuntarily for treatment but not as punishment merely for his or her addiction.

Impact

This decision is important in that it prevented the simple fact of drug addiction from making a person a criminal. It also acknowledged the growing belief that drug addiction was a disease appropriately treated by medical means. This does not mean that an addict who actually possesses drugs cannot be held criminally responsible for that possession, however.

SCHMERBER V. CALIFORNIA, 384 U.S. 757 (1966)

Background

The defendant, Schmerber, had been injured in a traffic accident. While he was being treated in the hospital, a police officer ordered a doctor to take a blood sample to be tested for alcohol. The results showed that the defendant had been legally drunk at the time of the accident. He was arrested. The test results were introduced as evidence in court; Schmerber was convicted and he appealed.

Legal Issues

The Fifth Amendment to the U.S. Constitution prohibits a person being compelled to incriminate him- or herself. The question is whether the forced blood test violates that prohibition. If so, the test results must be excluded from evidence.

Decision

In a unanimous decision written by Justice William J. Brennan, the Court ruled that the Fifth Amendment only prohibited forcing a person to give an incriminatory statement or testimony. Because the blood test evidence was neither "testimony nor evidence relating to some communicative act or writing by the petitioner, it was not inadmissible on privilege grounds."

Impact

This decision meant that involuntary alcohol blood tests (and by extension, blood or other tests for drugs) were not unconstitutional in themselves. Roadside and other testing of suspected drunk drivers would later become routine.

LEARY V. UNITED STATES, 395 U.S. 6 (1969)

Background

LSD "guru" Dr. Timothy Leary and his daughter were denied entry into Mexico and were driving back into Texas when their car was stopped and searched by U.S. Customs officials. They found some marijuana in the car and on the daughter's person. Leary was indicted under the 1937 Marijuana Tax Act.

At his trial Leary said he had acquired the marijuana in New York but said he did not know where it had been grown. The tax act requires registration of all marijuana "transfers" and payment of a small tax, or payment of a much higher tax for an unregistered transfer. The law also makes it illegal to transport marijuana without having complied with those provisions. Leary was convicted and appealed his case.

Legal Issues

Leary argued that the Marijuana Tax Act violated the Fifth Amendment to the Constitution because it compelled individuals to incriminate themselves. That is, complying with the tax law by paying the higher tax for an "unregistered" transfer would also provide evidence of illegal possession of marijuana.

The government's response was that because the law was administratively interpreted to allow payment of the tax only by someone whose possession of marijuana was legal, no self-incrimination occurred. Further, a provision of the U.S. Code (21 USC 176a) made it illegal to "transport or facilitate the transportation of illegally imported marijuana" and further said that it would be presumed that the possessor of marijuana knew it had been illegally imported unless he or she could furnish to the jury an adequate explanation of the drug's origin.

Decision

In an opinion delivered by Justice John Marshal Harlan, the Court ruled that the Marijuana Tax Act did violate the Fifth Amendment protection against self-incrimination:

Since the effect of the Act's terms were such that legal possessors of marihuana were virtually certain to be registrants or exempt from the order form requirement, compliance with the transfer tax provisions would have required petitioner as one not registered but obliged to obtain an order form unmistakably to identify himself as a member of a "selective group inherently suspect of criminal activities," and thus those provisions created a "real and appreciable" hazard of incrimination.

As for the presumption that the possessor of marijuana knows that it had been illegally imported, the Court noted that such a legal presumption must be "rational" and reasonably based on the underlying facts. The Court noted that even if most marijuana in the United States has been imported, "a significant amount may not have been imported at all." Because of this, the possessor cannot reasonably be assumed to know that his or her marijuana had been imported. Further, there was no evidence in the legislative record that it had been ascertained that the majority of possessors of marijuana would have learned that their marijuana had originally come from abroad.

The Court therefore concluded that Leary had been denied due process of law, reversed part of the conviction, and returned the rest to the lower court for further consideration. Leary was subsequently convicted of marijuana possession and sentenced to 10 years in prison.

Impact

This decision limited the ability to use the Marijuana Tax Act or the presumption of knowledge of importation to convict people for possession of marijuana. However, possession of marijuana is illegal under other federal and state laws.

NEW JERSEY V. T.L.O., 469 U.S. 325 (1985)

Background

A teacher in a New Jersey public school noticed that T.L.O. (a 14-year-old girl identified in court documents only by her initials) and another student were smoking in the school lavatory. The teacher took T.L.O. to the vice principal, to whom she denied that she had been smoking. The vice principal demanded to see T.L.O.'s purse, which proved to contain both a pack of cigarettes and a pack of cigarette paper, of a type commonly used by marijuana smokers. Continuing to search her purse, he found a pipe, some marijuana, and a list of students and two letters that suggested that T.L.O. was selling the drug.

The Law and Drug Abuse

Legal Issues

In juvenile court T.L.O.'s attorney argued that the search by the vice principal had violated the girl's privacy under the Fourth Amendment. However, while the court did agree that the Fourth Amendment did apply to searches in schools, the search of T.L.O.'s purse met the standard of being reasonable under the circumstances. The appeals court also upheld the search, but the New Jersey Supreme Court reversed the decision, calling the search unreasonable. The case then went to the U.S. Supreme Court.

Decision

The Supreme Court's decision, written by Justice Byron White, noted that while parents are not bound by the Fourth Amendment, teachers are not just substitutes for parents, but also representatives of the State. As such they are bound by the restrictions imposed by the Fourth Amendment.

The Court noted, however, that the need for "striking the balance between schoolchildren's legitimate expectations of privacy and the school's equally legitimate need to maintain an environment in which learning can take place requires some easing of the restrictions to which searches by public authorities are ordinarily subject." Thus school officials, unlike police, do not have to obtain a warrant before conducting a search, and do not have to meet the stricter standard of having "probable cause" to believe that there is criminal activity. Instead, they need only "have reasonable grounds for suspecting that the student has violated or is violating either the law or the rules of the school. And such a search will be permissible in its scope when the measures adopted are reasonably related to the objectives of the search, and not excessively intrusive in light of the nature of the infraction." Under this standard it was reasonable for the vice principal to look for smoking materials and, having found the cigarette papers, to look for marijuana.

Impact

This case reiterated that students do have some expectation of privacy, but schools have a wider scope than police officers, because of the need for schools to be a safe learning environment. In addition to a search where there is some particular suspicion (as in T.L.O.'s case), generalized searches such as the use of metal detectors to keep weapons out of schools have also been held to be permissible. For example, in *Zamora v. Pomeroy* (1981), the Supreme Court upheld a warrantless search of school lockers by trained police dogs, and in *State v. Moore* (1992) it was held to be "reasonable" for a school administrator to search a student's bookbag because a guidance counselor had been tipped off by another student that the student in question had drugs, and the suspected student had a previous instance of drug possession.

CALIFORNIA V. CIRAOLO, 476 U.S. 207 (1986)

Background

After receiving an anonymous tip that Ciraolo was growing marijuana, police in Santa Clara, California, tried to look into his backyard. If they could see the plants, they could get a search warrant. However, the fence around the yard was too high, so they hired a private plane and flew over the house at an altitude of 1,000 feet. Being able to confirm the presence of marijuana plants, they secured a search warrant and then arrested Ciraolo, who pled guilty to cultivation of marijuana. An appeals court, however, ruled that the fly-over constituted an illegal search and reversed Ciraolo's conviction. The case eventually reached the U.S. Supreme Court.

Legal Issues

The question is whether aerial observation of someone's property without a warrant is allowed by the Fourth Amendment. If so, is there some altitude at which it becomes unacceptable?

Decision

The majority decision by Justice Warren Burger ruled that the aerial search was acceptable. He noted that police officers have always been able to look into people's homes from the street. He also noted that the police observations were made "from public navigable airspace" and that "any member of the public flying in this airspace who glanced down could have seen everything that these officers observed."

The dissenting justices, led by Justice Lewis F. Powell, argued that the Court had previously, in *Katz v. United States* (1967), established a standard based on peoples' reasonable expectation of privacy, not on the technology or means used for surveillance. Allowing an observation just because someone else might have seen it seemed to the dissenters to be an unwarranted erosion of Fourth Amendment privacy rights.

Impact

This decision cleared the way for aerial surveillance as a tool in the war on drugs. In *Florida v. Riley* (1989), the Court said it was permissible for authorities to search for drugs from planes or helicopters at altitudes as low as 400 feet. Thus far the Supreme Court has not said there is a lower limit of altitude for flyovers.

UNITED STATES V. DUNN, 480 U.S. 294 (1987)

Background

Suspecting that residents were operating an illegal drug lab, DEA agents entered defendant Ronald Dale Dunn's property without a warrant. They went to a barn about 180 feet away from the ranch house, shined flashlights into its windows, and discovered the lab equipment inside. After conviction, the defendant appealed, arguing that the agents' actions had violated his Fourth Amendment right to privacy in his home. The appeal eventually reached the U.S. Supreme Court.

Legal Issues

What must be determined here is the extent of the area around a home (but within the owner's property) that is protected by the Fourth Amendment and thus requires a search warrant for entry.

Decision

The Court established four criteria for determining whether a given location was within a resident's "curtilage," or legally protected area: its proximity to a home, whether it is in an enclosure that includes the home, how the area is used, and whether there are fences or other barriers screening the area from passersby. The Court concluded that the barn was not within the curtilage because 1) no common fence surrounded both fence and barn, 2) the use of the barn (as a drug lab) was not related to the use of the house, and 3) the type of fence surrounding the barn was designed to keep animals in but not people out.

Impact

Many drug operations such as "meth labs" and marijuana growing areas are in barns, sheds, and so on that are not part of the residents' home. This decision made it easier for drug enforcers to obtain access to and search such places. (Open fields already did not have Fourth Amendment protection because they do not have a reasonable expectation of privacy, as found in *Oliver v. U.S.* (1984).)

Drug Abuse

NATIONAL TREASURY EMPLOYEES UNION V. VON RAAB, 489 U.S. 656 (1989)

Background

The U.S. Customs Service established a policy of requiring urine drug tests for employees who applied for positions involving the interdiction of drugs, carrying of firearms, or access to classified materials. The employees' union sought to overturn the testing requirement, arguing that it violated the workers' rights under the Fourth Amendment. The federal district court upheld the employees' position and ordered the Customs Service to stop requiring the drug tests. However, the court of appeals disagreed and overturned the lower court's order.

Legal Issues

This case pits the Customs Service's need to exclude from sensitive positions workers who might be compromised by their drug use against the employees' Fourth Amendment privacy rights.

Decision

The Court's 5-4 majority opinion, written by Justice Anthony M. Kennedy, noted that the Fourth Amendment ordinarily mandates that conducting a search of an individual requires a warrant based on a suspicion that the particular individual probably committed an illegal act. The Court noted that drug use was endemic in our society, and that a Customs agent who used drugs was in danger of being compromised (such as by being bribed or blackmailed). An agent with drug-impaired judgment who carried a firearm might misuse that firearm with tragic consequences. The Customs Service only tested employees who applied for sensitive positions, and set up their procedures so that the test was administered in privacy.

Therefore, the majority ruled that the Customs Service had a compelling interest that justified infringing on the applicants' expectation of privacy. However, in the case of employees applying only for jobs involving classified material, the Court decided that there was insufficient evidence on the record to make a determination.

In dissenting opinions Justices Thurgood Marshall and William Brennan argued that the majority had too quickly and easily dismissed the Fourth Amendment's requirement that there be probable cause before conducting a search. The Court's liberals were joined in dissent by conservative justice Antonin Scalia, who noted that the Customs Service had never presented actual evidence of actual or likely harm arising from failing to conduct the tests.

The Law and Drug Abuse

Impact

This case, which was decided along with *Skinner v. Railway Labor Executives Association*, showed that the Court believed that the dangers of drug use in certain sensitive or high-risk occupations justifies giving more latitude to an employer in requiring drug testing.

UNITED STATES V. SOKOLOW, 490 U.S. 1 (1989)

Background

Federal drug enforcement agents stopped defendant Sokolow at the Honolulu International Airport because they believed he showed a number of characteristics typical of drug smugglers. These included use of a false name, his paying for his ticket with cash, his having made a brief stop in Miami, his lack of checked luggage, and his apparent nervous demeanor. They arrested Sokolow and searched him without a warrant, finding 1,063 grams of cocaine.

Sokolow moved to suppress this evidence as being the fruit of an unlawful search. The district court denied his motion, but the court of appeals sided with Sokolow. It ruled that some more definite sign of "ongoing criminal activity" such as evasive movement was needed, not just characteristics that indicate some probability of criminality but were likely shared by many innocent persons as well. The case then went to the U.S. Supreme Court.

Legal Issues

The issue here is whether a warrantless search based on probabilistic rather than specific evidence violates the Fourth Amendment.

Decision

The Court's majority opinion, written by Chief Justice William H. Rehnquist, said that the lower court had applied too strict a standard. The Court ruled that the agents had a "reasonable suspicion that the respondent was engaged in wrongdoing." The decision referred to earlier cases such as *Terry v. Ohio* (1968), which ruled that police with a reasonable suspicion of criminal activity (not necessarily probable cause) could stop someone for questioning, and *United States v. Cortez* (1981) in saying that police could base their decision to search "on the totality of the circumstances." The characteristics observed by the agents in Sokolow's behavior had "probative value" even aside from the question of whether they amounted to use of a profile.

Drug Abuse

Impact

The principle of using "the totality of the circumstances" to determine whether the decision to search is reasonable may indicate judicial deference to the practical difficulties of making such decisions in a matter of moments (such as when a person will soon have left the area). In *United States v. Arvizu* (2002), the Court in a unanimous decision came to a similar conclusion involving a stop made by a border patrol officer.

At the same time, these decisions do not mean that use of a "smuggler profile" is automatically acceptable, especially if the profile is poorly designed, has a discriminatory effect, or is applied mechanically and without regard for individual circumstances.

EMPLOYMENT DIVISION V. SMITH, 494 U.S. 872 (1990)

Background

Two counselors working for a private drug rehabilitation agency were fired because they used peyote in ceremonies as members of the Native American Church. They applied for unemployment benefits, but the Employment Division of the State of Oregon turned them down because they considered the counselors' dismissal to have been the result of work-related misconduct. The ex-employees appealed their decision in state court all the way to the Oregon Supreme Court, which ruled in favor of the government. They then appealed to the U.S. Supreme Court, which vacated the Oregon Supreme Court's judgment and ordered the state courts to determine whether religious use of drugs was prohibited by state law.

The Oregon Supreme Court then decided that although the state law did forbid use of controlled drugs even for religious purposes, this prohibition violated the First Amendment to the U.S. Constitution, which guarantees the "free exercise of religion." Upon appeal by the government the case returned to the U.S. Supreme Court for a final decision.

Legal Issues

The issue is whether prohibiting the use of drugs associated with religious traditions violates the free exercise of religion guaranteed by the First Amendment.

Decision

The U.S. Supreme Court 6-3 majority opinion, written by Justice Antonin Scalia, began by noting the general principle that free exercise of religion does not mean that a person acting on religious beliefs has the right to do something that is forbidden to all by a valid law. Scalia observed that if there had to be exceptions for any law that somehow impinged on someone's religious beliefs, it "would open the prospect of constitutionally required exemptions from civil obligations of every conceivable kind." Some examples he gave include military service, compulsory vaccinations, and child neglect laws. In other words, religion may not be targeted for special burdens but also confers no special rights.

The dissenting view in this contentious issue sees the free exercise of religion in the First Amendment as something more substantial than just a guarantee of neutrality—something more akin perhaps to rights such as freedom of speech. In that view a law that infringed on a religious practice would have to be justified by a compelling state interest (such as, for example, public health in the case of vaccinations).

Impact

In response to this decision a number of religious groups lobbied Congress, which responded by passing the Religious Freedom Restoration Act (RFRA) in 1993. This law required that courts use a "compelling interest" standard to justify laws that infringe on the exercise of religion. However, the RFRA was in turn challenged and eventually overturned in *City of Boerne v. Flores* (1997), when the Supreme Court ruled that Congress had in essence gone too far in creating what amounted to a special status for religion and imposing it on the states.

VERONIA SCHOOL DISTRICT V. ACTON, 515 U.S. 646 (1995)

Background

A school district in Veronia, a small town in Oregon, believed that it faced a problem of rampant drug use in school, particularly among athletes. The district instituted a program of random drug tests for all middle and high school athletes. Any student who refused to take a test would be banned from participation in sports for two years. A student who tested positive would also be suspended from sports and would have to undergo drug counseling. School board officials hoped that by starting with the athletes and reducing their drug use, other students who looked to the athletes as role models would also avoid drug use.

James Acton, a seventh grader with excellent grades and no record of drug use, applied to try out for the football team. His parents, believing as a matter of principle that the testing requirement violated his and their privacy, refused to sign a consent form for the test. Instead, the family sued the school board. When their suit was dismissed by the federal district court, they appealed to the Ninth District Court of Appeals. That court reversed the district court's decision and declared that the school district's testing program violated the Fourth Amendment. The school district then appealed the case to the U.S. Supreme Court.

Legal Issues

The question was whether students for which the school had no particular suspicion of drug use could be forced to take random drug tests if they wanted to participate in athletics. Attorneys for the Acton family argued that the Fourth Amendment requires that before a search (or by extension, an intrusive test) could be conducted, there had to be an individualized, reasonable suspicion of drug use. The school district, however, argued that it had a compelling interest in reducing drug abuse as much as possible.

Decision

The Supreme Court's 6-3 majority opinion, written by Justice Antonin Scalia, squarely supported the school district's contentions. It noted that the testing was highly reliable and the tests provided some privacy. At any rate, schools had the right to exercise "a degree of supervision and control that could not be exercised over free adults." When this was coupled with the importance and reasonableness of the school's approach to reducing drug use by starting with the athletes, the testing was justified.

In dissent Justice Sandra Day O'Connor did not reject the whole idea of drug testing of students. However, she argued that there had to be some individualized suspicion. It might, for example, be reasonable to test students who had a sufficiently serious record of disciplinary infractions.

Impact

This decision emphasized both the Court's high regard for the seriousness of the drug problem and its general principle that minors, while having some privacy rights, did not have as high a threshold of Fourth Amendment protection as adults. While this case involved only athletes, the principle would, in *Board of Education v. Earls* (2002), later be extended to uphold drug tests for students who participated in any form of extracurricular activity.

WILSON V. ARKANSAS, 514 U.S. 927 (1995)

Background

On New Year's Eve, in 1992, the door to the home of Sharlene Wilson of Malvern, Arkansas, suddenly burst open. A police informant had previously made several narcotics purchases from Wilson. On this basis the Arkansas State Police had entered Wilson's home without knocking or otherwise announcing their presence. They found a gun, ammunition, and a large quantity of drugs. They also caught Wilson in the act of flushing drugs down the toilet. Wilson was arrested, convicted, and sentenced to 31 years in prison.

Wilson appealed to the Arkansas Supreme Court, claiming that both the common law and the requirements of the Fourth Amendment dictated that police "knock and announce" themselves before entering a home. The Arkansas high court disagreed, finding that the language of the Fourth Amendment about search and seizure did not require that such an announcement be made. Wilson appealed to the U.S. Supreme Court. Because there were conflicting federal decisions about whether knock-and-announce was required, the Supreme Court agreed to hear the appeal.

Legal Issues

There is strong support in the Anglo-American common law for the idea that "a man's home is his castle" and that the poorest person as well as the king has the right to confront the police and verify their identity and warrant before allowing them to enter. However, many drug enforcement officials have argued that a "no knock" warrant is necessary in cases where drug possession is suspected, because if the police announce themselves, the suspect might have time to destroy the evidence—such as by flushing it down the toilet. Further, a warning would give an armed suspect enough time to grab a gun and use it against the police.

Decision

The opinion, written by Justice Clarence Thomas and reflecting a unanimous 9-0 decision, ruled that there was a strong basis in history to conclude that the Fourth Amendment included the common law requirement that police "knock and announce." However, there were circumstances where a no-knock entry might be justified if necessary to prevent evidence from being destroyed, police being endangered, or a suspect escaping. However, the police would have to show, based on the facts of the case, that these considerations should apply. Therefore, the case was returned to the lower court for a factual determination of whether the entry was reasonable.

Impact

This decision made indiscriminate use of no-knock entries less likely, because police now know they will have to justify such an entry in court. However, in practice a knock followed almost immediately by a rapid entry can be made in time to prevent suspects from reacting effectively.

Police received further support for rapid entries with the Supreme Court's unanimous ruling in *United States v. Banks* (2003). Here the Court ruled that the police did not have to wait more than 15 or 20 seconds before breaking down the door to a suspected drug dealer's apartment. Even though the defendant said he did not hear the police because he was taking a shower, Justice David H. Souter's opinion emphasized that the rapid forced entry was reasonable in circumstances where it was likely the suspect would try to destroy evidence.

NEAL V. UNITED STATES, 516 U.S. 284 (1996)

Background

The defendant Meirl Gilbert Neal was sentenced by a federal district court for possession of LSD with intent to distribute. The LSD doses were in the form of pieces of blotting paper impregnated with a solution of the drug. Following guidelines from federal statute and from the U.S. Sentencing Commission, the amount of the drug in question was determined to include the weight of the paper, not just of the LSD itself. As a result, defendant Neal was given a mandatory minimum sentence of 10 years.

The sentencing guidelines were subsequently revised so they specified a fixed weight for each dose of "blotter acid." Under the new guidelines, a lower sentence would apply. Neal's appeal asked the court to apply the new rules and revise his sentence downward. However, the district court ruled that the statute specifying that the weight of the drug plus paper be used took precedence over the revised sentencing guidelines. Neal's appeal then came to the U.S. Supreme Court.

Legal Issues

The question to be decided was whether the statute or the sentencing guidelines should determine how the amount of drugs is calculated.

Decision

By a 6-3 decision written by Justice Anthony Kennedy, the Court ruled that the U.S. Code section 841(b)(1) takes precedence over the sentencing guidelines for determining the drug weight and thus the sentence.

Impact

This decision seems highly technical, but it speaks to a common criticism that the drug laws are often arbitrary and not rationally related to their stated objectives. One might presume that the number of doses of LSD, not the weight of the drug and paper, would be the most important factor in assessing the seriousness of the crime. The complexity involved in determining the severity of drug offenses and of their punishment gives great scope for plea bargaining and an advantage to defendants who can obtain a lawyer who is familiar with arcane nuances.

WHITNER V. SOUTH CAROLINA, 492 S.E. 2D 777 (S.C. 1997)

Background

The defendant, Cornelia Whitner, pled guilty to having caused her baby to be born with cocaine metabolites in its system by reason of her use of crack cocaine during the third trimester of pregnancy. Despite her being in drug counseling at the time and her child being apparently healthy, the circuit court judge sentenced Whitner to eight years in prison. Whitner subsequently appealed for post-conviction relief on grounds that her lawyer had not given her effective representation. In particular, she said the lawyer should have realized that she should not have taken a plea because the abuse of a fetus was not covered by the child neglect statute—because a fetus was not legally a child. (A plea is ineffective if the underlying offense is nonexistent.) Whitner's appeal was accepted, so the state in turn appealed to the Florida Supreme Court.

Legal Issues

The primary issue here is whether a fetus is a legal person such that damaging it through drug addiction is child neglect.

Decision

The Florida Supreme Court began by reviewing case law and concluding that a fetus is a person for purposes of the child neglect statute. (For example, it looked at situations where a fetus had been hurt or killed in an assault.)

Whitner had also argued that her right of reproductive privacy could not be "overly burdened" by regulations, according to the U.S. Supreme Court. She argued that avoiding a jail sentence by not carrying her pregnancy to term was an undue burden on her reproductive choice (that is, of continuing the pregnancy). The Florida Supreme Court ruled that the state had a compelling interest in the life and health of a fetus. The right of privacy does not protect drug use, so there is no reason why an additional penalty cannot be attached for drug use that affects a fetus.

Impact

This decision drew a rapid response from defenders of women's reproductive privacy, who saw it as part of a trend to undermine *Roe v. Wade* by acknowledging fetuses as persons and restricting women's rights correspondingly.

Many experts on drug abuse treatment agree that punitive sanctions against addicts for effects of their drug use on fetuses are unlikely to prevent their drug use. Instead, they may deter pregnant drug abusers from seeking drug treatment or proper prenatal or postnatal care.

FERGUSON V. CITY OF CHARLESTON, 532 U.S. 67 (2001)

Background

Having observed what they believed to be an alarming increase in incidence of cocaine use among their pregnant patients, the public hospital operated by the Medical University of South Carolina at Charleston instituted a program of identifying and testing pregnant patients suspected of drug use. Patients who tested positive were offered substance abuse counseling, but depending on their stage of pregnancy, could also be arrested on drug charges or for various offenses such as child neglect. However, no special prenatal or postnatal care was offered for patients testing positive.

Several patients who had tested positive and had been arrested on drug charges shortly after delivery of their babies filed a suit claiming that the drug testing had been illegal because it had been done without a warrant and without the patients' consent. The district court instructed the jurors to find for the patients unless the tests had been consensual. The jury found for the hospital, saying that the tests had indeed been consensual.

The patients then appealed. The Fourth Circuit Court of Appeals did not consider consent but said the tests were reasonable because of the "special need" to address drug abuse by pregnant women. (The Supreme Court had already established a "special needs" test allowing relaxation of Fourth Amendment protection in certain venues such as public schools, as found in *New Jersey v. T.L.O.* (1985).

Legal Issues

When the Supreme Court agreed to hear the case, it said it would address the following question: "Whether the 'special needs' exception to the Fourth Amendment's warrant and probable cause requirements was properly applied to a discretionary drug testing program that targeted hospital patients and was created and implemented primarily for law enforcement purposes by police and prosecutors?"

Decision

The Supreme Court's 6-3 decision ruled that such use of a nonconsensual test did violate the Fourth Amendment. However legitimate the hospital's interest might be in deterring drug use because of its dangers to the fetus, a nonconsensual search used for law enforcement purposes requires a warrant. The fact that the hospital was actively cooperating with police and turning over test results for prosecution meant that the tests served a law enforcement function. The Supreme Court returned the case to the lower court to determine whether the patients had given consent; the lower court then ruled the searches had not been consensual.

The key distinction here is that patients neither were informed about nor consented to the tests, and that the hospital, a state institution, was ultimately using the results for law enforcement purposes. In other cases such as *Chandler v. Miller* (1997), the persons (such as employment applicants) took the tests voluntarily and knew their purpose. Also, the results were not turned over to law enforcement authorities. As a result, in those cases the interest in minimizing the harm brought about by drug abuse could be balanced against the rights of the persons being tested.

Impact

This decision affirmed the general principle that the state (and law enforcement) cannot accomplish indirectly an objective that if pursued directly would have required a warrant. State hospital patients (who tended to be poor and/or minorities) would not have their status result in diminished privacy rights. (It should be noted that the patients lost a separate suit on a different contention—that because the majority of patients in that situation were black, the testing program amounted to illegal racial discrimination.)

KYLLO V. UNITED STATES, NO. 99-8508 (2001)

Background

When an agent of the U.S. Department of the Interior suspected that Danny Kyllo was growing marijuana in his home in Florence, Oregon, he and a colleague used a thermal imager to scan Kyllo's home at night. The imager detects infrared (heat) radiation, giving outlines of areas or sources that are relatively warmer than their surroundings. The scan showed that the roof over Kyllo's garage and one wall of his house were hotter than the rest of his home or neighboring homes. The agent concluded that Kyllo was using halide lights ("grow lights") to grow marijuana. Based on the imagery and other evidence such as excessive utility bills, the agent obtained a warrant, entered Kyllo's home, and discovered more than 100 growing marijuana plants. When Kyllo was indicted for growing marijuana, he moved to have the evidence seized from his home suppressed on grounds it was based on an unlawful search.

The Court of Appeals for the Ninth Circuit ordered the district court to determine whether the device used was "intrusive." The district court concluded that because the device showed only a crude image of heat sources and "did not show any people or activity within the walls of the structure," use of the device was not intrusive. The Court of Appeals eventually affirmed the district court's opinion, and Kyllo appealed to the U.S. Supreme Court.

Legal Issues

The issue here is whether use of a "passive" surveillance technology (a thermal imager in this case) is intrusive enough to amount to a "search" under the Fourth Amendment. The district court had concluded that the crude and limited nature of the imagery obtained meant that it did not show the kind of activities for which Kyllo had a legitimate expectation of privacy.

Decision

The Supreme Court disagreed in an order delivered by Justice Antonin Scalia. The opinion observed that the Court had previously declared that a mere visual inspection from outside is not a "search" in the meaning of the Fourth Amendment. However, in *Katz v. United States* (1967), the Court ruled that use of a listening device attached to the outside of a phone booth did violate the Fourth Amendment because the user of the booth has a reasonable expectation of privacy. Similarly, aerial surveillance of a house was not considered a "search" because a resident has no reasonable expectation that the outside and surroundings of a house will not be seen from the air.

Next, the Court considered how much "technological enhancement" of a search from the outside of a house might be permissible. For example, the court reserved the question of whether "enhanced aerial photography" might be too intrusive, especially when the area searched is directly outside or adjacent to a house (such as a backyard).

The Court concluded that

> *obtaining by sense-enhancing technology any information regarding the interior of the home that could not otherwise have been obtained without physical "intrusion into a constitutionally protected area" . . . constitutes a*

search—at least where the technology in question is not in general public use. This assures [sic] preservation of that degree of privacy against government that existed when the Fourth Amendment was adopted. On the basis of this criterion the information obtained by the thermal imager in this case was the product of a search.

The majority opinion rejected claims by the government that use of the imager was permissible because it only detected heat from "off the wall" and did not penetrate "through the wall." It also rejected the idea that the limited amount of information obtained should be a criterion for whether a search violates the Fourth Amendment. The case was therefore returned to the Circuit Court of Appeals to determine if evidence other than that obtained from imagery was sufficient to have obtained a warrant.

Impact

With the ever-growing capability of surveillance technology and the impetus of the war on drugs (and today, the war on terrorism), the Supreme Court seems in recent years to be trying to draw some sort of line to protect the privacy in and around a home that people expect and need. Such an effort would seem necessary if the Fourth Amendment is to continue to have meaning in the 21st century.

UNITED STATES V. OAKLAND CANNABIS BUYERS COOPERATIVE, NO. 00-151 (2001)

Background

In 1996, California voters enacted a ballot proposition called the Compassionate Use Act of 1996. This initiative exempted from California anti-marijuana laws a patient or his or her primary caregiver who cultivates or possesses marijuana for medical purposes, providing such use had been recommended by a physician.

A number of cannabis buyers' clubs or cooperatives were organized to carry out the distribution of marijuana to patients. In January 1998 the U.S. government sued one such group, the Oakland Cannabis Buyers Cooperative, seeking to enjoin them from growing or distributing the drug. They argued that regardless of state law, the federal Controlled Substances Act prohibited such activities. The federal district court granted a preliminary injunction against the cooperative.

Rather than appeal the case further, the cooperative simply continued to operate in defiance of the injunction. The federal government responded by asking the court for a contempt citation. The cooperative responded by arguing medical necessity—that is, that marijuana was the only way that certain seriously ill patients could relieve their severe pain, nausea, loss of appetite, and other symptoms. (Necessity is a rather rare legal defense that claims that a violation of the law is justified because it is the only way to prevent some greater harm from occurring.)

The district court acknowledged that some harm might come to the patients if they were deprived of marijuana, but that they were bound to follow federal law. It refused to modify the original injunction, and in addition, a contempt citation was issued, along with authorization to seize the cooperative's facilities.

Although the cooperative eventually agreed to follow the original injunction and stop operations, the issue of medical necessity remained "alive" in an appeal to modify the original injunction. The Ninth Circuit Court of Appeals reversed the lower court and acknowledged that the medical necessity defense was likely to be applicable to this case. It also argued that the district court had (and should have used) the discretion to consider the potential harm to the patients and the public interest, rather than being bound by the terms of the federal Controlled Substances Act. Following these instructions, the district court modified the injunction to allow distribution of marijuana in cases of medical necessity. The federal government petitioned to have the U.S. Supreme Court decide whether the medical necessity defense was applicable.

Legal Issues

The basic question is whether a medical necessity defense is applicable to the federal Controlled Substances Act. Put another way, do patients who believe (or whose doctors believe) that marijuana is necessary for their treatment have the right to receive the drug even though it is illegal under federal law?

Decision

The Supreme Court's opinion, delivered by Justice Clarence Thomas, seems to start by being dubious about the use of any necessity defense that is not actually allowed by the law in question. (The Controlled Substances Act allows use of marijuana only in federally authorized research projects and has no provision for medical necessity.) The Court noted that the creation of exceptions to legislation is properly a function of the legislature, not of the courts.

That general principle aside, the Court concluded that Congress had, through the language of the Controlled Substances Act, made a "determination of values." By defining marijuana as a Schedule 1 drug, it had clearly implied that it has no accepted medical value, even if it did not make an explicit determination of that fact.

The cooperative had also argued that even if the necessity defense is not allowed, the Controlled Substances Act exceeds the power of Congress under the constitution's Commerce Clause, and that enforcing this law against medical marijuana patients would deprive them of the right to due process and infringe on liberties guaranteed by the Fifth, Ninth, and Tenth Amendments. However, because these constitutional issues were not raised earlier in the appeals process, the Court declined to consider them.

In a concurring opinion Justices John Paul Stevens, David Souter, and Ruth Bader Ginsburg noted that the ruling had a narrow scope and disallowed the medical necessity defense only for producing and distributing marijuana, not for possession of the drug. According to this opinion, the opinion of the Court should not have gone beyond this to state that medical necessity was not available as a defense to possession of the drug by "a seriously ill patient for whom there is no alternative method of avoiding starvation or extraordinary suffering." That "is a difficult issue that is not presented here."

Impact

This ruling suggests that the necessity defense is unlikely to be permitted in federal court, even when bolstered by a local community's or even state's decision to support medical marijuana use. However, substantive constitutional challenges to federal drug regulations may be more successful. See the case of *Raich v. Ashcroft*, discussed later. In that case the question is whether the constitutional power of Congress to regulate interstate commerce properly extends to local, noncommercial medical use of marijuana.

MARYLAND V. PRINGLE, DOCKET NO. 02-809 (2003)

Background

Joseph Pringle, the defendant, and Donte Partlow, the owner and driver of the car, were pulled over by a Maryland police officer. When Partlow opened the glove compartment to get his car registration slip, the officer saw some money (which turned out to be $763). When the officer asked the men whether they were hiding drugs or weapons in the car, they denied it. He then searched the car with Partlow's permission and found cocaine hidden in the back seat armrest. Pringle and Partlow both denied that the drug was theirs, and they were arrested. Pringle later admitted possession of the cocaine. However, Pringle then argued in court that his statement should be suppressed because the police officer had arrested him without probable cause.

Drug Abuse

Legal Issues

Does finding contraband in a vehicle where no one admits to possession automatically provide probable cause to investigate or arrest all of the passengers?

Decision

Pringle's motion was denied by the trial and lower appeals courts, but the Maryland Court of Appeals ruled that the police officer did not have probable cause for the arrest because there was no reason to assume that Pringle, who was only a front seat passenger, had any knowledge of the drugs hidden in the back seat. The state appealed further, and the U.S. Supreme Court agreed to hear the case.

In a unanimous opinion the Court ruled that arresting all the occupants of the car met the requirement for probable cause. Writing for the Court, Chief Justice William H. Rehnquist declared that "we think it an entirely reasonable inference from these facts that any or all three of the occupants had knowledge of, and control over, the cocaine." Because of this the Court ruled that the officer had probable cause to believe Pringle, alone or with the others, was in possession of the cocaine.

Impact

Passengers in a vehicle or nonresidents in a dwelling are sometimes "scooped up" by police if they cannot determine who owns drugs or other contraband. This creates a conflict between the practical problem of the police not being able to immediately determine ownership and the individualized right of each person under the Fourth Amendment not to be arrested without probable cause to believe that he or she has engaged in criminal activity.

In its *Pringle* ruling the Supreme Court unanimously and definitely declared that under circumstances where contraband is found in a small space like a car, the fact that police cannot know for sure who knows about or has control of the illegal object does not in itself mean there is no probable cause to arrest any or all individuals. This can be read as a decision in favor of practical necessity.

Traffic stops have led to other thorny legal issues. In December 2002, the Illinois Supreme Court ruled that using drug-sniffing dogs during traffic stops was unconstitutional unless officers already had specific reasons to suspect drug involvement. In April 2004, the U.S. Supreme Court agreed to review the case.

The Law and Drug Abuse

RAICH V. ASHCROFT, 03-15481 (2003)

Background

Two California women suffering from serious health problems sued U.S. Attorney General John Ashcroft in order to try to win an injunction barring the federal government from prosecuting them for growing marijuana within the state for their own medical use. (Medical use of marijuana is legal under California law.) In district court a federal judge threw out the suit, saying that the federal Controlled Substances Act (CSA) had already determined the medical status of marijuana and precluded his issuing any such order. The women then appealed to the Court of Appeals for the Ninth Circuit.

Legal Issues

Besides medical necessity, the appeal to the circuit court also argued that because the women were growing marijuana within the state (and were thus not involved in interstate commerce), the federal Controlled Substances Act should not apply to their activities.

Decision

The Circuit Court panel, by a 2-1 vote, ruled that the Controlled Substances Act was intended to apply to interstate commercial trafficking in illicit drugs. It did not apply to drugs produced entirely within a state for personal medical purposes. The panel ordered the case returned to the district court for final determination, with a preliminary injunction issued barring enforcement of the CSA. Meanwhile, federal prosecutors appealed to a full panel of the Ninth Circuit.

Impact

This decision potentially opens up a new front in the legal battle for medical marijuana. The U.S. Supreme Court has in recent years more narrowly interpreted the power of Congress to regulate interstate commerce (which is the constitutional basis for the CSA), so it might be receptive to upholding the Ninth Circuit. The latter's distinction between commercial and personal medical use of marijuana is also interesting. Together, these arguments might carve out a "safe haven" from federal prosecution for states that have passed medical marijuana laws.

Ideological contradictions make the outcome especially difficult to predict. Conservative justices might generally be expected to uphold federal drug laws, but they have also supported narrowing the federal power to regulate interstate commerce. Liberals, on the other hand, have generally supported a broad interpretation of federal regulatory power in order to carry out social and economic objectives, but they are also more likely to be sympathetic to the plight of medical marijuana users.

On the other hand, the Supreme Court might more narrowly follow the thread of its decision in *United States v. Oakland Cannabis Buyers Cooperative* and uphold the enforcement of the CSA.

RAYTHEON COMPANY V. HERNANDEZ, DOCKET NUMBER 02-749 (2003)

Background

In 1991, Joel Hernandez was an employee of Hughes Missile Systems, which was later bought by Raytheon Company. When he tested positive for cocaine in a drug test, he was given the choice of resigning or being fired. Hernandez resigned, but after undergoing drug rehabilitation, he reapplied with the company in 1994. However, his application was denied.

Hernandez sued the company, claiming that the Americans with Disabilities Act (ADA) did not allow discrimination against rehabilitated alcohol or substance abusers. The district court dismissed the suit, but it was then appealed to the Ninth Circuit Court of Appeals.

Legal Issues

The Americans with Disabilities Act is intended to ensure that disabled people are provided equal access to employment and other facilities, and to prevent discrimination against the disabled. The question is whether the plaintiff's past drug addiction constituted a disability, making it unlawful to discriminate against him. Although the ADA specifically considers recovered or recovering substance users to be disabled under the law, Raytheon argued that its blanket policy of not rehiring anyone who broke any company rule was not discriminatory since it applied to all employees, disabled or not.

Decision

The Ninth Circuit ruled that Raytheon's blanket policy did not shield it from the obligation not to discriminate against former drug abusers. The company was obligated to take Hernandez's "protected status" (as disabled) into account and could not deliberately avoid learning about that status. The court ruled that the case should go to trial to determine whether Hernandez had been discriminated against. Raytheon appealed to the U.S. Supreme Court.

The Supreme Court, in an opinion written by Justice Clarence Thomas, overturned the Ninth Circuit ruling. The Court said that because Raytheon's policy applied to anyone who had been dismissed for breaking a company rule, not just cases of drug abuse, it could not be assumed that the policy was discriminatory on its face. For Hernandez to prevail, there would have to have been a showing that Raytheon had refused to rehire him specifically because of his disability.

Impact

Employers welcomed the Supreme Court's ruling because it suggested that as long as their policies did not actively discriminate against recovering drug abusers, they were not vulnerable to a discrimination lawsuit under the ADA. Employee advocates, however, point to the difficulty of proving intent to discriminate and are concerned that more employment doors might now be closed against addicts who have been rehabilitated and are trying to resume a productive career.

U.S. V. ROSENTHAL, 266 F. SUPP. 2D 1068, N.D. CAL. (2003)

Background

Medical marijuana activist and writer Ed Rosenthal had been authorized to distribute marijuana to persons claiming medical need for the drug. He operated one of several "marijuana clubs" that provided marijuana to patients. California voters had earlier passed a ballot proposition authorizing the distribution of marijuana to persons suffering from glaucoma, AIDS, cancer, and other diseases whose doctors documented their need for the drug. The city of Oakland, California, had also authorized Rosenthal to distribute marijuana.

The federal government, however, has continued to maintain that marijuana (except in Marinol, a pill form) has no legitimate medical use, and that federal laws would continue to be enforced. Indeed, in recent years federal agents seem to have stepped up their campaign against marijuana "clubs" and cooperatives. They arrested Rosenthal and charged him with cultivating and distributing marijuana.

In his trial in district court, Rosenthal wanted to explain to jurors that he was acting with the blessing of California voters and of the city of Oakland, and that there was a medical necessity for patients to receive marijuana. However, federal district judge Charles Breyer refused to allow any such testimony to be presented at trial, deeming it irrelevant to a federal case.

Legal Issues

There are several large issues that impinge on this case, even though the rules of the legal process ensured that they would not be resolved at the level of a jury trial. First, there is the question of whether a patient has a right to obtain a drug that he or she believes is essential to maintaining health and quality of life. It has been widely reported that marijuana, for example, controls nausea in chemotherapy patients and improves appetite in AIDS patients. However, there is a lack of rigorous scientific testing of these claims, in part because the government has been reluctant to authorize such research. Second, does a state have the right to make its own decision about the legality of a drug, based on its perception of medical necessity? Finally, does the jury have the right to hear the arguments about state authorization and medical necessity?

Decision

The jury voted to convict Rosenthal. However, after jurors learned about the information they had been denied, many of them expressed outrage and said that they would have decided differently if they had known about the state authorization. Judge Breyer decided not to give Rosenthal any jail time. Federal prosecutors objected to what they saw as too lenient a sentence and have appealed.

Impact

This decision probably seems to have had more of a political impact than a legal one. It has energized medical marijuana advocates as well as supporters of jury nullification—the idea that jurors should be able to decide whether a law is being fairly applied in a particular situation. Barring the acknowledgement of a medical necessity defense, the well-established principle that federal laws take precedence when in conflict with state laws means that the medical marijuana dispute would have to be ultimately resolved on the national level.

CHAPTER 3

CHRONOLOGY

circa 5000 B.C.

- Early Sumerian tablets refer to a substance that is probably opium.

circa 3500 B.C.

- An Egyptian papyrus describes the process of brewing beer.

circa 300 B.C.

- Theophrastus, a Greek philosopher and naturalist, writes about the use of poppy juice, a form of opium.

1493

- Christopher Columbus returns to Spain from the New World. Among the wonders he brings back is tobacco.

1525

- The alchemical philosopher and physician Paracelsus writes about the use of tincture of opium as a medicine.

1551

- A council of Spanish missionaries in Peru condemns the native practice of chewing coca leaves.

1561

- Jean Nicot introduces tobacco to the court of Catherine de' Medici in France, touting its alleged medicinal properties. The plant's active stimulant ingredient, nicotine, will eventually be named for him.

Drug Abuse

1604

■ King James I of England expresses a rather different opinion in his *Counterblast to Tobacco*, which denies the substance has any real medicinal value. The king also tries to reduce the growing popularity of smoking by taxing tobacco, a practice that is soon taken up by other European nations.

1611

■ Virginia colonists begin to plant hemp (marijuana). Its main use, however, will be making rope for ships.

1613

■ The Virginia colonists send the first shipment of tobacco back to England.

1620

■ The Catholic Inquisition condemns peyote, a hallucinogenic substance used by some Native Americans, for creating "fantasies [that] suggest intervention by the devil."

1642

■ Pope Urban VIII issues an encyclical condemning the use of tobacco.

1729

■ In China, the Manchu dynasty takes a drastic approach to curbing the use of opium: Those who deal opium are to be strangled.

1736

■ The British Gin Act taxes the cheap, potent spirit in an attempt to reduce its widespread use among the poor. The law has little effect.

1776

■ Pioneering British chemist Joseph Priestley discovers nitrous oxide—laughing gas. In coming decades, parties where the intoxicating gas is inhaled will become popular among medical students and others.

1785

■ In his "Inquiry into the Effects of Ardent Spirits on the Human Body and Mind," pioneer American physician Benjamin Rush refers to the intemperate use of alcohol as "a disease." He estimates that at least 4,000 people die annually from alcohol abuse—this is out of a total population of approximately 6 million.

1790

- Benjamin Rush and other members of the Philadelphia College of Physicians urge Congress to tax alcoholic spirits heavily enough to "restrain their intemperate use."

1792

- An opium-induced reverie inspires British poet Samuel Taylor Coleridge to write his poem "Kubla Khan."

1800

- Returning from its Egyptian campaign, Napoleon's army introduces cannabis (hashish and marijuana) into French society.

1805

- A German pharmacist's assistant discovers how to isolate morphine from opium. The resulting narcotic is about 10 times more potent.

1822

- British essayist Thomas De Quincey publishes *Confessions of an Opium Eater*. It is one of the first accounts of the process of addiction.

1839 to 1842

- In the first Opium War, Britain forces China to continue to allow British companies to sell the highly profitable drug to millions of addicts in Asia. In addition to the British legal monopoly, there soon develops a flourishing illegal trade controlled by powerful criminal groups.

1852

- Susan B. Anthony founds the New York Women's State Temperance Society. Throughout the rest of the century there will be a close connection between temperance (antialcohol), feminist, and women's suffrage movements.

1856 to 1860

- In the second Opium War, Britain and France force additional concessions from China for distributing the drug.

Drug Abuse

1859

- An Italian doctor named Paolo Mantegazza had been living in Peru, where he became acquainted with the "restorative" properties of coca leaves. His book helps popularize the substance cocaine, which finds its way into popular teas, wines, and chewing gum.

1869

- The Prohibition Party is founded. It declares that its objective is to continue the spirit of abolition by freeing the millions of "involuntary slaves" to alcohol.

1874

- The Women's Christian Temperance Union is founded in Cleveland, Ohio.

1880s

- John Pemberton of Atlanta, Georgia, markets Coca-Cola as an alternative to alcohol, which had been banned in the city. The new drink includes extracts of the coca leaf and kola nuts.

1884

- Sigmund Freud treats his own depression with cocaine and reports that it produces "exhilaration and lasting euphoria." He says he cannot detect any deleterious effects.
- New York State passes a law requiring public schools to teach students about the evils of alcohol abuse. By the end of the century, the rest of the states will have followed suit.

1894

- A voluminous report from the Indian Hemp Commission concludes that hemp (marijuana), when used moderately, does not lead to excess and causes no more injury than moderate use of alcohol.

1898

- The Bayer Company begins marketing a powerful new cough suppressant and painkiller under the trade name Heroin. The powerful opium derivative had been discovered in 1874.

Chronology

1900

- An article in the *Journal of the American Medical Association* entitled "The Cocaine Habit" warns of growing abuse of the drug among poor people, especially blacks. A racist stereotype of "cocaine-crazed Negroes" begins to develop.

1903

- Coca-Cola replaces coca extract (cocaine) with caffeine.

1906

- The landmark federal Pure Food and Drug Act requires that medicines list the nature and amounts of any narcotics they contain. Many medical organizations and temperance groups pressure drug companies to replace narcotics with safer alternatives.

1909

- The International Opium Commission meets to discuss ways to stop drug trafficking. Two years later a treaty signed at The Hague requires signatories to limit the use of narcotics to specific medical purposes. Meanwhile, the United States bans the importation of smoking opium.

1912

- The first in a series of conventions on the international control of opium traffic is held at The Hague, Netherlands.

1914

- The federal Harrison Narcotics Act outlaws the sale of narcotics without a prescription. In addition to narcotics, the law also covers some stimulants such as cocaine.

1919

- Mescaline, a powerful hallucinogen, is isolated from the peyote cactus.
- Methamphetamine, a powerful stimulant, is synthesized.

1920

- The Volstead Act, prohibiting use of alcohol, takes effect. It had been authorized by ratification of the Eighteenth Amendment to the U.S. Constitution the previous year.

Drug Abuse

1924

- The manufacture of heroin in the United States is prohibited.

1925

- In *Linder v. U.S.*, the Supreme Court rules that the Harrison Narcotics Act notwithstanding, physicians may use controlled doses of narcotics to help patients through withdrawal from addiction.

1929

- In an article entitled "Waging the War Upon Narcotics," the *New York Times* first uses a metaphor that will later become popular in describing the struggle against drug abuse.

1930

- President Herbert Hoover creates the Federal Bureau of Narcotics, headed by former Prohibition agent Harry Anslinger. Anslinger focuses much of his efforts on combating the growing popularity of marijuana among Mexican immigrants and jazz aficionados.

1932

- The amphetamine Benzedrine first appears on the market in the form of an inhaler for treating nasal congestion. The inhalers are soon abused. Amphetamine pills will soon appear as "pep pills" and for treating obesity.
- Congress passes the Uniform Narcotic Act. It requires that drug prescriptions and sales be recorded using standard forms.

1933

- Alcohol Prohibition is repealed by ratification of the Twenty-first Amendment to the U.S. Constitution. The focus of federal agencies shifts increasingly to combating illicit drug use.

1935

- Alcoholics Anonymous (AA) is founded. Although the group will have its critics, its quasi–religious group self-help model will prove effective for many people.
- The American Medical Association (AMA) passes a resolution declaring that "alcoholics are valid patients."

Chronology

1937

- The federal Marijuana Tax Act is passed. Ostensibly a tax, in reality the law forces dealers to choose between not paying the tax and revealing their illegal activity.

1938

- The Food, Drug, and Cosmetic Act gives the Food and Drug Administration (FDA) the authority to declare which drugs could only be used under prescription. Amphetamines and barbiturates are soon put in this category.

1941 to 1945

- During World War II illicit drug use declines. However, soldiers are offered free cigarettes, leading to a great increase in tobacco addiction. Amphetamines are also distributed to soldiers and pilots to prolong their effectiveness under extreme combat conditions.

1943

- A Swiss researcher, Albert Hoffman, accidentally takes some LSD. The drug, which had been first synthesized in 1938, sends him on a vivid hallucinogenic "trip." Some psychologists find the drug intriguing and begin to study its effects.

1945

- The newly founded United Nations establishes a Commission on Narcotic Drugs.

1948

- The United Nations turns over responsibility for its antidrug efforts to the World Health Organization.

1950

- Barbiturate abuse is on the rise. In addition, some U.S. soldiers in Korea concoct "speedballs," a mixture of amphetamines and heroin.
- The American Medical Association publishes the first report linking tobacco with cancer. However, the impact of this and subsequent studies on public attitudes toward smoking will be only gradual.

Drug Abuse

1951

- Mandatory federal sentences for drug abuse and trafficking are imposed by the Boggs Act.

1958

- Synanon, a therapeutic community for treating drug addiction, is founded by Charles Dederich. A number of similar groups follow.
- A joint commission of the American Bar Association and American Medical Association recommends that sentences for drug use be more lenient and that more treatment options be offered.

1959

- The drug PCP (phencyclidine) is developed and approved as an anesthetic for use in animals only. It later becomes a drug of abuse, often producing violent outbursts in users.

1960

- The Federal Trade Commission (FTC) begins to take more of an interest in cigarette advertising. It rules that tobacco companies cannot claim that filtered cigarettes are safer for health.

1963

- The President's Commission on Narcotics and Drug Abuse recommends greater use of drug treatment instead of jail for narcotics offenders.

1964

- A report by U.S. surgeon general Luther Terry definitively links smoking with cancer and other serious diseases.
- The use of methadone maintenance for heroin addicts is developed by Rockefeller University researchers Vincent Dole and Marie Nyswander.

1965

- After a legislative battle between anti-smoking activists and tobacco companies, Congress requires that a warning label be placed on cigarette packs. The first, tepid version of the warning says that smoking "may be hazardous" to health.

Chronology

1966

- In *Schmerber v. California*, the U.S. Supreme Court upholds blood alcohol tests for suspected drunken drivers, provided authorities have clear indications that evidence will be found.

1967

- The United States signs the United Nations Single Convention on Narcotic Drugs.

1968

- Responsibility for federal enforcement of drug laws is shifted from the FDA to the Department of Justice.
- As U.S. involvement in Vietnam increases, a growing number of GIs are exposed to the temptations of cheap marijuana and heroin. On their return, some veterans help swell the growing numbers of street drug addicts.
- In his campaign for the presidency, Richard Nixon calls for a "war on drugs." Soon after his election he forms the President's National Commission on Marijuana and Drug Abuse.

1969

- *September 21:* The U.S. Customs Department launches Operation Intercept. For a period of two weeks every vehicle crossing the border between the United States and Mexico is searched. Traffic bogs down for miles, and businesses on both sides of the border are severely impacted. The operation is stopped, but Mexico agrees to more aggressively pursue marijuana traffickers.

1970

- The organization NORML (National Organization for Reform of Marijuana Laws) is founded by Keith Stroup. Its objective is to decriminalize the use of the drug.
- Congress passes the Controlled Substances Act. Among other things, the law establishes "schedules" for classifying drugs according to their dangerousness. Penalties for marijuana use are reduced, but the law also allows for "no knock" warrants to prevent suspects from disposing of incriminating evidence.
- Required cigarette warning labels are changed to read that smoking "is dangerous" to health. Cigarette ads disappear from television and radio after tobacco companies are required to finance antismoking commercials if they continue to advertise.

Drug Abuse

1971

- **May:** Congressmen Robert Steele (R-CT) and Morgan Murphy (D-IL) release a report that warns that many U.S. servicemen in Vietnam are using heroin.
- **June 17:** President Nixon declares that drugs are "public enemy number one in the United States." He establishes a Special Action Office for Drug Abuse Prevention. For the first time more federal funds are being spent on prevention and treatment than on drug law enforcement.

1972

- The "French Connection" is broken by a series of raids. It had involved a drug trafficking ring in Marseilles, France, working with Corsican gangsters and the Mafia in the United States.
- **January:** The Nixon administration steps up the enforcement side of the drug effort by establishing the Office of Drug Abuse Law Enforcement. Its purpose is to establish joint federal and local task forces to fight street-level drug crime.

1973

- Eradication of opium poppies in Turkey appears to be successful, but production shifts to Southeast Asia.
- Researchers discover that special receptors in the brain are responsible for the effects of opiates. This discovery paves the way for research into ways to block these effects.
- Researchers discover fetal alcohol syndrome, a constellation of problems such as low birth weight and developmental disabilities associated with infants whose mothers had drunk excessively during pregnancy.
- Two thirds of the respondents in a nationwide Gallup poll "support the proposal of New York Governor Nelson Rockefeller that all sellers of hard drugs be given life imprisonment without possibility of parole."
- **July:** The Drug Enforcement Administration (DEA) is established. It consolidates existing federal drug agencies and works closely with U.S. Customs and the FBI. It soon becomes known for aggressive "no knock" drug raids that critics argue violate Fourth Amendment privacy rights.

1974

- The National Institute on Drug Abuse (NIDA) becomes the research arm of the federal antidrug effort.

Chronology

1975

- *September:* Under President Gerald Ford the Domestic Council Drug Abuse Task Force issues a report that recommends that enforcement be concentrated on the most dangerous drugs such as heroin, amphetamines, and barbiturates, while marijuana should be given a low priority.
- *November 25:* After Colombian police seize an unprecedented 600 kilos of cocaine at the Cali airport, Drug traffickers assert their power by killing 40 people in the city in one weekend.

1976

- Campaigning for the presidency, Jimmy Carter calls for removing federal penalties for possession of up to one ounce of marijuana.
- *August:* The first parent's antidrug organization, Families in Action, is founded.

1977

- *May:* A *Newsweek* story about the use of cocaine in chic society leads to charges that the publication is glamorizing use of the drug and minimizing its dangers.

1978

- Congress amends the Comprehensive Drug Abuse Prevention and Control Act to allow law enforcement officials to seize all money or other things of value related to illegal drug transactions.

1979

- Drug kingpin Carlos Lehder establishes a refueling point in the Bahamas to allow small planes to transport cocaine between Colombia and the United States.
- *July 11:* The extent of reach of the Colombian cartels into the United States is seen in a shootout between rival traffickers in Dadeland Mall in Miami.

1980s

- The federal antidrug budget rises from $1.5 billion in 1981 to $4.2 billion in 1989.

1981

- In Colombia the Ochoa family, Pablo Escobar, Carlos Lehder, and Gonzalo Rodríguez Gacha form what becomes known as the Medellín cartel. In response to the growing power of the Medellín drug cartel, the United States and the Colombian government sign an extradition treaty. The cartels will use violence to try to intimidate the government into not extraditing traffickers.

- At President Ronald Reagan's urging, Congress amends the 1878 Posse Comitatus Act to allow the military to provide surveillance planes and ships for drug interdiction purposes.
- Crack, an inexpensive but powerfully addictive form of smokable cocaine, becomes increasingly popular. Meanwhile, heroin becomes less popular as fear of overdoses and AIDS make needle use seem much more risky.

1982

- Colombian drug lord Pablo Escobar and Panamanian strongman General Manuel Noriega agree to allow Escobar to ship cocaine through Panama in exchange for a payment of $100,000 per shipment.
- *January 28:* Responding to the growing drug activity and violence in Miami, the Reagan administration creates a special interagency task force headed by future president George Herbert Walker Bush.
- *March:* Pablo Escobar's search for political legitimacy and cover leads him to build low-income housing and give money to Medellín slum dwellers. Escobar is elected to the Colombian Congress but will be driven out of office in 1983 by Colombia's Minister of Justice, Rodrigo Lara Bonilla.
- *March 9:* The seizure of a record 3,906 pounds of cocaine from a hangar at Miami International Airport leads U.S. drug enforcers to the realization that the organization of Colombian drug traffickers is much larger and more elaborate than they had realized. Subsequent raids against drug activity in Florida and the Caribbean will result in drug traffic increasingly moving to the U.S.-Mexico border.

1984

- The Crime Control Act of 1984 drastically increases federal penalties for drug trafficking and use.
- Nancy Reagan popularizes the "just say no!" slogan, urging children to avoid drugs.
- *March 10:* Colombia authorities and U.S. Drug Enforcement Administration agents discover a huge drug manufacturing operation deep in the Colombian jungle. They destroy 14 laboratory complexes containing a total of 13.8 metric tons of cocaine and 11,800 drums of chemicals (such as ether), plus seven airplanes. The total value of the assets, which belong to the Medellín cartel, is estimated at $1.2 billion or more.

- *April 30:* Colombian Minister of Justice Rodrigo Lara Bonilla, who had long crusaded against the Medellín cartel, is assassinated. In response Colombian president Belisario Betancur, who had previously opposed extradition of Colombian drug traffickers, announces he will extradite top members of the cartel. The Ochoa family, Pablo Escobar, and Rodríguez Gacha flee to Panama but soon return and reestablish their power.
- *July 17:* DEA informant Barry Seal, who had infiltrated the Medellín cartel's operations in Panama, is featured in a story leaked to the *Washington Times* by Col. Oliver North, in order to implicate the Nicaraguan Sandinista leftists in the drug trade. Seal will be assassinated in 1986 by gunmen working for the Medellín cartel.
- *November 6:* In the so-called "Bust of the Century," DEA agents and Mexican officials seize a large marijuana plantation and processing center in the Chihuahua desert. Owned by Rafael Caro Quintero, the complex has about 7,000 workers and stored as much as 10,000 tons of marijuana worth up to $2.5 billion.
- *November 15:* Medellín cartel leader Jorge Ochoa is arrested in Spain. He is extradited to Colombia rather than the United States and will serve only a one-month sentence.

1985

- MDMA, popularly known as ecstasy, is banned by the federal government.
- A synthetic nonsmoked form of marijuana, Marinol, is approved as an antinausea drug.
- San Francisco enacts a regulation banning workplace drug tests unless an employer has a reasonable suspicion of drug use that poses a "clear and present danger."
- *January 15:* Colombia extradites four drug traffickers to the United States. The Medellín cartel responds by creating a "hit list" of U.S. diplomats, businesspersons, and journalists.
- *February 15:* After U.S. DEA agent Enrique Camarena is kidnapped and murdered by Mexican drug traffickers and there is a cover-up by corrupt Mexican officials, the United States cracks down on border traffic.
- *July 23:* Colombian Superior Court judge Talio Manuel Castro Gil, who had indicted Pablo Escobar for the murder of Lara Bonilla, is assassinated. Drug traffickers step up their campaign to harass and intimidate the Colombian judiciary.
- *November:* A *New York Times* cover story highlights the growing use of inexpensive, powerful crack cocaine in inner city neighborhoods.
- *November 6:* A guerrilla group affiliated with the Medellín cartel attacks the Colombian Palace of Justice. At least 95 people are killed, including

11 Supreme Court justices. Judicial records, including pending extradition requests, are destroyed in a fire.

1986

- The growing development of "designer drugs" is addressed by the Controlled Substances Analogue Reinforcement Act, which puts similar synthetic forms of controlled drugs on the highest control level (Schedule 1).
- A report from the U.S. surgeon general declares that secondhand smoke also causes lung cancer.
- *June 19:* College basketball star Len Bias dies from a cocaine overdose. The death of an apparently healthy athlete highlights the potential dangers of the drug.
- *October 27:* President Reagan signs the Anti-Drug Abuse Act of 1986. The bill appropriates $1.7 billion, including $97 million for prisons, $200 million for drug education, and $241 million for drug treatment. However, the law also imposes mandatory minimum sentences for possession of specified amounts of drugs. This policy will be criticized for its disproportionate effect on inner city blacks arrested for crack cocaine possession.
- *November 18:* A federal grand jury in Miami indicts the Medellín cartel leaders (including the Ochoa family, Escobar, Lehder, and Gacha) under the RICO (Racketeer-Influenced and Corrupt Organizations) statute.
- *December 17:* The assassination of Colombian newspaper editor Guillermo Cano Isaza leads to widespread outrage and a government crackdown on traffickers.

1987

- Supreme Court nominee Douglas Ginzburg's revelation of past marijuana use dooms his chances of getting on the Court.
- *February 3:* Medellín kingpin Carlos Lehder is captured by Colombian police and extradited to the United States. The following year he will be sentenced to life in prison without parole.
- *June 25:* The Colombian Supreme Court annuls the country's extradition treaty with the United States by a vote of 13-12. Many view this as a victory for the cartels, which had killed or threatened justices for several years.
- *November 21:* The indictment of Medellín cartel leader Jorge Ochoa leads to the emergence of "the Extraditables," a narcoterrorist group that threatens to kill Colombian leaders if Ochoa is extradited. Ochoa is not extradited.

1988

- The Anti-Drug Abuse Act of 1988 is signed into law.

Chronology

- *February 5:* Panamanian general Manuel Noriega is indicted by a federal grand jury in Miami.

1989

- President George Herbert Walker Bush appoints William Bennett to head the new Office of National Drug Control Policy. He becomes the first "drug czar." A cultural conservative, Bennett will emphasize efforts to make drug abuse socially unacceptable.
- The U.S. Supreme Court upholds mandatory drug testing for U.S. Customs Service employees in sensitive positions.
- *April 8:* Mexican drug lord Miguel Angel Felix Gallardo is arrested in Guadalajara and charged with involvement in the 1985 kidnapping and murder of U.S. DEA agent Enrique Camarena.
- *April 14:* A report of a congressional subcommittee chaired by Senator John Kerry (D-Mass) concludes that the U.S. antidrug effort had been compromised by the Reagan administration's ignoring evidence of drug trafficking by its Nicaraguan contra allies.
- *August 18:* The war between the Colombian government and drug traffickers heats up. After presidential candidate Luis Carlos Galán, who had supported extradition, is assassinated, President Virgilio Barco Vargas declares an emergency and reinstates extradition. The narcoterrorist Extraditables respond with a campaign of shootings and bombings against officials.
- *December 15:* Medellín cartel leader Gonzalo Rodríguez Gacha is killed by Colombian police during a drug raid.
- *December 20:* U.S. military forces invade Panama after months of tension between U.S. and Panamanian forces. Panamanian leader General Manuel Noriega's government is quickly overthrown. He eludes capture at first but is arrested about two weeks later by DEA agents and is brought to Miami.

1990s

- During this decade the federal drug-control budget increases from $4.2 billion to $12.2 billion.
- A federal law requires warning labels on alcoholic beverage containers. They state that women should not drink during pregnancy due to the risk of birth defects, and that alcoholic beverages "impair your ability to drive a car or operate machinery and may cause other health problems."
- Lower costs and the availability of a smokable version leads to a resurgence in heroin use.

Drug Abuse

1990

- The U.S. Supreme Court rules that the First Amendment protection for religious freedom does not require states to allow use of peyote.
- *September:* The three Ochoa brothers who had been major Medellín cartel leaders agree to surrender to Colombian authorities in exchange for a reduced prison sentence and no extradition to the United States.

1991

- *June 19:* The Colombian legislature secretly adds a ban on extradition to the nation's new constitution. Probably not coincidentally, cartel leader Pablo Escobar surrenders to the authorities.
- *November:* Mexican federal police attempting to stop a cocaine shipment are killed by Mexican soldiers who are in the pay of drug traffickers. An investigation results in the arrest and temporary imprisonment of an army general.

1992

- *July 10:* Panamanian General Noriega is convicted on charges of drug trafficking, racketeering, and money laundering. He will be sentenced to 40 years in federal prison.

1993

- Upon taking office President Bill Clinton initiates a modest shift away from drug law enforcement to treatment programs. However, five years later the ratio between enforcement and treatment will remain about 2 to 1.
- *December 2:* Pablo Escobar, most notorious of the Colombian drug lords, is killed in a shootout with Colombian police after they hone in on his cell phone.

1995

- Five leaders of the Cali cartel are arrested. It marks the beginning of the end of the organization, which had supplanted the Medellín cartel after the arrest or killing of the latter's leaders.
- In *Veronia School District v. Acton,* the U.S. Supreme Court rules that schools' compelling interest in reducing drug use justified administering drug tests to student athletes.
- *May:* The U.S. Sentencing Commission notes the discrepancy in sentences for powder cocaine, used mainly by whites, and crack, used mainly by inner city blacks. The commission recommends making the sentences more nearly equal, but Congress refuses to agree.

Chronology

1996

- *February:* President Clinton appoints General Barry McCaffrey to be the new drug czar.
- *November:* California voters approve the Compassionate Use Act, allowing medical use of marijuana.

1997

- *September 24:* A federal grand jury indicts Ramón Arellano Félix, head of a violent Mexican drug cartel, on charges of drug smuggling. Arellano Félix remains at large and is added to the FBI's 10 Most Wanted List.

1998

- *May:* The United States launches an undercover anti–money laundering effort called Operation Casablanca. 167 persons are arrested, and three Mexican and four Venezuelan banks are indicted. However, Mexico and Venezuela both strongly object to what they consider to be a violation of their national sovereignty.
- *July:* In response to Mexican concerns about U.S. undercover operations, the two nations agree to inform one another about their operations in the border area.

1999

- *October 13:* In "Operation Millennium," police in Mexico, Colombia, and Ecuador launch simultaneous raids. Thirty-one drug traffickers are arrested, including Fabio Ochoa.

2000

- *January:* The Fox, ABC, CBS, NBC, and WB broadcast networks admit they had allowed the White House Office of Drug Control Policy to review about 100 scripts for popular prime-time shows. The controversial program made payments to networks that agreed to include antidrug themes in their programs.
- *May 11:* Benjamín and Ramón Arellano Félix are indicted for 10 counts of drug trafficking, conspiracy, money laundering, and aiding and abetting violent crimes. The U.S. State Department posts a $2 million reward for the fugitives.
- *August:* President Clinton delivers a $1.3 billion aid package to Colombia as part of Colombian president Andres Pastrana's "Plan Colombia." Among other things, the money will be used to buy 60 combat helicopters and to train the Colombian military to fight leftist insurgents.

Drug Abuse

2001

- In *Ferguson v. City of Charleston*, the U.S. Supreme Court declares that forcing pregnant patients in a state hospital to take drug tests and turning the results over to law enforcement authorities violated the Fourth Amendment.
- The U.S. Supreme Court rules that use of infrared imaging systems to search for evidence of a marijuana-growing operation in a home violates the expectation of privacy provided for in the Fourth Amendment.
- In a defeat for medical marijuana advocates, the U.S. Supreme Court rules that the federal Controlled Substances Act precludes a "medical necessity" defense on the part of the Oakland, California, Cannabis Buyers' Club.
- *February:* Officials at the popular drug education program DARE admit that some of the techniques they have been using may be ineffective. They begin a process of reviewing research and revising the curriculum.

2002

- Establishment of the new Department of Homeland Security is expected to have a significant impact on drug enforcement policy. Although the Drug Enforcement Agency is not affected, other agencies involved in dealing with drug trafficking, such as the Coast Guard, Border Patrol, and U.S. Marshal Service, become part of the new organization. For the FBI and CIA, fighting terrorism, not drugs, will be the main priority for the foreseeable future.
- Federal authorities close several medical marijuana "clubs," mainly in California. Operators such as Ed Rosenthal in Oakland, California, are arrested and charged under federal laws, which do not recognize the smoked form of marijuana as a medical drug.
- *November:* Attorney General John Ashcroft announces the arrest of two Pakistani men and a naturalized U.S. citizen. They are charged with trying to trade a large quantity of hashish and heroin to FBI agents posing as weapons dealers. The men claimed they wanted the Stinger missiles to sell to al-Qaeda. This month other "narcoterrorism" arrests are also announced; suspects include two leaders of a Colombian paramilitary group.

2003

- The U.S. Supreme Court rules that police can have "reasonable suspicion" and can arrest any or all occupants of a vehicle in which drugs are found, even if they cannot determine who actually owns the drugs.
- Overturning the Ninth Circuit Court of Appeals, the U.S. Supreme Court rules that a corporate policy barring rehiring of employees who violated company rules does not necessarily violate the rights of recovering drug addicts under the Americans with Disabilities Act.

Chronology

- *January:* California medical marijuana activist Ed Rosenthal is convicted in federal court of growing marijuana and of conspiracy. Many of the jurors, who had not been allowed to hear that Rosenthal had permission from the state to operate his dispensary, react angrily after the verdict. Rosenthal does not receive any jail time.
- *February:* Thailand launches a major campaign against producers of heroin and other drugs. The campaign will yield more than 13,000 arrests but also give rise to charges by human rights organizations such as Amnesty International that authorities had murdered perhaps hundreds of innocent people and planted drugs on their bodies.
- *April:* Congress passes the Illicit Drug Anti-Proliferation Act, popularly known as the "Rave Act." It makes operators of nightclubs and other venues responsible for drug violations by partygoers. Civil libertarians worry that it might have a chilling effect on political or cultural gatherings.
- *August:* Texas governor Rick Perry pardons 35 of 38 persons who had been convicted of drug offenses in Tulia, Texas, in 1999. Tom Coleman, the undercover agent who had made all the arrests, has been charged with perjury. It is alleged that he had made up descriptions of drug-related activity. No money or drugs had actually been found on the suspects, who are nearly all black (Coleman is white).
- *September 11:* Comedian Thomas Chong, half of the duo of Cheech & Chong, is sentenced to nine months in jail for selling marijuana pipes, bongs, and other "drug paraphernalia." The duo had been famous for its portrayal of stoned marijuana users.
- *October 14:* The U.S. Supreme Court lets stand an appeals court decision that doctors and patients have a constitutional right to discuss all health-related matters, including medical marijuana. Federal authorities had sought to revoke prescription licenses for physicians who discussed the matter.
- *November 13:* In response to new reports of steroid use among professional baseball players, Major League Baseball announces new penalties for offenders. Players receiving a second positive test will receive a 15-day suspension or a fine of up to $10,000; penalties increased to a year's suspension or a $100,000 fine for a fifth positive test.
- *December 16:* The Ninth Circuit federal court of appeals rules that Congress lacks the power under the Interstate Commerce clause to prevent California patients from growing marijuana for personal medical use. The government is expected to appeal to the U.S. Supreme Court.
- *December 30:* The Food and Drug Administration announces that it will ban ephedra, an herbal dietary supplement with amphetamine-like effects that has been popular with dieters and athletes. The government has included that the substance poses "an unreasonable risk of illness and injury."

- *December 30:* The U.S. Olympic Committee releases results showing that seven top American athletes—six track and field athletes and a cyclist—had tested positive for banned substances the previous summer.

2004

- *February 6:* A federal appeals court rules that the DEA cannot ban the sale of food made with natural hemp without significant THC content.
- *April 5:* The U.S. Supreme Court agrees to review the ruling of the Illinois Supreme Court that drug-sniffing dogs cannot be used in routine traffic stops unless officers have specific reasons to suspect there are drugs.
- *April 6:* The federal Substance Abuse and Mental Health Services Administration (SAMHSA) announces proposed rules allowing federal agencies to use hair, sweat, and saliva tests to screen employees in security-related positions for drug use.

CHAPTER 4

BIOGRAPHICAL LISTING

The following listing is a selection of individuals who have played an important role in drug trafficking, antidrug efforts, or drug policy and reform. The entries are not complete biographical sketches but rather highlight the person's relevant activities and significance.

Harry J. Anslinger, pioneer in federal drug-law enforcement. Born in 1892 in Altoona, Pennsylvania, Anslinger acquired a variety of law enforcement experience. He worked as an investigator for the Pennsylvania Railroad and then as an arson investigator for the fire department. After World War I, Anslinger worked for the State Department. He discovered a drug ring in Hamburg, Germany, that was using American soldiers to smuggle heroin into the United States. His success in breaking up this ring and a rum-running operation in Venezuela during Prohibition led to Anslinger being appointed chief of the Foreign Control Section of the Treasury Department's Prohibition enforcement unit. However, by the 1930s Prohibition was unpopular with the public and on its way out. Anslinger turned his attention to narcotics. Anslinger became the first federal commissioner of narcotics and vigorously pursued drug traffickers until his retirement in 1962. Supporters saw him as a stalwart fighter against an insidious social problem, while critics accused him of being more interested in building a bureaucratic empire through criminalizing what might better be treated as a medical problem.

Ramón Arellano Félix, together with his brothers, heads the powerful Tijuana drug cartel called the Arellano Félix Group. The group is believed to have brought more cocaine, marijuana, heroin, and other drugs into the United States via the Mexican border than any other traffickers during the 1990s. In 2000, Félix was charged with drug conspiracy in a sealed indictment; the State Department offered a $2 million reward for his arrest. The Arellano Félix Organization reportedly responded by offering money for the murder of any police officer in San Diego County. Arellano is also sought in connection with the murder of Cardinal Juan Jesus Posada Ocampo, as well as the killing of Mexican police officials and numerous other persons.

William Bennett, educator, cultural conservative, and first "drug czar." Born in 1943 in Brooklyn, New York, Bennett maintained a distinguished academic career as a teacher, professor of religion and philosophy, university administrator, and director of the National Endowment of the Humanities. When Bennett was appointed by President George Herbert Walker Bush in 1988 to become the head of the Office of National Drug Control Policy, the new drug czar saw education as a key component in the fight against drugs. Besides promoting increased emphasis on drug treatment, in addition to interdiction and enforcement, Bennett tried to craft messages that would convince young people that drugs were not "cool," and he urged media organizations not to glamorize narcotics use. Bennett resigned the drug post in 1990 to concentrate on writing and promoting cultural literacy through publications such as *The Book of Virtues*. In 2003, he admitted to a gambling problem and was criticized by some for hypocrisy for his harsh condemnation of drug users.

George W. Bush, Jr., president of the United States, 2001– . The terrorist attacks of September 11, 2001, would lead the former Texas oil executive and governor to face unexpected challenges and to make controversial policy decisions. The "war on drugs" would be largely eclipsed by a new "war on terrorism," with federal law enforcement and intelligence agencies changing focus and shifting priorities and resources from drugs and organized crime to detecting, apprehending, or thwarting international terrorists. Many agencies on the front lines in the drug war, such as the Border Patrol and Coast Guard, would become part of the new Department of Homeland Security in 2002. However, Bush and senior officials such as Attorney General John Ashcroft would attempt to link drugs and terrorism, and new powers granted in the USA PATRIOT Act in response to the terrorist threat are starting to be used in drug and organized crime cases, raising civil liberties concerns. As of early 2004 the president has yet to promote significant new antidrug initiatives, although promised new aid for Colombia and other countries could have an impact on both drugs and terrorism.

George Herbert Walker Bush, president of the United States, 1989–1993. Bush reaffirmed the "war on drugs" as national policy. When Congress established the Office of National Drug Control Policy Bush appointed educator William Bennett to be its first head, a position that became popularly known as the "drug czar." Bush and Bennett promoted a ramping up of the antidrug effort, including more prosecutions, stiffer penalties, and programs to eradicate drug production in drug-exporting countries. In 1989 Bush ordered the U.S. invasion of Panama, whose leader, General Manuel Noriega, had been indicted for drug trafficking. Similarly Bush promoted an "Andean Strategy," in which the United States would provide military aid for the governments of Colombia, Peru, and Bolivia to fight drug traffickers. However, assessment of these efforts suggests they had little ultimate impact on the supply of drugs available to users in the United States.

James Earl Carter (Jimmy Carter), president of the United States, 1977–1981. President Carter initially took a lower-key approach to the drug war than had his predecessors Gerald Ford and Richard Nixon. During the presidential campaign of 1976, Carter had come out in favor of decriminalizing the use of small amounts of marijuana. He believed that use of the drug had become so widespread and socially acceptable that the government could no longer effectively suppress it, especially given limited federal resources. When Carter also downplayed the dangers of cocaine (partly at the urging of his adviser, Dr. Peter Bourne), many conservatives objected. The revelation of Bourne's own cocaine use caused great embarrassment to the administration. Further, the United States soon became involved in supplying aid to Afghan guerrillas fighting the Soviet invaders, but many guerrillas were also associated with opium production, leading to fear that foreign policy expediency was compromising international control of narcotics. Meanwhile, cocaine use had grown considerably, the Colombian cartels were becoming well established, and most observers would consider the drug war to be a failure by the time Carter's administration ended.

William Jefferson Clinton (Bill Clinton), president of the United States, 1993–2001. During the 1992 presidential campaign Clinton pledged to change U.S. drug policy to make it more effective by increasing domestic treatment and prevention programs and promoting social aid to drug-producing countries. He thus proposed reducing both the supply and demand for drugs rather than focusing on interdiction. However, during Clinton's first term there was a resurgence in heroin use. Conservatives attacked Clinton for what they saw as a lax attitude toward drugs, especially when he explained to a young audience that he had tried marijuana but "didn't inhale." In the 1996 presidential campaign Republican candidate Robert Dole attacked Clinton for being soft on drugs. In response Clinton promised a new initiative, with $75 million in helicopters and other military aid to be given to Latin American and Caribbean nations for fighting drug traffickers. Clinton won reelection handily, but his administration seemed unable to come up with any substantially new antidrug strategies.

Charles Dederich, founder of Synanon, an influential but controversial drug abuse rehabilitation program. Born in Toledo, Ohio, while still a boy Dederich experienced the death of his father, an alcoholic, in a car crash. Dederich also became a heavy drinker in his college years but received help through Alcoholics Anonymous (AA). Dederich became an enthusiastic supporter of the self-help group and its Twelve Step method. When he encountered a drug addict in his AA group in 1958, Dederich struggled to adapt the group's methods to dealing with other kinds of substance abuse. He found that he could help addicts who had been written off by many experts. Dederich started his own organization, Synanon (the name came from a member's mispronunciation of the word seminar). Synanon combined the traditional Twelve Steps with lectures and intense encounter sessions where participants challenged each other to get at the psychological roots of their addiction. (This was similar to techniques being developed in what became known as the human potential movement.) The group achieved national prominence, but Dederich became embroiled in a series of disputes with the Internal Revenue Service. In the mid-1970s, Dederich reorganized Synanon as a church—in part, perhaps, to gain a more favorable tax status. Many critics, however, charged the group with having taken on cultlike characteristics, with members living in a commune and working at various businesses to support the organization. Dederich was also accused of a bizarre murder attempt on an attorney by means of putting a rattlesnake in his mailbox. In 1980, Dederich entered into a plea bargain on conspiracy charges. He served no jail time but was required to give up control of the organization. Both he and the group lost much of their reputation. Dederich died in 1997.

Pablo Escobar, probably the most notorious of the Colombian drug lords and a major leader of the Medellín cartel. Born in 1949 near Medellín, Colombia, Escobar spent his youth as a petty criminal. In his twenties he became involved in the increasingly profitable cocaine trade, which he eventually dominated. Escobar was willing to threaten or use violence and intimidation to stop authorities from interfering with his business, but he also became popular with many poor Colombians because he built them housing and provided money and other support. In 1991, with Colombia under increasing U.S. pressure to do something about the drug trade, Escobar negotiated his surrender to Colombian authorities in exchange for a sentence in a luxurious custom-built prison and no extradition. He continued to direct the Medellín cartel from prison. The next year, however, fearing that the arrangement would be revoked, Escobar escaped from prison. He was killed in a gun battle with police on December 2, 1993.

Ken Kesey, writer, cultural activist, and proponent of drug use as a path to greater consciousness. Born in 1935 in Colorado, Kesey, as an aide at the Menlo Park Veterans' Hospital, volunteered for a government experiment in which he received various psychedelic drugs. The experience convinced Kesey that such drugs could be a powerful tool for treating psychiatric disorders as well as for expanding "normal" consciousness. After writing a best-selling novel about psychiatric abuses *(One Flew Over the Cuckoo's Nest)*, Kesey began to tour the country in the early 1960s in an old bus whose destination sign read "Furthur." Kesey began to conduct public "acid tests," in which people were encouraged to take LSD and other psychedelic drugs. After two arrests for possession of marijuana, Kesey fled to Mexico but returned to serve his sentence. By the 1970s, Kesey had abandoned drugs, saying they had accomplished their purpose and were no longer needed for expanding consciousness.

Rodrigo Lara Bonilla was the Colombian Minister of Justice (comparable to attorney general) who in 1983 uncovered ties between the Medellín cartel and prominent politicians. He organized raids on cartel facilities, seizing airplanes and other equipment. His denouncing of cartel kingpin Pablo Escobar forced the latter to give up a seat he had won in the Colombian Congress. Enraged, Escobar threatened to assassinate Lara Bonilla, who at first did not take the threat seriously. Finally, however, plans were made to send Lara Bonilla to Czechoslovakia as Colombian ambassador, but he was killed before he could take the post.

Timothy Francis Leary, LSD activist and "guru" to a generation of young drug experimenters. As a Harvard psychologist Leary became convinced of the value of psychedelic drugs such as LSD and performed experiments with students. After the university dismissed him Leary set up a commune where he continued his experimentation. In 1970, Leary was arrested and imprisoned for drug possession, but he escaped with the aid of underground radical groups. Leary fled to Algeria, where he was hosted by expatriate Black Panthers until they had a falling out over the use of drugs. Leary was expelled from Algeria and then from Switzerland, which refused his request for political asylum. Finally, he went to Afghanistan but was extradited to the United States, where he served a year in prison. In his later years Leary became interested in a variety of esoteric subjects, including space migration, immortality, and cybernetics. As he was dying of prostate cancer in 1996, he recorded and shared his experiences via a web site.

Rush H. Limbaugh, conservative radio talk show host who attracted a legion of followers in the 1990s. Limbaugh's attacks on the "liberal elite" and demands for personal accountability appealed to many people who identified themselves as "ordinary Americans." In turn, Limbaugh energized many of his listeners to work for conservative candidates and issues. By the mid-1990s, Limbaugh's influence seemed to be peaking; many political pundits give him considerable credit for mobilizing thousands of his followers (self-proclaimed "ditto-heads") to go to the polls in 1994 and vote the Republicans into control of Congress. However, in 2003 Limbaugh revealed to his listeners that he had become addicted to Oxy-Contin, a powerful painkiller, in the course of dealing with prolonged back pain. Federal authorities announced they were investigating persons who might have supplied him the drug. Limbaugh entered a one-month drug rehab program, then returned to the airwaves. Many critics, however, focused on Limbaugh's lack of sympathy for drug users in the past, and his urging that the way to deal with disparities in treatment between black and white drug abusers was to jail more whites. It is unclear whether Limbaugh's personal experience with drugs will change his views on drug policy.

Barry McCaffrey, army general and the Clinton administration "drug czar." McCaffrey's distinguished career spans the highest ranks of military command (he headed the U.S. Army Southern Command, which was responsible for operations in Latin America). A graduate of Philips Academy in Andover, Massachusetts, and the U.S. Military Academy at West Point, he also earned an M.A. in civil government from American University. McCaffrey has held a number of academic posts in government and national security studies. Thus when President Clinton was looking for a "commander in chief" for the "war on drugs," McCaffrey's dual military and academic background made him an attractive candidate. As head of the Office of National Drug Control Policy, McCaffrey advocated expanded treatment options for drug users and decried the lack of priority given to the treatment of drug abuse and the related area of mental health. McCaffrey left his post in 2001 and as of 2004 served as a consultant and national security analyst, as well as and on the boards of a number of organizations including the Phoenix House drug treatment center.

Carry Nation (Carry Amelia Moore), temperance crusader and demolisher of saloons. Born Carry Amelia Moore in Kentucky in 1846, Nation married an alcoholic. That experience convinced her that alcohol was an evil that had to be rooted out of American society. In the early 1900s, Nation began a series of "hatchetations," where she would enter a saloon, axes in hand, and break liquor bottles, windows, and furniture. Arrested some 30 times, Nation would lecture between jail stints and sell souvenir hatchets. Although she typified the personal initiative that neighborhood crusaders would later bring to fighting drug use, her eccentric and arguably counterproductive efforts also contributed to the passage of Prohibition nine years after her death in 1911.

Elliot Ness, well-known to viewers of television's *The Untouchables*, spearheaded street-level anti-alcohol enforcement during the Prohibition era of the 1920s. After graduating from the University of Chicago, Ness was hired in 1929 as a special agent of the U.S. Department of Justice. The energetic Ness was made head of the Prohibition Bureau in Chicago and charged with breaking up bootlegging rings such as that headed by organized crime kingpin Al Capone. Ness and his picked team of officers raided distilleries, bootleg warehouses, and speakeasies (clandestine bars). The group refused bribes from the bootleggers, thus earning them the "Untouchables" label. Eventually Ness was able to obtain evidence that led to Al Capone's conviction—not for bootlegging but for tax evasion. After the repeal of Prohibition, Ness's career with the government continued but on a quieter note.

Richard Nixon, president of the United States, 1969–1974. Nixon launched the modern "war on drugs" in response to a surge in heroin use in the early 1970s. There was a significant increase in the federal budget for narcotics enforcement. New agencies established included the Office for Drug Abuse Law Enforcement. The administration also supported congressional passage of the Drug Abuse and Treatment Act of 1972, which brought new emphasis to prevention and treatment. Critics, however, charged that these efforts were never properly implemented.

Manuel Antonio Noriega, Panamanian dictator turned drug trafficker. A career soldier, Noriega was placed in charge of military intelligence after his mentor, General Omar Torrijos, came to power in a coup in 1968. By the early 1980s, however, it was Noriega who held the reins of power as a self-proclaimed general. Although Noriega was soon suspected of being involved with narcotics trafficking, his supposed antidrug efforts and his support for the Nicaraguan U.S.-backed contra rebels shielded him from U.S. government antidrug efforts throughout most of the decade. However, in 1988, Noriega was indicted by the United States on drug charges. The following year U.S. forces removed him from power and brought him back to the United States. In 1992, Noriega was convicted and sentenced to 40 years in prison on various drug charges.

Jorge Luis Ochoa Vasquez, a founding member of the Medellín cartel and member of a family deeply involved in drug trafficking in the 1970s and early 1980s. When his sister Marta Nieves Ochoa Vasquez was kidnapped in 1981 (and later released), Ochoa decided to forge protective links with other major traffickers, especially Pablo Escobar and Carlos Enrique Lehder, who together formed the organization known as the Medellín cartel. Ochoa led the intimidation against Colombian officials, resulting in the murder of the justice minister, Rodrigo Lara Bonilla. Eventually Ochoa and other cartel leaders were forced out of Colombia but were able to buy protection from Panama's General Manuel Noriega. Ochoa was briefly arrested in Spain in 1984, extradited to Colombia, but soon released. However, in January 1991 he turned himself in to Colombian authorities in exchange for leniency.

Drug Abuse

Ronald Wilson Reagan, president of the United States, 1981–1988. In 1982, Reagan made the drug problem a major campaign issue in the 1982 midterm election, beefing up enforcement, particularly in Florida, which had become the arrival point for much of the flood of cocaine entering the country. Reagan decided to make the FBI rather than the DEA the lead agency in the drug fight and also involved U.S. intelligence agencies and the military in the effort. Meanwhile, Reagan's wife Nancy became a spokesperson for drug education efforts, urging that young people "just say no" to offers of drugs. However, the participation of senior administration officials in the Iran-contra scandal (where shipments of weapons and drugs were used to support the anti-Sandinista rebels in Nicaragua) raised widespread concern. By the end of Reagan's term, even though unprecedented amounts of drugs were being confiscated, drug prices had actually fallen and the ranks of drug abusers had scarcely declined.

Ed Rosenthal, California medical marijuana activist. A magazine columnist and author, he has written extensively on "Cannabis culture," with his book *Marijuana Grower's Handbook* selling over a million copies and being reviewed by the *New York Times*. Rosenthal has written a syndicated advice column for marijuana growers and users. In recent years Rosenthal has also become a national spokesperson for the effort to allow the legal medical use of marijuana for cancer and AIDS patients and others who say the drug is essential for fighting pain, nausea, and loss of appetite. In 2002 federal authorities closed a medical marijuana dispensary that Rosenthal had been operating with the blessing of California voters, who had passed a proposition in favor of medical marijuana. In January 2003 Rosenthal was tried and convicted on marijuana growing and conspiracy charges. The jury was not allowed to hear Rosenthal's defense that he was operating under state authority. Although the judge ruled such evidence inadmissible as a matter of law, he did not sentence Rosenthal to any prison time.

Hamilton Wright, a pioneer in U.S. narcotics control policy. A physician and specialist in tropic diseases, Wright was appointed in 1909 by President Theodore Roosevelt as part of the U.S. delegation to the first worldwide convention on narcotics control, held in Shanghai, China. Wright would continue to emphasize international cooperation to fight drug traffic, as well as tough domestic laws and publicizing the dangers of drugs. His efforts were largely responsible for the passage of the Harrison Narcotic Acts of 1914.

CHAPTER 5

GLOSSARY

The following terms, organizations, and events are frequently found in discussions of drugs, drug abuse, and drug policy. For a list of acronyms referring to organizations and laws, see Appendix A. For a list of "street names" of drugs, see Appendix B.

abuse   Inappropriate use of a psychological, legal or illegal drug in such a way that the user experiences physiological, social, or legal problems.

addiction   The state in which a user is physically or psychologically dependent on a drug and is compelled to keep taking it.

amphetamines   A family of stimulant drugs. The first was Benzedrine, marketed in the 1930s for asthma and then used during World War II to keep soldiers and pilots alert.

analgesic   A drug that relieves pain but does not make the user unconscious.

Arellano-Felix Organization   An extremely active (and violent) Mexican drug trafficking group that has shipped huge quantities of cocaine, heroin, and methamphetamine into the United States. The group is based in Tijuana but has affiliates throughout Mexico and the United States.

asset forfeiture   Legal provision allowing authorities to seize property used by people involved in drug trafficking. While hailed as an additional deterrent to drugs, critics argue asset forfeiture (particularly as a civil proceeding) violates constitutional property and due-process rights and often amounts to disproportionate or unfair punishment.

barbiturates   A family of depressant, sedative drugs, originally marketed as calming or sleep aids but proving to be highly addictive.

bong   An often elaborate water pipe used for smoking marijuana or hashish.

Brownsville Agreement   An agreement signed by the United States and Mexico to inform one another about undercover operations in the border area. It arose from Mexican anger over the U.S. undercover Operation Casablanca in 1998.

Drug Abuse

Cali cartel A Colombian drug-trafficking organization that emerged as the dominant player in the cocaine trade after the demise of Pablo Escobar and the rival Medellín cartel. The Cali cartel became famous for cultivating contacts with all levels of society and using intelligence-gathering, bribery, and legal action in preference to direct violence.

Campaign Against Marijuana Planting (CAMP) A largely unsuccessful effort to eradicate marijuana cultivation in California during the 1980s. Growers became more adept at concealing their product and some operations moved to Oregon.

cartel In business, the term refers to an organization of independent producers who seek to control prices and limit competition. Drug cartels are similar but use intimidation and violence to maintain control of their market.

certification Under federal law, determination by the president that one of the 32 recognized major drug-producing countries has complied with U.S. policies on drug trafficking. Countries that fail to reply face withdrawal of U.S. financial assistance.

cocaine An addictive stimulant that appears as a white powder. Cocaine can be inhaled through the nose (snorted) or injected.

codeine A narcotic painkiller. In the 1960s use of the drug was more tightly controlled when it was discovered that cough syrup containing the substance was being abused.

crack Cocaine processed into the form of small "rocks" for smoking. Crack produces a quicker, more intense "high" than powder cocaine. The high is followed by a "crash"—depression and an urgent need for another dose.

crack babies Common term for children born to mothers who used crack cocaine during pregnancy. Although the extent of the problem is somewhat controversial, there is evidence that such children experience developmental problems and a higher risk of Sudden Infant Death Syndrome (SIDS).

crop substitution A program in which people growing opium poppies or coca are urged and helped to replace them with legal, benign crops such as grain or vegetables. One problem with the policy is that legal crops pay much less to producers; another is that one drug-producing area will simply be replaced by another in order to meet the profitable demand.

decriminalization An approach to drug use that falls short of full legalization but reduces or removes criminal sanctions against users while keeping penalties for trafficking. About a dozen states decriminalized marijuana during the 1970s, but most restored penalties under pressure from the federal government.

dependency The state in which a drug user's body has adapted to a drug such that discontinuing use of the drug will result in painful and sometimes dangerous symptoms.

Glossary

depressants   Drugs such as barbiturates or tranquilizers that suppress or reduce the activity of the central nervous system. Depressants can produce sedation or euphoria but prolonged use can bring increasing dependence and addiction.

designer drugs   Drugs synthesized to have effects similar to existing illegal drugs but are often more potent and sold at a lower cost. Originally another motive in creating designer drugs was that they would not be found in lists of drugs banned by law, but laws were amended to make "chemical analogs" of illegal drugs or drugs with similar effects also illegal.

detoxification ("detox")   The process of managing drug withdrawal so that physical dependency on the drug is removed.

downers   Slang term for barbiturates or other depressant drugs.

drug   Any substance (other than food) that alters the functioning of the body or mind.

Drug Abuse Resistance Education (DARE)   A program introduced in 1983 to help kids resist the temptation of drugs by boosting self-esteem, decision-making ability, and the ability to resist peer pressure. Experts differ about the efficacy of the program.

drug czar   Colloquial term for the head of the federal Office of National Drug Control Policy. He or she is the chief administration spokesperson on issues related to drug abuse.

Drug Enforcement Administration (DEA)   Established in 1973 as a consolidation of existing federal drug enforcement agencies, the DEA is now responsible for enforcement of all federal drug laws.

drug-free zone   A defined area such as around a school, where penalties for dealing drugs are substantially increased.

drug legalization   The movement to remove criminal sanctions for the use of a particular drug, or of all drugs. Advocates for legalization believe that by removing incentives for criminal activity, drug use would become much more manageable and less destructive. Opponents believe the lack of deterrence would increase drug use. Legalization advocates would retain restrictions on access to drugs by minors.

ecstasy (MDMA)   One of the first "designer drugs" appearing in the 1980s, a member of the amphetamine family. The drug produces a feeling of energy and social "closeness" and became popular at all-night dance parties called raves.

eradication   Reduction of the supply of drugs by destroying the raw crops from which they are made, such as by burning or the use of herbicides.

Extraditables   A terrorist group associated with the Colombian drug cartels. In the late 1980s the group killed or threatened Colombian leaders in order to prevent extradition of drug traffickers to the United States.

extradition   The act of turning over a criminal suspect to the country that has placed charges against him or her. Not all countries have extradition treaties with one another, but a UN convention against drug trafficking that provides for extradition of suspects has 43 signatories. Some countries such as Colombia have wavered in extradition policy, depending on the resolution of the government and the ability of traffickers to intimidate it.

fetal alcohol syndrome (FAS)   A set of conditions (such as poor development and learning disabilities, including problems with concentration and memory) experienced by children whose mothers drank alcohol during pregnancy.

French Connection   A large heroin-trafficking ring based in Marseilles, France, and run by French and Italian gangsters. It was the main source of street heroin in the United States until 1973, when the ring was smashed by a coordinated international law enforcement operation.

gateway drug   The assertion that one drug (such as marijuana) predisposes users to try another drug (such as cocaine or heroin).

Golden Crescent   An area containing portions of Pakistan, Afghanistan, and Iran that has been a major opium-growing (and heroin-producing) region since the 1970s. Drugs produced there usually reach the United States via Turkey and Europe.

Golden Triangle   An area ranging from Myanmar (Burma) into the Yunan province of China to parts of Laos and Thailand. The area has long been known for opium cultivation and production under control of various regional groups.

hallucinogen   Drugs such as marijuana and LSD that produce changes in perception, imagery, or mood. In the 1960s such drugs were often called psychedelics.

harm reduction   A policy that seeks to minimize the harm caused by drug use to both user and society rather than focusing on deterrence or punishment. Harm reduction advocates believe that drug use is inevitable and should be made as safe as possible, such as through needle exchanges or even provision of drugs to registered addicts.

hashish (hash)   A resinous extract of the female *cannabis* or marijuana plant. Because it has a higher concentration of the active ingredient (THC), it is considerably more potent than regular marijuana. It is no longer widely used in the West.

hemp   The fiber of the *cannabis* plant. Hemp has little or no THC and therefore cannot be used as a drug. The plant has found many creative uses, notably in the making of fiber and paper, and was grown in the American colonies. Activists decry the fact that it is illegal to grow hemp in the United States, although it is legal in many other developed countries.

110

heroin A narcotic produced by chemically treating morphine. It is a powerful drug that after its introduction in 1898 was marketed as a painkiller and cough suppressant. Evidence of its highly addictive nature led to heroin being completely banned by 1922.

hypnotic A depressant drug that induces sleep, such as methaqualone and chloral hydrate. Sometimes the same drug in different dosages can produce both sedative and hypnotic effects.

inhalants Substances that abusers inhale in order to obtain an intoxicating effect. Many ordinary products including glue and paint thinner can be used in this way, and the results can include liver or brain damage or even death.

interdiction The attempt to stop illegal drugs from reaching users by disrupting drug production in other countries (such as by aiding their government's antidrug efforts) or intercepting shipments.

intravenous (IV) Injection of a drug directly into the bloodstream.

just say no A slogan and campaign popularized by Nancy Reagan in the mid-1980s. It tried to get young people to make and stick to a simple decision to avoid drugs, but critics have viewed the idea as too simplistic.

lysergic acid diethymalide (LSD) A powerful hallucinogenic drug first synthesized in 1938, although its psychedelic properties were not discovered until 1943. In the 1960s the drug spread from experimenters' labs to the street, where countercultural figures such as Ken Kesey and Timothy Leary promoted its use as a tool for expanding consciousness.

marijuana A hallucinogenic drug prepared from the buds, leaves, and stems of the *Cannabis sativa* plant. It is usually smoked in a hand-rolled cigarette (joint) or a pipe, although it can also be incorporated in food and eaten. Marijuana is by far the most popular illegal drug in the United States.

Medellín cartel Named after the Colombian city, this cartel was probably the most successful drug trafficking organization from the late 1970s to the end of the 1980s, when Pablo Escobar and other major cartel leaders were arrested, imprisoned, or killed.

medical marijuana The assertion that marijuana has medical value (such as for treating glaucoma or nausea, or increasing appetite) and should be legally available to patients. Nine states currently have some form of medical marijuana provision, but it is not recognized by the federal government, which has prosecuted marijuana dispensaries.

methadone A synthetic narcotic that satisfies the physical need of an addict for heroin and prevents symptoms from heroin withdrawal. Methadone is addictive itself, but advocates of methadone maintenance believe it allows addiction to be managed in a safe, controlled environment.

methamphetamine A stimulant similar to, but stronger than an amphetamine. Various forms of the drug can be injected, taken as a pill, snorted, or smoked. The last form, "crystal meth," is particularly potent and addictive.

money laundering The process of concealing the illegal source of money so it can be introduced into normal commerce. Large drug trafficking organizations are faced with the problem of laundering revenues in the millions of dollars, such as by making many smaller bank deposits, forming illicit relationships with financial institutions, creating dummy corporations, or converting the money into some other portable form of wealth.

morphine A narcotic produced from opium and developed in the mid-19th century as a painkiller. It has been replaced by safer painkillers for many applications.

narcoterrorism The alleged link between drug trafficking and terrorism, such as the use of drugs to obtain funding for terrorist groups. Also, terrorism conducted on behalf of drug traffickers, as with "the Extraditables" in Colombia.

needle exchange A program in which addicts are provided with clean hypodermic syringes in exchange for their used ones, in order to reduce the spread of AIDS and other diseases.

neuroadaptation Chemical and physiological changes in brain structure or function in response to continued use of a psychoactive drug.

opiate An opium derivative.

opium The first narcotic in widespread use (since antiquity), with many derivatives such as morphine and heroin. Opium was a common ingredient in over-the-counter medicines until the early 20th century.

paraphernalia Legal term for implements used for preparing or taking drugs, such as pipes, hypodermic syringes, and so on.

peyote A spineless cactus found in northern Mexico and southern Texas. The top of the plant, shaped like a button, contains a hallucinogenic substance. Some Native Americans have used the substance in healing and other rituals, and it was taken up by various seekers of psychedelic experience in the late 1950s and 1960s.

phencyclidine (PCP) Introduced as an anesthetic in the 1950s and often known on the street as "angel dust." The drug's effects are quite unpredictable, ranging from a dreamy euphoria to hallucinations and erratic behavior.

Prohibition The period from 1920 to 1933 when use of alcoholic beverages was illegal throughout the United States.

psychoactive drugs Drugs that alter perception or consciousness, such as by inducing hallucinations or psychotic behavior.

Quaalude (methaqualone) A prescription sedative and sleep aid that was removed from the legal market in the early 1980s because of widespread abuse.

Ritalin An amphetamine (methylphenidate) in widespread use for treating hyperactivity or Attention Deficit Disorder (ADD) in children because of its calming effect, but actually acts as a stimulant in adults and older teenagers, leading to abuse.

sedative   A depressant drug that produces a feeling of calm or relaxation, as with alcohol and barbiturates.

stimulant   A drug, such as amphetamines and cocaine, that increases the activity of the brain and central nervous system.

subcutaneous   Injection of a drug under the skin.

tolerance   A characteristic of certain drugs where the effects diminish after prolonged use, requiring that the user take increasingly large dosages to achieve the desired effects.

tranquilizers   General name for a class of drugs that have a sedating or relaxing effect. Examples include diazepam (Valium) and chlordiazepoxide.

trip   A drug experience, particularly one involving hallucinogens such as LSD.

uppers   Slang term for stimulant drugs such as amphetamines.

"war on drugs"   General term for the coordinated efforts in the United States and around the world to fight narcotics trafficking and to deal with drug addiction. The metaphor has been criticized as simplistic, since it implies a definable enemy and the possibility of a definitive victory.

withdrawal   The symptoms that occur when a habitual drug user abruptly stops taking the drug.

PART II

GUIDE TO FURTHER RESEARCH

CHAPTER 6

How to Research
Drug Abuse Issues

This chapter presents a guide to resources and techniques for students and others who are researching topics relating to drug abuse and treatment, the war on drugs, and drug policy. As might be expected with such an important and controversial subject, the amount of material available is staggering.

Today most researchers will turn first to the Web rather than to the local library. The Web is now a primary source for news stories and feature articles (even those also available in print). It is also often the first place to look for resources about a subject, such as topic guides, bibliographies, and lists of additional Web links. Summaries of ongoing research programs or forthcoming papers are often available online months ahead of print publication.

WEB RESOURCES

There are a number of web sites that offer extensive resources on many aspects of drug abuse and related issues. Here are some suggested starting points. Of course, many sites will provide extensive lists of links to other sites.

- The American Civil Liberties Union (ACLU) is the nation's foremost civil liberties organization. As such it has serious concerns about the effects of the war of drugs on civil liberties. Its web site at http://www.aclu. org/ has a topical page linked under Drug Policy. There one can find sections on topics such as asset forfeiture, decriminalization of drugs, drug testing, harm reduction, medical marijuana, racial justice and drugs, and sentencing.
- DRCNet Online Library of Drug Policy, sponsored by the Drug Reform Coordination Network at http://www.druglibrary.org, bills itself as the "world's largest online library of drug policy," and the claim is

117

plausible. It includes links to a number of archives of drug policy advocacy, including the Schaffer Library, Cannabis Research, the Carl Olsen Archive (including information on medical use of marijuana), and the Psychedelic Library.

- Drug Abuse Resistance Education (DARE) is the nation's largest and best-known drug abuse prevention and education organization. Its web site at http://www.dare.org offers reports of national and local DARE activities, resources, testimonials, and studies on the effectiveness of the program. (The latter should be balanced with critical studies, some of which are listed in chapter 7 under Drug Education.)

- The U.S. Drug Enforcement Administration is the principal federal enforcer of laws against possession and trafficking in controlled substances. Its web site at http://www.usdoj.gov/dea/ provides news and statistics about enforcement activity (including state-by-state summaries of drug seizures and other activities), as well as background on drug trafficking.

- The Drug Policy Alliance is a major organization that declares as its goal an end to the war on drugs. Its web site at http://www.dpf.org includes a state-by-state status report on drug-law reform efforts, information about legislation regarding specific drugs, harm reduction strategies, civil liberties issues, and much more.

- Drugtext, sponsored by the International Harm Reduction Association at http://www.drugtext.org/, is a research resource emphasizing harm reduction and other alternatives to existing drug abuse policy. It includes extensive listings of articles, research reports, and books, which are accessible by author, drug, category, or topic.

- The Indiana Prevention Resource Center of Indiana University at http://www.drugs.indiana.edu/ offers extensive resources on alcohol, tobacco, and illegal drug use. Although some resources are geared to users in the state of Indiana, many, especially the statistics links page, would be of use to any student or researcher.

- The National Clearinghouse for Alcohol and Drug Information is operated by the federal Substance Abuse and Mental Health Services Administration (SAMHSA). Among this web site's offerings at http://www.health.org/ are links to "quick facts" on various topics such as drug abuse statistics for different racial or ethnic groups, addiction, various types of drugs, the role of parents in fighting drug abuse, and drugs in the workplace.

- The National Commission Against Drunk Driving at http://www.ncadd.com/ provides resources and practical information about one of the most serious consequences of drug abuse. There are also practical suggestions—

for example, how to deal with party guests who should not be driving themselves home.

- On the National Criminal Justice Reference Service web site at http://www.ncjrs.org, in addition to news, statistics and archives on just about every aspect of criminal justice and law enforcement, access to hundreds of thousands of annotated articles throughout the abstracts database is provided.

- The National Association for the Reform of Marijuana Laws (NORML) is one of the major organizations working to decriminalize marijuana. Its web site at http://www.norml.org/ provides news of court cases and other developments, as well as background materials for drug-policy reform advocates.

- The National Inhalant Prevention Coalition (http://www.inhalants.org/) deals with the persistent problem of abuse of inhalants (such as paint thinner, glue, nail polish, and even correction fluid). Their web site describes inhalant abuse and gives tips for parents on how to spot its presence in children.

- The National Institute on Alcohol Abuse and Alcoholism (NIAAA) of the U.S. National Institutes of Health at http://www.niaaa.nih.gov/ is a good source of background information and news about current clinical trials and research studies, as well as access to various databases and treatment referrals.

- The National Institute on Drug Abuse (NIDA) is the federal government's principal direct research effort in this field. The organization supports more then 85 percent of the world's research on drug abuse and addiction. Its web site at http://www.nida.nih.gov gives news about research results and ongoing studies. There are also fact sheets on general trends in drug abuse as well as information about specific groups such as youth and women. However, because of the government affiliation, research supporting alternatives to current drug policy is not emphasized.

- The Office of National Drug Control Policy of the White House is charged with formulating the national drug control strategy. Its web site at http://www.whitehousedrugpolicy.gov/ includes annual reports on the international fight against drug trafficking, as well as a variety of other links relating to drug abuse and drug policy.

- The Partnership for a Drug-Free America is a leading drug-abuse education organization. Its web site at http://www.drugfreeamerica.org includes features on current topics (such as the use of "E," or ecstasy, by young people), provides a "drug challenge" quiz for high school students, and includes drug information that can be looked up in different ways, including by regular and slang, or "street," name.

- Quitnet at http://www.quitnet.com/ provides resources and encouragement to individuals who seek to stop smoking. The web site includes information about tobacco addiction and various methods for quitting smoking, as well as an interactive facility for creating one's own "Quit Plan."
- Transactional Access Records Clearinghouse (TRAC) at Syracuse University compiled publicly accessible records of federal law-enforcement activity. Its web site at http://trac.syr.edu/ offers links to databases for the Drug Enforcement Agency, U.S. Customs, the FBI, and other agencies.
- Virtual Chase is an Internet research guide that has a relevant page at http://www.virtualchase.com/resources/drugs_and_alcohol.html. This page links to many accessible databases such as from government agencies.

NEWS RESOURCES

When breaking news such as a major drug "bust," a court decision, or a major federal policy announcement occurs, the Web is a good place to go for coverage that is more detailed than that available on television and timelier than that found in magazines. The major broadcast and cable networks, news (wire) services, most newspapers, and many magazines have web sites that include news stories and links to additional information. For breaking news, the following sites are also useful:

- **Associated Press (AP) wire:** http://wire.ap.org/public_pages/WirePortal. pcgi/us_portal.html
- **Cable News Network (CNN):** http://www.cnn.com
- *New York Times:* http//www.nytimes.com
- **Reuters:** http://www.reuters.com
- *Time* **magazine:** http://www.time.com
- *Wall Street Journal:* http://online.wsj.com/public/us
- *Washington Post:* http://www.washingtonpost.com/

Yahoo! also maintains a large set of links to many newspapers that have web sites or online editions at http://dir.yahoo.com/News_and_Media/ Newspapers/Web_Directories/.

Another useful site for tracking down recent news stories is Google News at http://news.google.com/. The site describes itself as "highly unusual in that it offers a news service compiled solely by computer algorithms without human intervention. While the sources of the news stories vary in perspective and editorial approach, their selection for inclusion is done without regard to political viewpoint or ideology. While this may lead to some occasionally unusual and contradictory groupings, it is exactly this variety that makes Google News a valuable source of information on the important issues of the day."

FINDING MORE ON THE WEB

Although the resource sites mentioned earlier provide a convenient way to view a wide variety of information, it will eventually be necessary for the researcher to look for information or views elsewhere. The two main approaches to Web research are the portal and the search engine.

WEB PORTALS

A Web guide or index is a site that offers what amounts to a structured, hierarchical outline of subject areas. This enables the researcher to zero in on a particular aspect of a subject and find links to web sites for further exploration. The links are constantly being compiled and updated by a staff of researchers.

The best known (and largest) Web index is Yahoo! (http://www.yahoo.com). The home page gives the top-level list of topics, and the researcher simply clicks to follow them down to more specific areas. Within Yahoo! there are two main paths to follow. For pursuing topics relating to drug law enforcement and the war on drugs, go to Society and Culture / Crime. Within that category is War on Drugs, which includes a variety of links, many of which relate to the struggle against international drug trafficking. Other subcategories under Crime that might be appropriate for information about drug law enforcement include asset confiscation, correction and rehabilitation, criminal justice, criminology, law enforcement, organized crime, and statistics. The other path runs through Health / Pharmacy / Drugs and Medications / Drug Policy. This includes topics such as drugs in sports, harm reduction, and marijuana, as well as general resource links. In addition to following Yahoo!'s outlinelike structure, there is also a search box into which the researcher can type one or more keywords and receive a list of matching categories and sites.

Web indexes such as Yahoo! have two major advantages over undirected surfing. First, the structured hierarchy of topics makes it easy to find a particular topic or subtopic and then explore its links. Second, Yahoo! does not make an attempt to compile every possible link on the Internet (a task that is virtually impossible, given the size of the Web). Rather, sites are evaluated for usefulness and quality by Yahoo!'s indexers. This means that the researcher has a better chance of finding more substantial and accurate information. The disadvantage of Web indexes is the flip side of their selectivity: The researcher is dependent on the indexer's judgment for determining what sites are worth exploring.

SEARCH ENGINES

Search engines take a very different approach to finding materials on the Web. Instead of organizing topically in a "top down" fashion, search engines work their way "from the bottom up," scanning through Web documents and indexing them. There are hundreds of search engines, but some of the most widely used include:

- **AltaVista:** http://www.altavista.com
- **Excite:** http://www.excite.com
- **Google:** http://www.google.com
- **Hotbot:** http://www.hotbot.com
- **Lycos:** http://www.lycos.com
- **Northern Light:** http://www.northernlight.com/news.html
- **WebCrawler:** http://www.WebCrawler.com

Search engines are generally easy to use by employing the same sorts of keywords that work in library catalogs. There are a variety of Web-search tutorials available online (try "web search tutorial" in a search engine to find some). One good one is published by Bright Planet at http://www.brightplanet.com/deepcontent/tutorials/search/index.asp.

Here are a few basic rules for using search engines:

- When looking for something specific, use the most specific term or phrase. For example, when looking for information about needle exchange programs, try the specific term *needle exchange*, but be aware that you might need to check the more general term *harm reduction* as well.
- Phrases should be put in quotes if you want them to be matched as phrases rather than as individual words. Examples include **"needle exchange," "harm reduction,"** and **"medical marijuana."**
- When looking for a general topic that might be expressed using several different words or phrases, use several descriptive words (nouns are more reliable than verbs). For example, **drug abuse statistics.** Most engines will automatically put pages that match all three terms first on the results list.

- Use "wildcards" (such as an asterisk) when a desired word may have more than one ending. For example, **abuse*** matches both "abuse" and "abuser"
- Most search engines support Boolean (and, or, not) operators that can be used to broaden or narrow a search. Use *and* to narrow a search. For example, **legalization and poll** will match only pages that have both terms. Use *or* to broaden a search: **legalization or decriminalization** will match any page that has either term, and since these terms are often used interchangeably, this type of search is necessary to retrieve the widest range of results. Use *not* to exclude unwanted results: **hallucinogen not LSD** should mostly find articles about hallucinogens other than LSD.

Since each search engine indexes somewhat differently and offers somewhat different ways of searching, it is a good idea to use several different search engines, especially for a general query.

Several "metasearch" programs automate the process of submitting a query to multiple search engines. These include Metacrawler at http://www.metacrawler.com and SurfWax at http://www.surfwax.com./ Note that metasearch engines tend to have two drawbacks: They may overwhelm you with results (and insufficiently prune duplicates), and they often do not use some of the more popular search engines (such as Google or Northern Light).

There are also search utilities that can be run from the researcher's own PC rather than through a web site. A good example is Copernic, available at http://www.copernic.com.

FINDING ORGANIZATIONS AND PEOPLE

Chapter 8 of this book provides a list of organizations that are involved with various aspects of drug enforcement, treatment, and policy, but new organizations will emerge now and then. Many of the resource sites listed earlier will have links to organizations, as will Yahoo! and the other general Web portals.

If such sites do not yield the name of a specific organization, the name can be given to a search engine. Generally, the best approach is to put the name of the organization in quote marks such as "Drug Policy Alliance."

Another approach is to take a guess at the organization's likely Web address. For example, the American Civil Liberties Union is commonly known by the acronym ACLU, so it is not a surprise that the organization's web site is at http://www.aclu.org. (Note that noncommercial organization sites normally use the *.org* suffix, government agencies use *.gov*, educational institutions have *.edu*, and businesses use *.com*.) This technique can save time, but does not always work. In particular, watch out for "spoof" sites that mimic or parody organizational sites. Such a site might, for example, have the same name as that of a government agency but end in *.org* instead of *.gov*. (Of course, such sites may be of interest in themselves as forms of criticism or dissent.)

There are several ways to find a person on the Internet:

- Put the person's name (in quotes) in a search engine and possibly find that person's home page on the Internet.

- Contact the person's employer (such as a university for an academic or a corporation for a technical professional). Most such organizations have Web pages that include a searchable faculty or employee directory.

- Try one of the people-finder services such as Yahoo! People Search at http://people.yahoo.com or BigFoot at http://www.bigfoot.com. This may yield contact information such as an e-mail address, regular address, and/or phone number.

PRINT SOURCES

As useful as the Web is for quickly finding information and the latest news, in-depth research still sometimes requires trips to the library or bookstore. Getting the most out of the library requires the use of bibliographic tools and resources. Bibliographic resources is a general term for catalogs, indexes, bibliographies, and other guides that identify the books, periodical articles, and other printed resources that deal with a particular subject. They are essential tools for the researcher.

LIBRARY CATALOGS

Many library catalogs can now be searched online. Access to the largest library catalog, that of the Library of Congress, is available at http://catalog.loc.gov. This page includes a guide to using the catalog and both basic and advanced catalog searches.

Yahoo! offers a categorized listing of libraries at http://dir.yahoo.com/Reference/Libraries/. For materials available at one's local public or university library, that institution will be the most convenient source.

Most catalogs can be searched in at least the following ways:

- An author search is most useful if you know or suspect a person has written a number of works of interest. However, it may fail if you do not know the person's exact name. (Cross references are intended to deal with this problem, but cannot cover all possible variations.)

- A title search is best if you know the exact title of the book and just want to know if the library has it. Generally, you need only use the first few words of the title, excluding initial articles *(a, an, the)*. This search will fail if you do not have the exact title.

- A keyword search will match words found anywhere in the title. It is thus broader and more flexible than a title search, although it may still fail if all keywords are not present.
- A subject search will find all works that have been assigned that subject heading by the library. The big advantage is that it does not depend on certain words being in the title. However, using a subject search requires knowledge of the appropriate subject headings (see below).

Here are some often useful Library of Congress subject headings relating to drug abuse and drug policy. If you browse the subject-headings catalog, you can find other related headings of interest.

The heading Drug Abuse covers abuse of drugs in general. Drug treatment can be found under Drug Abuse—Treatment.

More specific headings include:

- Medication abuse: Abuse of prescription and other therapeutic (medical) drugs.
- Narcotic habit: Addiction to narcotics such as opiates or cocaine.

There are also some headings for abuse of specific drugs or specific types of drug abuse such as

- Aerosol sniffing
- Alcoholism
- Amphetamine abuse
- Hallucinogenic drugs
- Marijuana abuse
- Solvent abuse
- Tobacco habit

The heading Drugs of Abuse is a general heading for discussion of drugs that are likely to be abused, including narcotics, hallucinogens, alcohol, and tobacco.

Other aspects of drug abuse include:

- Brain drug effects
- Doping in sports

- Drug testing
- Drugged driving
- Drugs overdosage
- Drug treatment centers
- Intravenous drug abuse

Works on particular drugs are listed under the drug in question, with subdivisions reflecting geographical locations, historical periods, and aspects. Note that the Library of Congress uses the rather archaic term *habit* instead of *addiction*, so materials on heroin addiction, for example, would be found under heroin habit. Note also that the Library of Congress does not use the heading War on Drugs but instead uses Narcotics, Control of. This heading is also used for such subjects as drug trafficking, drug enforcement, and drug policy, although there is a separate heading for Narcotics dealers. There are also headings for drug legalization (also used for decriminalization). Harm reduction, however, is currently listed as a "proposed" heading.

Social aspects of drug abuse can be found under such headings as

- Drugs and mass media
- Drugs and sex

Many of these headings can be further qualified by geographical location, as in Drug Abuse—Study and Teaching—United States and/or by period (such as 20th century).

Once the record for a book or other item is found, it is a good idea to see what additional subject headings and name headings have been assigned. These in turn can be used for further searching.

AN ALTERNATIVE: BOOKSTORE CATALOGS

Many people have discovered that online bookstores such as Amazon.com (http://www.amazon.com) and Barnes & Noble (http://www.barnesandnoble. com) are convenient ways to shop for books. A lesser-known benefit of online bookstore catalogs is that they often include publisher's information, book reviews, and readers' comments about a given title. They can thus serve as a form of annotated bibliography.

Amazon in recent years has added a feature called "search inside the book" that applies to an increasing proportion of available titles. By default, this means a standard search will also retrieve books that contain the keyword or phrase somewhere in the text. This can be a mixed blessing—it can help one find obscure topics that might not otherwise be indexed, but it can also retrieve irrelevant titles. If that happens, one can try the "advanced search" with more specific criteria or try Barnes & Noble's web site instead.

BIBLIOGRAPHIES, INDEXES, AND DATABASES

Bibliographies in various forms provide a convenient way to find books, periodical articles, and other materials. How far to go back in one's reading depends, of course, on one's research topic and goals. Obviously material about illicit drug sales on the Internet is not likely to be found earlier than the mid-1990s, while references to various forms of drug smuggling go back considerably further.

Popular and scholarly articles can be accessed through periodical indexes that provide citations and abstracts. Abstracts are brief summaries of articles or papers. They are usually compiled and indexed—originally in bound volumes, but increasingly are available online.

Some indexes likely to be available in academic or large public libraries include:

- Applied Social Sciences Indexes and Abstracts
- Biological Abstracts
- Criminal Justice Abstracts
- Criminal Justice Periodical Index
- Psychological Abstracts
- Public Affairs Information Service (PAIS)
- Social Sciences Index
- Social Work Abstracts
- Sociological Abstracts

Most researchers will want to search indexes online. Generally, however, you can access them only through a library where you hold a card, and they cannot be accessed over the Internet (unless you are on a college campus). Consult with a university reference librarian for more help.

The Criminal Justice Abstracts available at http://www.ncjrs.org do offer free access to thousands of annotated citations. There is also a good general index that has unrestricted search access. UnCover Web at http://www.ingenta.com/ contains brief descriptions of about 13 million documents from about 26,000 journals in just about every subject area. Copies of complete documents can be ordered with a credit card, or they may be obtainable for free at a local library.

Depending on the degree of specialization involved in the subject being studied, a number of other databases may prove useful, especially general medical databases. These include:

- Clinical Alerts from the National Institutes of Health at http://www.nlm. nih.gov/databases/alerts/clinical_alerts.html provides reports on recent research findings.
- The Combined Health Information Database at http://www.chid.nih. gov/index.html, which brings together research studies from all federal agencies.
- MEDLINE Plus at http://www.nlm.nih.gov/medlineplus/ combines one of the largest and more comprehensive databases in the health field with additional resources, including an online medical encyclopedia and links to other resources.
- The NLM Gateway from the National Library of Medicine at http://gateway.nlm.nih.gov/gw/Cmd allows for searching a number of databases (including MEDLINE/PubMed and ClinicalTrials.gov) using a single search.

GENERAL PERIODICAL INDEXES

Most public libraries subscribe to database services such as InfoTrac and EBSCO that index articles from hundreds of general-interest periodicals (and some moderately specialized ones). The database can be searched by author or by words in the title, subject headings, and sometimes words found anywhere in the article text. Depending on the database used, "hits" in the database can result in just a bibliographical description (such as author, title, pages, periodical name, issue date), a description plus an abstract (a paragraph summarizing the contents of the article), or the full text of the article itself. Before using such an index, it is a good idea to view the list of newspapers and magazines covered and determine the years of coverage.

Many libraries provide dial-in, Internet, or telnet access to their periodical databases as an option in their catalog menu. However, licensing restrictions usually mean that only researchers who have a library card for that particular library can access the database (by typing in their card number). Check with local public or school libraries to see what databases are available.

For periodicals not indexed by InfoTrac or another index, or for which only abstracts rather than complete text is available, check to see whether the publication has its own web site (most now do). Some scholarly publications are putting all or most of their articles online. Popular publications tend to offer only a limited selection of articles. Major newspapers typically offer current and recent articles (up to a week old perhaps) for free, and provide an archive from which older articles can be purchased for a few dollars.

PERIODICALS

Relevant specialized periodicals can be found in general university libraries or departmental libraries. Good departments to check are psychology, sociology, criminology, and public policy. Medical and legal libraries are also a possibility, although such materials may be too technical or specialized for most researchers. Some example periodical titles include:

- *Addictive Behaviors*
- *Alcohol Research & Health*
- *Alcoholism: Clinical and Experimental Research*
- *Alcoholism Treatment Quarterly*
- *Behavioral Health Management*
- *Journal of Child and Adolescent Substance Abuse*
- *Journal of Drug Education*
- *Journal of Psychoactive Drugs*
- *Journal of Studies on Alcohol*
- *Journal of Substance Abuse Treatment*

LEGAL RESEARCH

It is important for researchers to be able to obtain the text and summary of laws and court decisions relating to drug abuse and the war on drugs. Because of the specialized terminology of the law, legal research can be more difficult to master than bibliographical or general research tools. Fortunately, the Internet has also come to the rescue in this area, offering a variety of ways to look up laws and court cases without having to pore through huge bound volumes in law libraries (which may not be easily accessible to the general public anyway).

FINDING LAWS AND REGULATIONS

When federal legislation passes, it eventually becomes part of the U.S. Code, a massive legal compendium. The U.S. Code can be searched online in several locations, but the easiest site to use is probably the Cornell Law

School at http://www4.law.cornell.edu/uscode/. The fastest way to retrieve a law is by its title and section citation, but phrases and keywords can also be used.

A good shortcut to researching legal issues is to check the various general resource and advocacy web sites listed at the beginning of this chapter. Many of these organizations regularly summarize or compile recent cases and documents.

KEEPING UP WITH LEGISLATIVE DEVELOPMENTS

The Library of Congress Thomas web site (http://thomas.loc.gov/) includes files summarizing legislation by the number of the Congress. Each two-year session of Congress has a consecutive number. For example, the 108th Congress is in session in 2003 and 2004. Legislation can be searched for by the name of its sponsor(s), the bill number, or by topical keywords. Laws that have been passed can be looked up under their Public Law number.

For example, selecting the 108th Congress and typing in the phrase *drug abuse* into the search box will retrieve a number of bills pertaining to that subject. Clicking on the highlighted bill number brings up a display that includes the bill's status and text as well as further details, including sponsors, committee action, and amendments.

FINDING COURT DECISIONS

The Supreme Court and state courts make important decisions every year that determine how the laws are interpreted. As with laws, legal decisions are organized using a system of citations. The general form is *Party1 v. Party2 volume reporter [optional start page] (court, year)*.

Here are some examples:

Brandenburg v. Ohio, 395 U.S. 44 (1969)
Here the parties are Brandenberg (the defendant who is appealing his case from a state court) and the state of Ohio. The case is in volume 395 of the *U.S. Supreme Court Reports*, beginning at page 44, and the case was decided in 1969. (For the Supreme Court, the name of the court is omitted.)

Fierro v. Gomez 77 F.3d 301 (9th Cir. 1996)
Here the case is in the 9th U.S. Circuit Court of Appeals, decided in 1996.

A state court decision can generally be identified because it includes the state's name. For example, in *State v. Torrance*, 473 S.E. 2d. 703,

S.C. (1996), the S.E. refers to the appeals district, and the S.C. to South Carolina.

Once the jurisdiction for the case has been determined, the researcher can then go to a number of places on the Internet to find cases by citation and sometimes by the names of the parties or by subject keywords. Some of the most useful sites are:

- The Legal Information Institute at http://supct.law.cornell.edu/supct/ has all Supreme Court decisions since 1990, plus 610 of "the most important historic" decisions.
- Washlaw Web at http://www.washlaw.edu has a variety of courts (including state courts) and legal topics listed, making it a good jumping-off place for many forms of legal research. However, the actual accessibility of state court opinions (and the formats they are provided in) varies widely.

LEXIS AND WESTLAW

Lexis and Westlaw are commercial legal databases that have extensive sources of information, including an elaborate system of notes, legal subject headings, and ways to show relationships between cases. Unfortunately, these services are too expensive for use by most individual researchers unless they are available through a university or corporate library. Consult with your librarian on gaining access to these databases.

MORE HELP ON LEGAL RESEARCH

For more information on conducting legal research, see the Legal Research FAQ at http://www.cis.ohio-state.edu/hypertext/faq/usenet/law/research/ top.html. After a certain point, however, the researcher who lacks formal legal training may need to consult with or rely on the efforts of professional researchers or academics in the field.

EVALUATING WEB SOURCES

Thanks to the Web there is more information from more sources available than ever before. There is also a greater diversity of voices, since any person or group with a PC and Internet service can put up a web site—in some cases a site that looks as polished and professional as that of an established group. One benefit is that dissenting views can be found in abundance.

However, the other side of the coin is that the student or researcher must not let the attractions of the Web override the need for the same kind of critical thinking that would be applied to printed materials. Further, the nature of the Web means that the researcher should take extra care to try to verify facts and to understand the possible biases of each source. Some good questions to ask include:

- Who is responsible for this web site?
- What is the background or reputation of the person or group?
- Does the person or group have a stated objective or agenda?
- What biases might this person or group have?
- Do a number of high quality sites link to this one?
- What is the source given for a particular fact? Does that source actually say what is quoted? Where did *they* get that information?

If one uses a good variety of the tools and resources that have been highlighted here, that will help ensure that the results of research are balanced and comprehensive.

CHAPTER 7

ANNOTATED BIBLIOGRAPHY

This chapter presents a representative selection of books, articles, and Web (Internet) documents relating to drug abuse and addiction, treatment, the war on drugs, drug policy, and related issues. Materials have been selected where possible to be accessible, substantial, and diverse in viewpoint. The bibliography is divided into four broad categories that are further divided into subtopics as follows:

Reference and Background
General Reference Works
Anthologies and Collections
Historical, Introductory, and Overview Works

Abuse, Addiction, and Treatment
Drug Abuse and Addiction
Treatment Programs and Methods
Drug Abuse Education

The War on Drugs
Drug War Policies
International Drug Trafficking
Drug Law Enforcement
Legal and Civil Liberties Issues

Drug Policy Issues and Alternatives
Drugs in Schools, Sports, and the Workplace
Medical Use of Marijuana
Legalization and Decriminalization of Drugs
Harm Reduction Strategies

Within each topic, the listings are divided according to books, articles, and Web documents. Note that although all Web addresses (URLs) have been checked, Web pages are often moved or removed. If an address is not found, a keyword search using a search engine is recommended. See chapter 6 for more information about Internet research and resources.

Reference and Background

GENERAL REFERENCE WORKS

This section includes reference books such as encyclopedias, dictionaries, and bibliographies.

BOOKS

Blachford, Stacey L., and Kristine Krapp, eds. *Drugs and Controlled Substances: Information for Students*. Detroit: Thomson/Gale, 2003. Provides detailed information on drugs of abuse and the physiological and psychological characteristics of addiction. The volume is arranged alphabetically with entries by drug name. The entries focus especially on teen drug use, since this is the target audience. However, the book is also a good general reference.

Bowers, Jean M. *Drug Abuse Prevention, Education, and Treatment: Selected References*. Washington, D.C.: Congressional Research Service, 1998. A bibliography of Web links, printed resources, and organization contacts. Materials covered include programs and policy discussions.

Brick, John, ed. *Handbook of the Medical Consequences of Drug Abuse*. New York: Haworth Press, 2003. This textbook provides clear and comprehensive explanations of the medical effects of the major drugs of abuse. It begins with basic explanations of the effects of drugs such as alcohol, marijuana, and opiates and then explains in detail how these drugs affect the major organ systems, the neural system and brain, cognition, and effects on the developing fetus.

Carson-DeWitt, Rosalyn, ed. *Drugs, Alcohol & Tobacco: Learning About Addictive Behavior*. New York: Macmillan Reference, 2003. This comprehensive three-volume reference makes the latest research and statistics on addictive drugs available to students starting at the junior high school level. More than 200 articles explore such concepts as binge drinking and the genetic basis of addiction. There is also a list of organizations and web sites, an annotated bibliography, and a glossary of terms.

Chepesiuk, Ron. *The War on Drugs: An International Encyclopedia*. Santa Barbara, Calif.: ABC-CLIO, 1999. An A–Z encyclopedia with 642 entries covering a wide range of drug abuse–related topics, including organizations, biographies of individuals (including major drug traffickers), and enforcement operations. Each entry includes brief bibliographical references; there is also a chronology, a list of selected web sites, and a general bibliography.

DrugScope Information & Library Service. *Books for Kids and Teens*. London: DrugScope Information & Library Service, updated Spring 2003. Also available online. URL: http://www.drugscope.org.uk/uploads/goodpractice/documents/kids.pdf. A bibliography of books and articles on drugs and drug abuse for young readers. Predominately covers British publications but includes some American works as well.

DrugScope Information & Library Service. *Books on Cocaine*. London: DrugScope Information & Library Service, updated September 2003. Also available online. URL: http://www.drugscope.org.uk/wip/7/pdfs/Cocaine.pdf. Presents a good variety of literature and articles about cocaine and cocaine use, including works for young people.

DrugScope Information & Library Service. *Books on Ecstasy*. London: DrugScope Information & Library Service, updated Autumn 2003. Also available online. URL: http://www.drugscope.org.uk/wip/7/PDFS/Ecstasy.pdf. A bibliography of books and periodical articles on the "club drug" ecstasy.

DrugScope Library & Information Services. *Drug Databases and Libraries*. London: DrugScope Library & Information Services, updated Spring 2003. Also available online. URL: http://www.drugscope.org.uk/library/librarysection/lib_results.asp?file=\wip\7\pathfinders.htm#. A guide to and listing of databases, libraries, and Web resource sites relating to drug abuse and drug policy. Coverage is international, with some emphasis on Great Britain.

DrugScope Library & Information Services. *Statistics Pathfinder*. London: DrugScope Library & Information Services, updated November 2003. Also available online. URL: http://www.drugscope.org.uk/library/librarysection/lib_results.asp?file=\wip\7\pathfinders.htm#. Provides a listing for data sources, studies, and statistics relating to drug abuse around the world.

Gahlinger, Paul M. *Illegal Drugs: A Complete Guide to Their History, Chemistry, Use and Abuse*. Las Vegas: Sagebrush Press, 2001. This comprehensive handbook begins with basic terminology and concepts and proceeds to the history of drug use, the war on drugs, drug laws, the nature of drug abuse and addiction, employee drug testing, drugs and the brain, and the illegal drug market. The second part of the book is a guide to the various types of illegal drugs, including history, users, chemical characteristics, withdrawal symptoms, and long-term effects.

Krasner, Steve. *Alcohol, Drug, and Substance Abuse Prevention/Intervention*. Connecticut State Department of Education, 2002 [?]. Also available online. URL: http://www.dmhas.state.ct.us/prevention/sabiblio.pdf. A bibliography of articles on drug abuse prevention and intervention, particularly concerning youth. The main listing covers 1988–95, but the included Addendum 1 brings the coverage up to May 2002. A rather extensive listing of web sites is included.

Llanes, Ninon. *Elsevier's Dictionary of Drug Traffic Terms*. New York: Elsevier, 1997. Provides definitions of terms relating to drug trafficking in five languages: English, Spanish, Portuguese, French, and German. Also includes relevant legal terms.

Nash, Jay Robert. *World Encyclopedia of Organized Crime*. New York: Marlowe, 1994. Since much international organized crime involves drug trafficking, this reference is useful for looking up historical background on groups (such as drug cartels) and individuals through the 1980s.

National Institute on Alcohol Abuse and Alcoholism, National Institutes of Health. *The Alcohol and Other Drug (AOD) Thesaurus: A Guide to Concepts and Terminology in Substance Abuse and Addiction*. 3rd ed. Washington, D.C: U.S. Dept. of Health and Human Services, 2000. Also available online. URL: http://etoh.niaaa.nih.gov/AODVol1/Aodthome.htm. This is an outline and list of terms used by researchers in the field. Looking up the appropriate terms can help with retrieving materials from scientific and medical databases such as MEDLINE.

Nordegren, Thomas. *The A–Z Encyclopedia of Alcohol and Drug Abuse*. Parkland, Fla.: Brown Walker Press, 2002. A comprehensive reference work covering more than 30,000 terms, slang words and phrases, organizations, and other entries relating to alcohol and drug abuse. Prepared in cooperation with the International Council on Alcohol and Addictions.

Parker, James N. and Philip M. Parker, editors. *Drug Abuse: A Medical Dictionary, Bibliography and Annotated Reference Guide to Internet References*. San Diego, Calif.: Icon Health Publications, 2003. This three-in-one reference work provides a complete dictionary of medical terms relating to drug abuse, extensive bibliographies, and a guide to Internet resources.

Ray, Oakley S., and Charles J. Ksir. *Drugs, Society, and Human Behavior with PowerWeb and HealthQuest CD-ROM*. 10th ed. New York: McGraw-Hill, 2003. This latest edition of a comprehensive guide to the pharmacological, behavioral, clinical, social, and legal aspects of drug abuse also includes a CD with powerful Web-searching and information-retrieval tools.

Sifakis, Carl. *Encyclopedia of American Crime*. New York: Facts On File, 2003. Defines nearly 900 terms used in the criminal underworld (and sometimes adopted into general language). Besides many of the terms being colorful and interesting in their own right, this reference will be helpful in reading interviews and other primary sources relating to drug trafficking.

Woods, Geraldine. *Drug Abuse in Society: A Reference Handbook*. Santa Barbara, Calif.: ABC-CLIO, 1993. This reference handbook includes a chronology, overview of laws, biographies, statistics, organizations, and bibliographies of print and nonprint resources.

WEB DOCUMENTS

Boston University Library. "Research Guides: Drug Abuse." Boston University Library. Available online. URL: http://www.bu.edu/library/guides/drugabuse.html. Updated December 9, 2003. Provides a useful list of subject headings, indexes, databases, statistics, and Internet resources on topics relating to drug abuse.

National Institute on Drug Abuse "Commonly Abused Drugs." National Institute on Drug Abuse. Available online. URL: http://www.nida.nih.gov/DrugPages/DrugsofAbuse.html. Updated May 28, 2003. Categorizes the main types of drugs of abuse and provides information and further links for each drug. Also includes a summary of basic principles of drug abuse treatment.

McCaul, Mary E. "Treatment Outcomes for Women Drug Abusers: Annotated Bibliography." National Institute on Drug Abuse. Available online. URL: http://www.nida.nih.gov/about/organization/DESPR/HSR/datre/McCaulTreatmentPartA.html. Posted April 1998. Summarizes NIDA funded studies and presentations that identify factors that determine the success or failure of substance abuse treatment for women, as well as developmental outcomes for drug-exposed infants. As with other NIDA summaries, although studies are rather technical, the basic conclusions can be understood by students and general readers.

Williams, Paul, and Tessa Piagno. "Annotated Bibliography of Pathways Theory of Drug Use." Australian Institute of Criminology. Available online. URL: http://www.aic.gov.au/research/drugs/pathway/bib.html#01. Updated January 8, 2003. This bibliography summarizes medical and other studies of the effects of drug abuse, particularly focusing on the question of whether alcohol, tobacco, or marijuana function as pathways or gateways leading to use of harder drugs.

ANTHOLOGIES AND COLLECTIONS

This section includes books that bring together writings from many contributors on broad themes relating to drug abuse or drug policy or that provide background for "pro/con" discussion or debates.

Drug Abuse

BOOKS

Cherry, Andrew, Mary E. Dillon, and Douglas Rugh. *Substance Abuse: A Global View.* Westport, Conn.: Greenwood Press, 2002. This collection has chapters by separate authors profiling the drug abuse situation in Burma, Canada, China, Colombia, England, France, India, Ireland, Mexico, the Netherlands, Russia, Switzerland, and the United States. For each country there is a historical perspective, current developments, and policy issues.

Egendorf, Laura K. *Chemical Dependency: Opposing Viewpoints.* 3rd ed. San Diego, Calif.: Greenhaven Press, 2003. A collection of sources and commentary arranged to illuminate major issues regarding chemical dependency or addiction. Topics discussed include the seriousness of the problem, the cause of chemical dependency, which treatments and prevention programs are effective, whether the war on drugs has been successful, and whether (and how) drug laws should be reformed.

Gaines, Larry K., and Peter B. Kraska, eds. *Drugs, Crime, & Justice,* Second ed. Prospect Heights, Ill.: Waveland Press, 2003. This collection of writings by experts in criminal justice and related fields begins with an overview and historical context. The remaining sections deal with the relationship between drug use and crime, illicit drug trafficking and markets, enforcement of drug laws, drug treatment, and various perspectives on illegal and legal drugs.

Goldberg, Raymond, ed. *Taking Sides: Clashing Views on Controversial Issues in Drugs and Society.* 6th ed. Guilford, Conn.: McGraw-Hill/Dushkin, 2004. A collection of pro/con articles with commentary. The volume is divided into three main sections: drugs and public policy, drugs and social policy, and drug prevention and treatment.

Hurley, Jennifer A., ed. *Addiction: Opposing Viewpoints.* San Diego, Calif.: Greenhaven Press, 2000. A collection of pro and con articles on various aspects of addiction, including factors involved in addiction, the seriousness of the problem, and methods of treatment. Includes bibliographies and a list of organizations.

Hyde, Stephen, and Geno Zanetti, eds. *White Lines: Writers on Cocaine.* New York: Thunder's Mouth Press, 2002. Understanding the history of drug use and its place in our culture also requires considering its reflection in literature and the arts. This volume brings together selections from well-known, notorious, and lesser-known writers on the cocaine experience from Victorian times to the present day. Authors of selections include Sigmund Freud, Aleister Crowley, William S. Burroughs, Timothy Leary, J.G. Ballard, Hunter S. Thompson, and Terry Southern.

Levinthal, Charles F. *Point/Counterpoint: Opposing Perspectives on Issues of Drug Policy.* Boston: Pearson Education, 2003. Provides overviews and "pro and con" documentary selections relating to nine drug policy questions. Issues covered include drug legalization, the priority for drug interdiction, needle exchanges, harm reduction as an overall policy approach, approaches to addiction and treatment, and legal medical use of marijuana.

Macoun, Robert, and Peter Reuter. *Cross-National Drug Policy.* Annals of the American Academy of Political and Social Science, vol. 582, July 2002. Thousand Oaks, Calif.: SAGE Publications, 2002. This volume is a collection of papers on drug policy issues in many nations. Topics discussed include drug law enforcement, harm minimization, and legalization, as well as the economic, social, and political aspects of black markets in illegal drugs in Colombia, Iran, and Russia.

Musto, David F. *Drugs in America: A Documentary History.* New York: New York University Press, 2002. Presents original documents relating to drugs in American history from colonial times to the end of the 1990s. Materials range from songs and speeches from 19th-century temperance organizations to medical studies and legal opinions and government documents.

Torr, James D. *Drug Abuse: Opposing Viewpoints.* San Diego, Calif.: Greenhaven Press, 1999. A collection of pro/con readings on drug policy issues, together with introductory commentaries. Topics covered include the seriousness of the drug abuse problem, effectiveness of drug education and testing, whether U.S. drug policy has been successful, and whether drugs should be legalized.

Wilson, Hugh T., ed. *Drugs, Society, and Behavior, 03/04.* Guilford, Conn.: McGraw Hill/Dushkin, 2003. This latest in a series of "Annual Editions" compilations includes articles arranged into the following categories: Living with Drugs; Understanding How Drugs Work; Major Drugs of Use and Abuse; Other Trends in Drug Use; Drugs and Crime; Measuring the Social Cost of Drugs; Creating and Sustaining Effective Drug Control Policy; and Prevention, Treatment, and Education. The volume also includes an introductory essay for each section, a guide to Web resources, and a glossary. The preceding volume (01/02) is also recommended, although there is a small overlap.

HISTORICAL, INTRODUCTORY, AND OVERVIEW WORKS

These books and articles present broad historical and general background to drug abuse and related issues, or deal with specific historical or cultural topics.

Drug Abuse

BOOKS

Abel, Ernest L. *Marihuana: The First Twelve Thousand Years.* New York: Plenum Press, 1980. This readable narrative explores one of humankind's oldest drugs and its use in "primitive" rituals, later abuse, and its characterization as a drug of abuse. There is also discussion of marijuana's portrayal in the arts and attitudes toward the drug in different cultures.

Bailey, William Everett. *The Invisible Drug.* Mosaic Publications, 1996. Written especially for junior and high school students, this book is a useful introduction to and overview of tobacco and smoking. Topics include tobacco regulation, the tobacco industry and its marketing efforts, the effects of secondhand smoke, and the influence of cigarette advertising on youth.

Barr, Andrew. *Drink: A Social History of America.* Carroll & Graf, 1999. According to this account, American society from colonial days to the 21st century is steeped in alcohol and its abuse—hence the story of drinking relates to the social history of America as a whole. The collective drinking binges were followed by equally ill-advised "binges" of prohibitionism.

Behr, Edward. *Prohibition: Thirteen Years That Changed America.* New York: Arcade Publishing, 1996. This engaging account begins with the rise of the temperance movement in reaction to widespread use of alcohol in 19th-century America and continues to the enacting of nationwide alcohol prohibition in 1920. The bulk of the book, however, covers the 13 years up to the repeal of Prohibition in 1933 and is filled with accounts of bootlegging, gang battles, law enforcers, and the people in both high society and the lower classes who continued to pursue the pleasures of alcohol.

Belenko, Steven R. *Drugs and Drug Policy in America: A Documentary History.* Westport, Conn.: Greenwood Press, 2000. Provides more than 250 primary source documents, including speeches, editorials, laws, and legal opinions. The documents are grouped into sections both chronologically and by topic, including special topics such as the escalation of punishment, the medicalization of addiction, and the debate over drug legalization.

Bonnie, Richard J., and Charles H. Whitebread. *The Marijuana Conviction: A History of Marijuana Prohibition in the United States.* New York: Lindesmith Center, 1999. This reprint from the Lindesmith Center contains a report originally written by a Nixon administration committee on the history, development, and effects of marijuana control policy in the United States up to the early 1970s. Rather surprisingly, given the time and place of its origin, the report is highly critical of marijuana policy, implicating it with charges of racism and recommending reform of marijuana laws.

Carnwath, Tom, and Ian Smith. *Heroin Century.* New York: Routledge, 2002. This history and overview puts heroin in perspective, including its development and use in the 20th century; how the drug is produced, distributed, and taken today; attempts at control and treatment; and prospects for the future.

Collin, Matthew. *Altered State: The Story of Ecstasy Culture & Acid House.* New York: Serpent's Tail, 1997. A social history of an underground culture that first developed during the 1970s in a mixture of psychedelic revival and disco music, and then began to flourish in the 1980s with raves and "house" music. Provides many sources, including interviews with people who were influential in the development of the culture, as well as documents reflecting governmental and medical response to the growing use of ecstasy and other club drugs.

Cooper, Edith Fairman. *The Emergence of Crack Cocaine Abuse in the United States: A Public Health Perspective.* Washington, D.C.: Congressional Research Service, 1998. This lengthy report gives background about crack cocaine use, including the development and spread of the "crack epidemic." The response of federal officials to the early stages of the epidemic is also evaluated.

Davenport-Hines, Richard. *The Pursuit of Oblivion: A Global History of Narcotics.* New York: W.W. Norton, 2002. In a wide-ranging survey a historian shows the use of intoxicating substances in the context of many eras and cultures in which human beings have sought their physical and psychological effects. Using vivid examples and quotations the author describes how opiates and other powerfully addictive substances were introduced in the 19th century for their real or supposed medical value, creating addiction in many cases. He then suggests that the struggle to control drug addiction throughout the 20th century has been considerably driven by class antagonisms and racial stereotypes, resulting in a war that cannot be won.

Durrant, Rossil, and Jo Thakker. *Substance Use and Abuse: Cultural and Historical Perspectives.* Thousand Oaks, Calif.: SAGE Publications, 2003. Presents (and argues for) a multidisciplinary understanding of drug use (not just abuse) that involves biological, psychological, cultural, and historical perspectives. The discussion includes some perspectives not often found in this field, such as an understanding of the evolutionary basis of drug-taking behavior.

Edwards, Griffith, and Malcolm H. Lader. *Alcohol: The World's Favorite Drug.* New York: St. Martin's Press, 2002. Alcohol is so familiar that many people do not really think of it as a drug. This book takes a balanced approach to the uses and abuses of alcohol throughout history and today. A number of common questions are addressed, including why people react differently to alcohol, why alcoholism is considered a disease, and the possible health benefits of moderate alcohol use.

Escohotado, Antonio. *A Brief History of Drugs: From the Stone Age to the Stoned Age.* Rochester, Vt.: Park Street Press, 1999. The author, a professor of philosophy and social science methodology at the University of Madrid, Spain, offers an eclectic social history of drugs that ranges widely in time and geography. The description of developments in Europe and elsewhere provides a useful complement to most American works on the subject.

Freud, Sigmund. *The Cocaine Papers.* New York: Stonehill Publishing Company, 1974. Collects the writings of the pioneer psychoanalyst on cocaine. Freud, at least at first, touted cocaine as a safe and effective treatment for depression and other problems. Today this naïve opinion remains an important document in the development of attitudes toward narcotics in the late 19th century.

Gordon, Susan M. *Heroin: Challenge for the 21st Century.* Wernersville, Pa.: Caron Foundation, 2001. Also available online. URL: http://www.caron. org/pdf/Heroin.pdf. An introduction to the problem of heroin addiction, including trends in use; the drug's appeal and threat; biological, psychological, and social aspects of addiction; treatment issues; and recovery options. The publisher is a nonprofit drug treatment center.

Hammersley, Richard, Furzana Khan, and Jason Ditton. *Ecstasy and the Rise of the Chemical Generation.* New York: Routledge, 2002. Drawing upon an extensive study funded by the British government, the author-researchers extensively interviewed participants in the Glasgow ecstasy scene in great detail. The authors want readers to understand that "Drug users are no longer a mad, bad or immoral minority. Using drugs is normal for the chemical generation, and the drug that defines them is Ecstasy." The book looks closely at the ways in which individuals began to use the drug, the different ways of using it, the connection between ecstasy and "clubbing," ecstasy use and sex, and many other topics. Problems encountered by users and cases of users who quit are also discussed, but the authors believe there is as yet no definitive answer to the question of whether ecstasy causes permanent damage to its users.

Himmelstein, Jerome L. *The Strange Career of Marijuana: Politics and Ideology and Drug Control in America.* Westport, Conn.: Greenwood Press, 1983. Drawing on both popular culture and official reports, the author provides an intriguing history of how law and policy about marijuana were shaped since the passage of the Marijuana Tax Act of 1937.

Holland, Julie, ed. *Ecstasy: The Complete Guide—A Comprehensive Look at the Risks and Benefits of MDMA.* Rochester, Vt.: Inner Traditions International, 2001. A collection of essays by experts exploring the benefits and risks of MDMA (ecstasy) for treating psychiatric disorders as well as the problems associated with recreational use of the drug. Suggestions are made for gaining the benefits of the drug while minimizing risks and harm.

Jackson-Jacobs, Curtis. *Illegal Drugs: America's Anguish.* Farmington Hills, Mich.: Gale Group, 2002. This volume in the Information Plus Reference Series is packed with background material, statistics, and charts, including characteristics of drugs of abuse, drug treatment, the war on drugs, and the issue of drug legalization.

Jay, Mike. *Emperors of Dreams: Drugs in the Nineteenth Century.* Sawtry, [Cambridgeshire, UK]: Dedalus, 2002. A fascinating account of how opium (laudanum), hashish, cocaine, and other drugs entered into European and American society in the 19th century and inspired the imagination in literature, the arts, and culture. The book explores the reaction to this drug explosion—calls for temperance and prohibition that grew increasingly strident into the early 20th century.

Jonnes, Jill. *Hep-Cats, Narcs, and Pipe Dreams: A History of America's Romance with Illegal Drugs.* New York: Scribner, 1996. A vivid investigation and narrative of the impact of drugs on American culture in the 20th century, from Prohibition to the psychedelic 1960s to the crack epidemic of the 1980s and 1990s and beyond. Discussion of controversial issues such as drug legalization is also woven into the account.

Kranz, Rachel. *Straight Talk About Smoking.* New York: Facts On File, 1999. A factual but engaging account of smoking-related issues for junior high and high school students. The author starts by quizzing readers on their knowledge of smoking and its effects, and then uses vignettes and facts to discuss such topics as health effects, effects of secondhand smoke, smoking as an addiction, ways to quit smoking, and tobacco marketing to young people and minorities.

Kuhn, Cynthia, et al. *Buzzed: The Straight Facts about the Most Used and Abused Drugs from Alcohol to Ecstasy.* 2nd Ed. New York: W.W. Norton, 2003. The authors, all knowledgeable researchers in the field, attempt to close the gap between current scientific understanding of the major drugs and their effects and widespread popular ignorance or misconceptions. Despite the complexity of the subject, the writing is straightforward and evenhanded. For each drug there is both a general discussion of effects and risks and specific details about interactions between drugs and special risks, such as to pregnant women.

Leary, Timothy. *Flashbacks: A Personal and Cultural History of an Era: An Autobiography.* New York: J.P. Tarcher, 1997. Leary provides a multifaceted account of his controversial career as a rogue psychologist, psychedelic guru, and spiritual explorer.

Leary, Timothy, and Beverly Potter. *Change Your Brain.* Berkeley, Calif.: Ronin Publishing, 2000. An account of Leary's early research on psychedelics in the 1950s and early 1960s. Includes Leary's discussion of the psychedelic experience and its relationship to behavior, creativity, and spirituality.

Levinthal, Charles F. *Drugs, Behavior, and Modern Society.* 3rd ed. Boston: Allyn and Bacon, 2002. A psychological textbook presenting biological, psychological, and public health perspectives on drug abuse. Different types of drugs and specific issues are explained at a level suitable for college and advanced high school students.

Massing, Michael. *Fix: Under the Nixon Administration, America Had an Effective Drug Policy. We Should Restore It. (Nixon Was Right).* New York: Simon & Schuster, 1998. The author makes the rather surprising assertion that the first emphasis in the drug war, under the Nixon administration, was actually the correct one. It focused on hard drug users—not users of marijuana—and it emphasized treating these hard-core addicts rather than imprisoning them. However, under Reagan, funding for treatment was drastically cut, and the author analyzes political reasons for this fateful turn.

Musto, David. *The American Disease: Origins of Narcotic Control.* 3rd ed. New York: Oxford University Press, 1999. This is an expanded edition of a classic work that traces the development of drug control laws in the United States from the mid-19th century to the present day. The author carefully traces the different interest groups (such as reformers in the Progressive era who saw drug abuse as a scourge and medical professionals seeking to protect their prescription rights), the influence of racism (as with stereotypes about Chinese opium users and Mexican-immigrant marijuana users), and political considerations.

National Center on Addiction and Substance Abuse. *National Survey of American Attitudes on Substance Abuse VI: Teens.* New York: National Center on Addiction and Substance Abuse at Colombia University, February 2001. Also available online. URL: http://www.casalibrary.org/CASAPublications/Survey%20VI.pdf. This survey attempts to probe deeply into teens' attitudes toward drugs in order to identify "factors that increase or diminish the likelihood that teens will use cigarettes, alcohol or illegal drugs." The survey found that "hands-on" parents who set expectations for their children's behavior and monitored them considerably reduced the risk of drug abuse. Teens are motivated far more by fear of physical harm or addiction than by the fact that drugs are illegal. Recent data suggests that cigarettes are becoming harder for teens to obtain, but marijuana is becoming somewhat more accessible.

National Center on Addiction and Substance Abuse. *National Survey of American Attitudes on Substance Abuse VII: Teens, Parents and Siblings.* New York: National Center on Addiction and Substance Abuse at Colombia University, August 2002. Also available online. URL: http://www.casalibrary.org/

CASAPublications/TeenSurvey2002.pdf. The report has the encouraging news that a majority of teens report they are attending "drug-free" schools. The report highlights a little known but important factor: Teens who believe their older siblings would strongly disapprove of their marijuana use are at substantially lower risk of substance abuse. On the other hand, when older siblings themselves use drugs, younger teens are at increased risk of becoming drug abusers.

Owen, Frank. *Clubland: The Fabulous Rise and Murderous Fall of Club Culture.* New York: St. Martin's Press, 2003. A detailed account interweaving the lives of the major "players" responsible for the "club" scene in New York in the 1990s, which featured drugs such as ecstasy and "Special K" (Ketamine, a veterinary anesthetic), as well as money, extravagant behavior, and crime.

Rawson, Jean M. *Hemp for Industrial Uses.* Washington, D.C.: Congressional Research Service, 2000. Describes the industrial uses of hemp (the inactive part of the cannabis plant) and summarizes arguments for and against legalization of hemp production in the United States.

Ryan, Elizabeth A. *Straight Talk About Drugs & Alcohol.* Revised Edition. New York: Facts On File, 1995. The author provides clear and practical advice to teens who are facing questions about their own drug or alcohol use or that of peers or even parents. The effects and risk of drugs are presented without being "preachy."

Sloman, Larry Ratso. *Reefer Madness: The History of Marijuana in America.* New York: St. Martin's Griffin, 1998. The first popular social history of the drug, this somewhat irreverent look at marijuana traces its use and popular attitudes from colonial times to the passionate dedication of anti-drug crusader Harry Anslinger and the enactment of marijuana prohibition and the proliferation of the weed in the 1960s and 1970s.

Sonder, Ben. *All About Heroin.* New York: Franklin Watts, 2002. Written primarily for high school students, this book describes the history of heroin use, effects of the drug, the experiences of addicts, and efforts to control use of the drug. Includes bibliographies and lists of web sites and organizations.

Stone, Jason, and Andrea Stone. *The Drug Dilemma: Responding to a Growing Crisis.* New York: International Debate Education Association, 2003. This sourcebook on drug policy issues includes a wide range of sources, including documents from the European Union and the United Nations. The major drug policy alternatives (including legalization) are presented; there is also a section on drugs and terrorism.

Streatfeild, Dominic. *Cocaine: An Unauthorized Biography.* New York: Picador, 2003. The author, a documentary film producer, has translated some of his techniques to the print medium. This book takes the unusual approach of tracing the "biography" or career of cocaine from pre-Columbian civilizations to its modern role as a drug of abuse through interviews with more than 150 traffickers, users, researchers, and law enforcement agents.

Tattersall, Clare. *Date Rape Drugs*. New York: Rosen Publishing Group, 2000. A clear explanation of GHB and its use as a "date rape" drug that incapacitates victims and even robs them of memory of the assault. The effects of the drug are explained and tips are given for avoiding exposure to situations where predators might be using the drug.

Tracy, Sarah W., and Caroline Jean Acker. *Altering American Consciousness: The History of Alcohol and Drug Use in the United States.* Amherst: University of Massachusetts Press, 2004. This collection of essays explores the changing perceptions of drug use in American history and culture. Such changes are perhaps most striking in the case of tobacco smoking, which once was considered glamorous and liberating by many but today borders on socially unacceptable. However, these essays point out that there have been important changes in the perception of alcohol, marijuana, and even cocaine and heroin.

Wolfe, Tom. *The Electric Kool-Aid Acid Test.* New York: Bantam Books, 1999. A classic account of the man that many came to consider the archetypal hippie. Wolfe, well-known for his achievements as a participant-writer, bases his account on a tour with Ken Kesey and his "Merry Pranksters" in the 1960s. The Pranksters traveled in a painted bus marked "Further," presiding over gatherings where people participated in "acid tests" by taking LSD.

Zimmer, Lynn, and John P. Morgan. *Marijuana Myths, Marijuana Facts: A Review of the Scientific Evidence.* New York: Lindesmith Center, 1997. Provides a comprehensive overview of what is known about marijuana from the scientific literature and applies it to current policy issues such as medical use and decriminalization.

WEB DOCUMENTS

Borio, Gene. "Tobacco Timeline." Tobacco.org. Available online. URL: http://www.tobacco.org/resources/history/tobacco_history.html. Downloaded December 7, 2003. A detailed chronological account of developments in tobacco use, advertising, marketing, and the movement against smoking.

"David F. Musto: Interview." *Frontline*, PBS Online. Available online. URL: http://www.pbs.org/wgbh/pages/frontline/shows/dope/interviews/musto .html. Posted in 1998. An eminent historian of drug use and drug policy in the United States provides an overview of the remarkable history of marijuana in America. It includes the activities of Harry Anslinger, the person probably most responsible for establishing the federal role in narcotics enforcement from the 1930s to the 1960s.

"Monitoring the Future: A Continuing Study of American Youth." University of Michigan. Available online. URL: http://www.monitoringthefuture.org/. Updated September 22, 2003. These ongoing studies are conducted under a grant from the National Institute on Drug Abuse of the National Institutes of Health. The reports include numerous data tables for the survey of youth use of and attitudes toward drugs, as well as an "overview of key findings."

Abuse, Addiction, and Treatment

DRUG ABUSE AND ADDICTION

This section deals with works that focus on the experience of drug users and abusers, including physiological and psychological aspects of the process of addiction.

BOOKS

Abel, Ernest L. *Fetal Alcohol Abuse Syndrome*. New York: Plenum Press, 1998. Describes the causes and consequences of fetal alcohol syndrome, including pregnancy-related problems (such as spontaneous abortion), birth defects, and neurological abnormalities. There is also discussion of how to diagnose the condition and how to estimate its prevalence.

Brigham, Janet. *Dying to Quit: Why We Smoke and How We Stop*. Washington, D.C.: National Academy Press, 1998. This accessible account explains the dynamics of tobacco addiction to both medical professionals and general readers. In addition to motivating smokers through a careful explanation of the horrendous health effects of smoking, the author explains how smokers can deal with withdrawal symptoms and how involvement in a social network can help prevent relapses in ex-smokers.

Colvin, Rod. *Prescription Drug Abuse: The Hidden Epidemic: A Guide to Coping and Understanding*. Omaha, Neb.: Addicus Books, 1995. Although abuse of illegal drugs seems to have received the lion's share of attention in the media and by policymakers, in recent years there has been increasing focus on the abuse of legal prescription drugs. This book is a practical guide that explains how use of prescription drugs can become abuse and then addiction. The author uses stories of affected individuals to show how treatment works and what is important in recovery from addiction and prevention of relapse.

DuPont, Robert L. *The Selfish Brain: Learning from Addiction.* Center City, Minn.: Hazelden, 2000. The author, a former "drug czar," provides an accessible explanation geared toward individuals and families facing the problem of drug addiction. The biological effects of drugs are described using real-life accounts.

European Monitoring Centre for Drugs and Drug Addiction (EMCDDA). *Annual Report 2003: The State of the Drugs Problem in the European Union and Norway.* Also available online. URL: http://annualreport.emcdda.eu. int/en/home-en.html. An annual report on drug abuse in the European Union nations and Norway, compiled from statistics provided by the various governments. An accompanying press release for the 2003 report offered "cautious optimism" with regard to the struggle against drug abuse.

French, Laurence Armand. *Addictions and Native Americans.* Westport, Conn.: Praeger Publishers, 2000. A useful introduction to the tragic role various addictions have played in Native American history and culture, as well as current problems and issues. Treatment must take into account the overall social and economic problems in Native American communities. The author also suggests that compulsive gambling is an emerging and troubling addiction problem for Native Americans.

Goldstein, Avram. *Addiction: From Biology to Drug Policy.* 2nd ed. New York: Oxford University Press, 2001. A systematic handbook on drugs, drug use, and drug policy. The book's three parts deal with the brain and drug addiction, the effects of the major types of addictive drugs, and questions of drug policy, including prevention and treatment. The author concludes with a discussion that endorses "harm reduction"—not as a disguised agenda for legalization, but as a way to better manage drug addiction, such as by providing drugs to existing addicts in a controlled way.

Grosshandler, Janet. *Coping with Drinking and Driving.* Revised ed. New York: Rosen Publishing Group, 1997. This book for high school students describes the terrible impact of drunken driving—more than a million people are injured, crippled, or killed each year in alcohol-related traffic accidents. The author also explains how alcohol affects the body and what this means in terms of driving skills.

Klee, Hilary, Marcia Jackson, and Suzan Lewis. *Drug Misuse and Motherhood.* New York: Routledge, 2001. There has been much controversy about the effects of drug abuse on mothers and their children. This book brings some concrete detail to the subject by presenting accounts from drug-using mothers and the professionals who seek to help them. There is also discussion of surveys and research and some conclusions about how policies and services can be improved.

Meier, Barry. *Pain Killer: The True Story of a Prescription Drug Disaster.* Emmaus, Penn.: Rodale Press, 2003. A *New York Times* reporter tells the story of OxyContin, showing how it became a major drug of abuse. Important issues arising out of the OxyContin debacle include the marketing, sale, and advertising of the drug and conflict between the drive for profit and the need to prevent abuse. Some critics, however, feel the author does not give sufficient weight to the importance of pain management as a legitimate medical specialty.

Murphy, Sheigla, and Marsha Rosenbaum. *Pregnant Women on Drugs: Combating Stereotypes and Stigma*. New Brunswick, N.J.: Rutgers University Press, 1999. Two sociologists reach beyond the data and stereotypes to work with interviews with 120 pregnant women who abuse drugs. The result is a much more individualized picture of how people see their choices and priorities, including decisions about whether to terminate the pregnancy or fight the addiction, keep the fetus, and deal with the possibility of not delivering a healthy baby.

National Institute on Drug Abuse. *Bringing the Power of Science to Bear on Drug Abuse and Addiction*. Revised ed. Bethesda, Md.: National Institute on Drug Abuse, 2000. Also available online. URL: http://165.112.78.61/PDF/StratPlan.pdf. Provides the institute's five-year plan for research on drug abuse and addiction. The introduction points out that rapid advances in both molecular biology and genomics are providing new paths to understanding the biological basis of addiction and how drugs work in (and on) the brain.

National Institute on Drug Abuse. *Drug Abuse Among Racial/Ethnic Minorities*. Revised ed. Bethesda, Md.: National Institute on Drug Abuse, 2003. Also available online. URL: http://165.112.78.61/pdf/minorities03.pdf. A compilation of surveys and studies on drug abuse by minorities, primarily from the mid- to late 1990s. Data sources include the U.S. Census and a variety of epidemiological studies.

Nevitt, Amy. *Fetal Alcohol Syndrome*. Revised ed. New York: Rosen Publishing Group, 1998. Written for students at junior high level and up, this book explains what can happen to children born to parents who use alcohol and how fetal alcohol syndrome can seriously affect an individual for a lifetime. There are suggestions for pregnant teens seeking help for their alcohol problems.

Peele, Stanton. *The Meaning of Addiction: An Unconventional View*. San Francisco: Jossey Bass, 1998. In another work attacking the generally accepted model of addiction, the author asks why, if addiction is a disease with a relentless effect on behavior, a large number of addicts "recover" and end their drug use without receiving treatment. He suggests that alcoholism and drug addiction, along with other compulsive behavior such as overeating, running, and sex, often represent a way of coping with life stresses. This suggests that individuals have considerable freedom to seek out better coping mechanisms.

Drug Abuse

Tan, Dawn. *Broken Mirror: True Stories About Drug Abuse.* Singapore: Angsana Books, 2000. In this unusual book the author, an award-winning journalist working in Singapore and the United Kingdom, provides vivid accounts of the predicaments of drug abusers and the people they interact with—parents, children, police, and counselors. The fact that Singapore sentences people to death for some drug offenses makes the stories particularly poignant and chilling.

Weatherly, Myra. *Inhalants.* Springfield, N.J.: Enslow, 1996. This book for young adults explains the dangers of "huffing" solvents and other inhalants, which can provide an accessible "high" for young people who might have trouble obtaining illegal drugs. Inhalant abuse can cause severe liver damage and other serious health problems.

ARTICLES

Adler, Jerry. "In the Grip of a Deeper Pain: Opioids." *Newsweek*, October 20, 2003, p. 48. Describes the double-edged sword that is opiates. These drugs have the strength to deal with agonizing, chronic, debilitating pain such as that of a slipped disk or even terminal cancer. However, opiates can also provide a tempting relief from depression or daily stress, and such use can lead to dependence and addiction. The author also describes two routes to drug treatment, a center called Hazelden that provides both medical and 12-step-based treatment, and the use of "rapid detox," where the patient is anesthetized in order to be able to undergo a rapid withdrawal that would otherwise be intolerable.

Baily, Cate. "Close-up: LSD: 'I'm Losing My Mind': A Young Woman's Experience with the Hallucinogenic Drug LSD." *Junior Scholastic*, vol. 106, October 27, 2003, pp. 16ff. Describes the story of Amanda Contadino, a former LSD abuser who recounts a time when she (unusually) took the drug almost daily. Today she is worried about the damage that may have been done to her brain, and she still experiences perceptual distortions. The article also includes background information and answers to frequently asked questions.

Begley, Sharon. "How It All Starts Inside Your Brain." *Newsweek*, February 12, 2001, pp. 40–42. Describes how brain scientists are gaining an understanding of the drug experience at the neural level. The most important factor is that drugs such as cocaine, heroin, alcohol, and amphetamines alter the brain's pleasure or reward "circuit" by increasing the concentration of the neurotransmitter dopamine in various ways. However, the brain also responds by cutting down the number of dopamine receptors, which means the addict has to keep increasing the drug dose to get the desired effects.

Carpenter, Siri. "The Changing Face of Marijuana Research." *Monitor on Psychology*, June 2001, pp. 40–42. Some people consider marijuana to be highly addictive and a gateway to harder drugs, while others believe it to be a social drug no more harmful than alcohol. Between these two positions lies the reality that marijuana affects individuals differently, as shown by variation in withdrawal symptoms. The identification of cannabis receptors in the brain has led to the realization that some marijuana users may be motivated to continue use in order to avoid withdrawal symptoms. However, about 40 percent of users seem not to experience drug dependence or withdrawal symptoms. Treatment plans need to take these different responses into account.

————. "Cognition Is Central to Drug Addiction." *Monitor on Psychology*, June 2001, pp. 34–35. Writing for a publication of the American Psychological Association, the author surveys recent research that suggests that drug abuse affects decision making, thinking, and inhibition. Some drug abusers lose the ability to consider long-term consequences, for example. These impairments of thinking in turn promote the transition to addiction. Persistent cognitive problems also make it more likely that recovering addicts will relapse.

Chua-Eoan, Howard. "Escaping from the Darkness." *Time*, May 31, 1999, pp. 44–49. Prescription drugs such as Prozac and Paxil can help clinically depressed kids get back on their feet and function normally. The problem is that the drugs' very effectiveness encourages their over-prescription and their application to emotional problems that fall well short of clinical depression. Besides contributing to a drug supply for illicit distribution and use, the over-prescription might also deprive teenagers of the opportunity to experience and overcome the challenges that are part of growing up.

Cloud, John. "It's All the Rave." *Time*, March 13, 2000, pp. 64–66. Reports that ecstasy, which was once a "club drug" used by the elite and the trendy sets, is now being widely used in fraternity houses and even in high schools. Producers are distributing huge quantities of the drug. The drug's socially enhancing effects combined with its lack of an obvious downside contributes to its popularity. Although the question of the drug's physical dangers has not yet been resolved, the entry of organized criminals into the trade brings potential violence as well as the danger of users getting contaminated or adulterated pills.

Cloud, John. "The Lure of Ecstasy." *Time*, June 5, 2000, pp. 62–68. Describes the background on ecstasy (MDMA), a drug that was actually developed about 80 years ago and today is widely used in clubs and raves. The history of psychiatric use of the drug is also recounted, and advocates for therapeutic use of the drug are again being heard. The author concludes that the drug is likely neither as dangerous as the government insists nor as safe and beneficial as proponents argue.

Duenwald, Mary. "A Scientist's Lifetime of Study into the Mysteries of Addiction." *New York Times*, August 19, 2003, p. F5. A profile of and interview with Dr. Nora Volkow, director of the National Institute on Drug Abuse. She has spent her career researching the brain and behavioral effects of drug abuse. She answers some common questions on topics such as drug abuse and free will. She explains that acknowledging that drug addiction is a disease does not absolve the individual from taking responsibility for his or her health, just as a person suffering from heart disease must take responsibility for diet and exercise.

Farrington, Jan. "Resisting Cocaine's Tragic Lure." *Current Health*, February 1999, pp. 6–12. Beginning with a description of the experience of "Zach," a 19-year-old whose life during high school spiraled downward into cocaine addiction, the article describes cocaine's use and effects. It also warns that kids are often enticed into using heroin by the same dealers who had been selling them cocaine. Powder heroin is tempting because it can be snorted like cocaine with no needle necessary.

Gard, Carolyn. "The Return of PCP: An Unpredictable Dangerous Drug of Abuse May Be Back." *Current Health 2*, vol. 30, November 2003, pp. 25ff. Reports a resurgence in use of phencyclidine (PCP), a drug originally developed in the 1950s as an anesthetic. PCP can cause hallucinations and violent, unpredictable behavior—users often become disassociated, unaware of what is happening to their bodies and impervious to pain. Many users who end up in emergency rooms say they did not realize they had taken PCP, because dealers frequently mix it with or sell it as other drugs such as ecstasy or LSD. However, PCP was used by only 1 percent of high school students in 2002.

Graham, Judith, and Michael Higgins. "Prescription Drug Abuse on the Rise in America." *Knight Ridder/Tribune News Service*, October 24, 2003, p. K2908. Reports that prescription drug abuse is the fastest growing form of drug abuse in the United States. In 2001, there were 2.1 million new prescription pain reliever abusers in the United States, and abuse of OxyContin "has taken hold across the country." The growth of illicit prescription drug sales on the Internet presents a major new challenge to drug law enforcers.

Hall, Carl T. "Research Finds Alcohol Tolerance Gene: UCSF Worm Study May Lead to Benefits for Human Drinkers." *San Francisco Chronicle*, December 12, 2003, pp. A1, A24. Reports that researchers have found a gene that seems to be associated with resistance to the effects of alcohol. In the course of the research, a clearer picture has emerged of how alcohol affects the brain—it increases the flow of potassium ions across the BK channel, a sort of gate in the outer membrane of nerve cells, leading to a disruption of neural activity. Researchers, however, caution that there is a long road between discovering this finding in worms in the laboratory and determining its relevance to human drinkers.

Inciardi, James A., and Jennifer L. Goode. "OxyContin and Prescription Drug Abuse: Miracle Medicine or Problem Drug?" *Consumers' Research Magazine*, vol. 86, July 2003, pp. 17ff. This comprehensive feature article begins with an introduction to OxyContin. When the drug was introduced into the market in 1996, it was hailed as a breakthrough because its time-release formula allowed for continuous, long-term relief for moderate to severe pain. However, the drug's active ingredient, oxycodone, has a high potential for abuse, and OxyContin users discovered they could crush the pills to take the dose all at once for a quick "high." Discussion and statistics are provided for criminal diversion of OxyContin and other painkillers, reports of death associated with oxycodone and OxyContin, and the regional focus of use in areas such as rural Maine and Appalachia. Recent media, government, and industry reactions to the OxyContin abuse "epidemic" are also summarized.

Jaffe, Harry. "New Coke." *Men's Health*, vol. 17, June 2002, pp. 129–133. Ritalin, a drug that has been widely prescribed to calm down hyperactive young children, has an opposite effect on teens and adults. Users claim that it sharpens focus, stimulates, and provides an energy boost for study or all-night partying. However, "Vitamin R" and a related drug, the amphetamine Adderall, have become full-blown addictions for a growing number of college students and young professionals.

Kalb, Claudia. "Playing with Painkillers." *Newsweek*, April 9, 2001, pp. 45–51. The growing movement toward demanding more effective pain management has its dark side—the flood of prescriptions that can be diverted into illegal channels and the growing number of abusers of painkillers and other drugs. Accompanying vignettes describe the impact of OxyContin abuse on a small Kentucky town, an ensuing crackdown, and ways in which the community is trying to cope with the aftermath.

Lacayo, Richard. "Are You Man Enough?" *Time*, April 24, 2000, pp. 58–64. Testosterone, the male sex hormone, has been widely sought by men who either had a deficiency in the substance or who wanted to boost their muscle mass or sex drive. Until recently testosterone had to be injected (leading to uneven dosage) or applied via an inconvenient patch, but it is now becoming available in a gel form that can be applied to any patch of bare skin. However, it is unclear what negative effects might occur from widespread use of supplementary testosterone—they might include an increase in aggression or faster growth of any existing prostate tumor.

Meadow, Michelle. "Prescription Drug Use and Abuse." *FDA Consumer Magazine*, September–October 2001, n.p. Also available online. URL: http://www.fda.gov/fdac/features/2001/501_drug.html. Using the example of a woman who came to depend on tranquilizers after the death of her infant son, the author describes typical patterns of prescription drug abuse. A number of drugs that are heavily abused are mentioned, including OxyContin and Ritalin (abused particularly among middle and high school students). The key to preventing abuse is to ensure appropriate use under close supervision by physicians, who need better training in recognizing signs of drug abuse. The article closes with advice to consumers on appropriate use of prescription drugs and sources for drug abuse treatment.

Morse, Jodie. "Women on a Binge." *Time*, vol. 149, April 1, 2002, pp. 56–61. The 125 percent increase in binge drinking by women college students is only one of a number of other behaviors that are growing in incidence among young women. These activities include smoking, drug abuse, dangerous driving, fighting, and violent crime. In part this behavioral shift may be an unintended consequence of the triumph of feminism, where some women believe that acting like (some) men and testing the limits affirms their freedom and equal opportunity.

Nestler, Eric J., and David Landsman. "Learning About Addiction from the Genome." *Nature*, vol. 409, February 15, 2001, pp. 834ff. The researchers look for signs of a genetic basis for addiction by finding genes that are associated with brain changes that take place after exposure to drugs. In particular, they find tentative connections to genes that regulate how a certain chemical receptor becomes less sensitive to the effects of drugs over time. This, in turn, is related to tolerance, sensitization, dependence, and other features of drug addiction.

Ola, Per, and Emily D'Aulaire. "A Dangerous Drug Hits the Heartland." *Reader's Digest*, April 1999, pp. 139–143. Reports that by the end of the 1990s, "meth" abuse was sweeping from its origins on the West Coast across the Heartland, reaching deeply into the middle class. Further, use is growing faster among women than among men. The drug's appeal to women includes its ability to control appetite and promote weight loss, as well as providing energy needed by working mothers. However, prolonged use often results in paranoid episodes and serious health and legal consequences.

Roche, Timothy. "The Potent Perils of a Miracle Drug." *Time*, vol. 157, January 8, 2001, p. 47. Describes the emergence of OxyContin, the opiate painkiller that is becoming one of the most widely abused prescription drugs. The time-release capsules are broken open and the drug can then be snorted or injected, producing an effect not unlike heroin. Federal authorities are starting to pressure doctors to look for signs of OxyContin abuse in their patients.

Rosenberg, Debra. "Oxy's Offspring." *Newsweek*, April 22, 2002, p. 37. The growing abuse of OxyContin is having a troubling effect: Pregnant "Oxy" users are more likely to contract HIV/AIDS and other infections through unsafe sex and then pass the disease on to their babies. If an Oxy-using mother goes through withdrawal (which can happen repeatedly during the struggle with addiction), the fetus can be stressed or even killed, or premature labor or a miscarriage can be induced.

"Rx Drug Abuse Posing Public Health Crisis." *Drug Topics* (National Institute on Drug Abuse), May 7, 2001, p. 58. This report warns that drug abuse is becoming "mainstream" through the abuse of prescription drugs by many segments of the population. National pharmacy and trade groups are now joining with the National Institute on Drug Abuse, medical groups, and the AARP to raise consumer awareness of the dangers of abusing prescription drugs. A newsletter and an expanded web site are the two major outreach efforts.

Solotaroff, Paul. "Killer Bods." *Rolling Stone*, February 14, 2002, pp. 53–59, 72–74. A look at the new high school bodybuilding and athletic culture around supplements such as "andro" (androstenedione), a precursor to sex hormones androgen and estrogen, creatine (an amino acid), and the stimulant ephedrine. Although banned by athletic programs, the supplements are widely available over the counter, and the supplement lobby defeated FDA attempts to regulate these substances as drugs. Steroids like andro may have long-term effects on fertility, as well as increasing the risk of heart or liver problems, while stimulants like ephedrine are more dangerous, with effects similar to amphetamines. Combined with intense exercise, the results can be stroke or heart failure.

Spartos, Carla. "Prescription: Euphoria: New Research Brings Ecstasy Back to the Couch." *Village Voice*, January 9–15, 2002, n.p. Also available online. URL: http://www.villagevoice.com/issues/0202/spartos.php. Before MDMA (ecstasy) became illegal in 1985, some psychiatrists believed the drug was an effective tool for promoting communication and openness in their patients, thus making therapy much more effective. In November 2002 the Food and Drug Administration approved a study of the medical use of ecstasy, leading to hopes that the drug might prove to again be an effective psychiatric tool. However, the FDA may be at odds with the Drug Enforcement Agency, and some researchers believe that even a single dose of ecstasy could impair the brain's ability to produce serotonin, a vital neurotransmitter.

Stocker, Steven. "Finding the Future Alcoholic." *The Futurist*, May/June 2002, pp. 41–46. Scientific research suggests that people whose brain is hypersensitive to stress due to a lack of natural opioids are more prone to becoming alcoholics because drinking restores balance in the brain. Antidepressant medications or drugs that block the release of stress hormones may provide an alternative for such persons. But compelling people to take genetic or brain tests to identify at-risk individuals would violate civil liberties.

Thomas, Evan. "'I am Addicted to Prescription Pain Medication': True Confessions." *Newsweek*, October 20, 2003, p. 42. A rather acerbic account of conservative broadcaster Rush Limbaugh's addiction to the pain reliever OxyContin and other prescription drugs, in which his housekeeper has turned over what is alleged to be damning evidence of Limbaugh's having received more than 30,000 pills. The author suggests that Limbaugh must now be honest with his audience if he wants to retain his popularity.

WEB DOCUMENTS

Colby, Lauren A. "In Defense of Smokers." Version 2.5. Available online. URL: http://www.lcolby.com. Posted in 2003. The author, apparently a contrarian independent scholar, argues that the connection between smoking and diseases such as lung cancer is not proved and is based on questionable assumptions. The author believes the case against second-hand smoke is even weaker. Although this is decidedly a minority view out of step with established medical opinion, some of the author's points about the "neo-Puritan" and prohibitionist impulse behind the anti-smoking movement seem worth considering.

"Drug Abuse." Crisis Intervention of Houston, Inc. Available online. URL: http://www.crisishotline.org/strategies/yourself/drugabuse.html Downloaded on December 6, 2003. Answers common questions about drug abuse, including how common it is, who is most at risk, signs of drug abuse, and how drug abuse treatment programs work.

"A Guide to Drugs and the Brain." National Families in Action. Available online. URL: http://www.nationalfamilies.org/brain/. Posted in 2001. Gives a brief overview of how addictive drugs affect the brain, with more detailed information about major drugs or types of drugs that are abused. There is also an interactive database for looking up drugs by street name.

Hanson, David J. "Binge Drinking." Alcohol Problems & Solutions. Available online. URL: http://www2.potsdam.edu/alcohol-info/BingeDrinking.html. Downloaded on December 6, 2003. Describes binge drinking as heavy drinking over at least several days, such that the drinker ignores work and other responsibilities and often engages in risky behavior. Although there has been considerable media attention to the problem, binge drinking among young people and college students actually declined during the 1990s. Exaggerating the problem can be counterproductive because it can give young people the impression that binge drinking is the norm among their peers.

———. "Zero Tolerance." Alcohol Problems & Solutions. Available online. URL: http://www2.potsdam.edu/alcohol-info/ZeroTolerance.html. Downloaded on December 6, 2003. The author argues that zero tolerance (suspending students for any consumption of alcohol, even such things as mouthwash) is counterproductive. Such policies can have grave consequences for students who, in fact, do not have a drinking problem, while doing little to deter alcohol abuse by other students. A better approach (often used in Europe) is to provide objective information and to emphasize that students who choose to drink must learn to do so responsibly.

Leshner, Alan. "Addiction Is a Brain Disease." *Global Issues,* June 1997. Available online. URL: http://usinfo.state.gov/journals/itgic/0697/ijge/gj-2.htm. In this electronic journal from the U.S. Information Agency, Lesher, head of the National Institute on Drug Abuse, describes drug addiction as brain disease that has behavioral components. Treatment therefore requires both medical and psychological/behavior therapy. Leshner believes that scientists now have sound principles for understanding addiction, but they must be applied flexibly and creatively, not turned into "cookie-cutter" programs.

"Marijuana: Facts for Teens." National Institute on Drug Abuse. Available online. URL: http://165.112.78.61/MarijBroch/Marijteenstxt.html. Revised March 2003. Questions and answers about marijuana written in straightforward language for young people. Coverage is generally objective, although some topics such as medical use of marijuana might be considered poorly covered by some advocates.

"NIDA Community Drug Alert Bulletin: Anabolic Steroids." National Institute on Drug Abuse. Available online. URL: http://165.112.78.61/SteroidAlert/SteroidAlert.html. Posted in 2002. Describes the increasing abuse and serious health effects of anabolic steroids, drugs that are related to male sex hormones. Suggests approaches to education and other ways to counteract steroid abuse among young athletes, such as in high school.

"NIDA Community Drug Alert Bulletin: Club Drugs." National Institute on Drug Abuse. Available online. URL: http://165.112.78.61/ClubAlert/ClubDrugAlert.html. Posted in 1999. Describes the use and effects of drugs commonly used in raves and club settings. Drugs covered are MDMA (ecstasy), gamma-hydroxybutyrate (GHB), Ketamine, Rohypnol, methamphetamine, and LSD.

TREATMENT PROGRAMS AND METHODS

Works in this section describe or evaluate drug abuse treatment methods or programs, or identify factors that are important for the success of treatment.

BOOKS

DuPont, Robert L., and John P. McGovern. *A Bridge to Recovery: An Introduction to 12-Step Programs.* Washington, D.C.: American Psychiatric Publishing, 1994. Explains the 12-step program popularized by Alcoholics Anonymous but now applied to many forms of addiction. The book draws on contributions of many professionals to integrate the 12-step approach into the practice of mental health professionals and the development of community groups.

Holder, Harold D. *Alcohol and the Community: A Systems Approach to Prevention.* New York: Cambridge University Press, 1998. Most approaches to alcohol and drug abuse focus on the abuser and his or her treatment. This book takes a quite different approach: It urges researchers and policy makers to look at the interaction between alcohol abusers and the community and treating the abuse as a matter of public health. By changing the way the community responds to alcohol or drug abuse, the framework within which treatment and prevention efforts are carried out can be made more effective.

Loue, Sana. *Diversity Issues in Substance Abuse Treatment and Research.* New York: Kluwer Academic, 2003. Different ethnic and other communities perceive drugs and drug abuse differently. The relationship between ethnic and gender groups and drugs is also perceived differently by the majority community, with a number of stereotypes often getting in the way of understanding and effective treatment. The author explains these differences and how clinicians, researchers, and, by implication, students can deal with them.

National Center on Addiction and Substance Abuse. *Crossing the Bridge: An Evaluation of the Drug Treatment Alternative-to-Prison (DTAP) Program.* New York: National Center on Addiction and Substance Abuse at Colombia University, March 2003. Also available online. URL: http://www. casalibrary.org/CASAPublications/Crossing_the_bridge_March2003.pdf. An evaluation of a program in Brooklyn, New York, that diverted persons convicted of nonviolent drug trafficking to treatment as an alternative to prosecution (or, after 1998, to sentencing). The program is effective as measured by re-arrest rates (25 percent less compared to those who receive prison sentences). The overall cost of putting someone in a DTAP program is only about half that of incarceration.

Peele, Stanton. *The Diseasing of America: How We Allowed Recovery Zealots and the Treatment Industry to Convince Us We Are Out of Control.* San Francisco: Jossey-Bass, 1999. A prominent iconoclast in drug research argues that there is no convincing evidence that drug and other addictions are genetically acquired diseases—or are diseases at all. He argues that the "disease model" has provided a self-serving justification for a "treatment industry" of doctors, counselors, and other specialists whose methods are largely unsuccessful in stopping drug abuse.

Peele, Stanton, and Charles Bufe. *Resisting 12-Step Coercion: How to Fight Forced Participation in AA, NA, or 12-Step Treatment.* Tucson, Ariz.: See Sharp Press, 2000. The authors argue that there is no evidence for the superiority of 12-step programs and no justification for courts coercing alcohol or drug abusers to participate in such programs. They give suggestions for preventing forced participation as well as discussing alternative types of programs that promote rational self-responsibility rather than dependence on a higher power for delivery from a "disease."

Perkinson, Robert R. *The Alcoholism and Drug Abuse Patient Workbook.* Thousand Oaks, Calif.: SAGE Publications, 2003. Provides a variety of simple, effective exercises that persons in alcohol or drug abuse treatment or counseling can use to reinforce what they are learning, motivate them to stick to the program, and prevent relapses.

———. *Chemical Dependency Counseling.* Second Ed. Thousand Oaks, Calif.: SAGE Publications, 2001. Although intended primarily for counselors and other treatment professionals, this well-organized guide is also useful to students and researchers who want to learn how various facets of a successful treatment program come together. Topics discussed include 12-step programs, cognitive and behavioral therapy, integrating treatment of mental disorders and of substance abuse, treatment of adolescents, and treatment of nonsubstance dependencies (such as gambling addiction).

Shavelson, Lonny. *Hooked: Five Addicts Challenge Our Misguided Drug Rehab System.* New York: New Press, 2002. Instead of taking the common "big picture" and analytical approach to drug policy, the author (a physician, journalist, and photographer) closely follows five addicts who are struggling to use "the system" to get free of their addiction. Observations and conclusions about the relationship between drug abuse, mental health, child abuse, and other factors are then teased out of these individual stories.

Sherman, Barry R., Laura M. Sanders, and Chau Trinh. *Addiction and Pregnancy: Empowering Recovery Through Peer Counseling.* Westport, Conn.: Praeger Publishers, 1998. Describes SISTERS, a pioneering peer-counseling program for women substance abusers who are pregnant or postpartum (having recently given birth). The authors present a framework for treatment and counseling and attempt to measure its success. They conclude that the treatment model is effective and should be more widely adopted.

Stimmel, Barry. *Alcoholism, Drug Addiction and the Road to Recovery: Life on the Edge.* New York: Haworth Press, 2001. The author provides a comprehensive look at drugs of abuse and the process of addiction and recovery, but the focus is on the reasons why people use different types of drugs, as well as providing guidance on important issues such as multiple drug use, drug abuse and AIDS, drugs and pregnancy, drug use in sports, and drug abuse testing.

Van Wormer, Katherine S., and Diane Rae Davis. *Addiction Treatment: A Strengths Perspective.* Belmont, Calif.: Wadsworth, 2002. The authors present a systematic approach to understanding addictions as well as compulsive behavior such as eating disorders and compulsive gambling. Rather than choosing between 12-step and abstinence-based approaches and the newer harm reduction model, these and other approaches are explained as tools that can be applied to different situations. There are also vivid narratives and useful background readings, as well as a summary of recent developments in drug law and policy.

White, William L. *Slaying the Dragon: The History of Addiction Treatment and Recovery in America.* Bloomington, Ill.: Chestnut Health Systems/Lighthouse Institute, 1998. A comprehensive history of the many movements and systems that have attempted to treat alcohol and substance abuse in the United States since the 19th century.

Wilcox, Danny M. *Alcoholic Thinking: Language, Culture, and Belief in Alcoholics Anonymous.* Westport, Conn.: Praeger Publishers, 1998. This volume will be of particular interest to anthropology students. It examines the language and thinking used in Alcoholics Anonymous in a larger context of how people think about substance abuse problems and, indeed, how they address the conflict between ideals of individualism and achievement and the feelings of alienation and isolation that helped lead them into dependency.

ARTICLES

"80% of Participants Complete Online Drug Abuse Treatment." *Health & Medicine Week*, October 20, 2003, p. 233. A national study of substance abuse treatment that is delivered online rather than in person reveals that 80 percent of participants completed the online treatment—about twice the rate for traditional outpatient treatment. Online treatment is being touted as a way to deal with access, stigma, privacy cost, and other problems associated with in-person treatment.

Annotated Bibliography

"Anticonvulsant Drug Is Promising Therapy." *Drug Week*, October 24, 2003, p. 97. Reports results of research funded by the National Institutes of Health that suggests that an anticonvulsant drug called GVG may also be effective in treating cocaine addiction. Because the drug reduces brain levels of dopamine (the substance responsible for cocaine's pleasurable feelings), it may also reduce the craving for the drug that is characteristic of addiction.

Byrne, Andrew. "Lessons from 20 Years of Addiction Treatment: Look After Individuals and Public Health Improvements Follow." *Journal of Addiction and Mental Health*, vol. 7, Autumn 2003, p. 20. Drawing on his considerable experience, the author suggests that standardization of treatment is important in order to make programs widely available, but that treatment strategies must also be tailored to the individual. Harm reduction and public health–oriented measures have reduced overdose deaths in Switzerland and HIV transmission rates in Australia, but the United States has been slow to adopt needle exchange programs.

Cloud, William, and Robert Granfield. "Many Paths Lead to Substance-Abuse Treatment." *Denver Post*, June 29, 2003, p. E05. Two experts on drug abuse provide a realistic assessment of the value of treatment. Studies suggest that drug abuse treatment is effective about 20 percent of the time—although perhaps higher in the case of high-profile persons who have plenty of resources and support. On the other hand, the number of drug abusers who overcome their addiction on their own is greatly understated—some estimates suggest that such recoveries outnumber cases of successful treatment by as much as 3 to 1. The authors conclude that factors such as strong relationships and regular employment increase the chances of recovery, and that treatment and other options must be tailored to individual needs.

Peele, Stanton. "Hungry for the Next Fix." *Reason*, vol. 34, May 2002, pp. 32–36. The author criticizes the view of drug abuse promoted by organizations such as the National Institute on Drug Abuse. This view is characterized by a belief that addiction has a purely biological explanation and is thus amenable to medical approaches such as the development of anti-addiction drugs and a treatment program aimed at achieving abstinence. The author believes that this dominant theory cannot account for the remarkable effectiveness of placebos in drug treatment studies—suggesting the social and psychological factors involved in drug use. These factors play an important role in determining whether someone is a drug abuser or a "responsible" moderate drug user.

"Research Summary on Relapse Makes Case for Tailored Treatment." *Alcohol & Drug Abuse Weekly*, vol. 15, July 28, 2003, pp. 1ff. Reports on a research study from the Caron Foundation that drug abusers who have relapsed back to drug use after treatment require a different mixture of treatment approaches than do first-time patients. Caron treats relapsing patients separately from first-timers and emphasizes helping the former overcome feelings of hopelessness and shame that often accompany a relapse. Treatment programs for women and men may also have to be approached differently; women tend to relapse less often, perhaps because they are more skilled at building social networks.

Satel, Sally L. "The Fallacies of No-Fault Addiction." *The Public Interest,* Fall 1999, pp. 52ff. The author presents a conservative perspective, beginning by taking issue with Alan Lesher and other researchers who consider addiction to be a "brain disease." Satel criticizes the implication that drugs "hijack the brain . . . relapse is normal." She argues that lack of success in finding medical treatments that will truly block addiction reveals a failure to "remedy the underlying anguish for which drugs like heroin and cocaine are the desperate remedy." An approach involving sanctions and rewards can help addicts expand the scope of their ability to control their actions and appetites.

"The War on Addiction: Abuse in America: Fresh Research and Shifting Views of Treatment Are Opening New Fronts in a Deadly Struggle." *Newsweek,* February 12, 2001, p. 36. This special report features modest but important shifts in the understanding and treatment of drug addiction. Successive "drug czars" have been giving greater emphasis to treatment, which is less expensive to society than incarceration and arguably more effective. California has passed a ballot proposition that provides treatment options for all nonviolent drug offenders. Another alternative growing in popularity is "coerced abstinence"—treatment with the threat of prison to back it up. However, the amount of resources spent on treatment still falls far short of the need.

Wright, Karen. "A Shot of Sanity: You'll Get No Kick from Cocaine if You Take this New Vaccine." *Discover,* June 1999, pp. 47–48. Reports on clinical trials of a "vaccine" that triggers an immune system reaction that blocks the absorption of cocaine. However, while the vaccine blocks the effect of the drug, it does not block the craving. Users may be able to circumvent the vaccine by taking very high doses of cocaine or they may simply decide to stop taking the vaccine.

WEB DOCUMENTS

Brown, Barry S. "Comorbidity of Mental Disorders with Drug Abuse/Dependence." National Institute on Drug Abuse. Available online. URL: http://www.nida.nih.gov/about/organization/DESPR/HSR/datre/BrownComorbid.html. Posted in May 1998. Some of the studies summarized here measure the incidence of psychiatric problems among clients in drug treatment programs, while others take the opposite tack and look for drug problems among patients in the mental health system. Studies also suggest ways of dealing with the fact that drug abuse and mental illness often go together and complicate each other's treatment.

————. "HIV/AIDS and Drug Abuse Treatment Services." National Institute on Drug Abuse. Available online. URL: http://www.nida.nih.gov/about/organization/DESPR/HSR/da-tre/BrownHIV.html. Posted September 1998. Treating drug abuse has been shown to be an effective way to control the spread of HIV/AIDS. However, drug abusers who are already infected by the virus have special needs that challenge conventional drug abuse treatment programs. The studies reviewed here explore innovations intended to meet this challenge in various ways.

Caroll, Robert Todd. "Substance Abuse Treatment." The Skeptic's Dictionary. Available online. URL: http://skepdic.com/sat.html. Updated on November 11, 2003. This contrarian approach to substance abuse treatment acknowledges the good intentions of pioneers such as Charles Dederich of Synanon but argues that a number of programs violate human rights. The author questions the role and self-interest of "professional interventionists" who try to get substance abusers into treatment. He also argues that there is an inherent contradiction between the disease model of substance abuse and the moral approach of 12-step organizations such as Alcoholics Anonymous.

"Drug War Facts: Treatment." Common Sense for Drug Policy. Available online. URL: http://www.drugwarfacts.org/treatmen.htm. Updated on July 26, 2002. A collection of sourced facts statistics, and quotes relating to drug treatment, including availability, efficacy, funding, and impact.

"Treatment Approaches." Drug Addiction [web site] Available online. URL: http://www.drug-addiction.com/drug_addiction_treatment_approaches.htm. Downloaded on January 6, 2004. Summarizes a variety of approaches to treating drug abuse, including cognitive-behavioral approaches to relapse prevention, the "matrix model" for integrated treatment, and various forms of special-purpose, limited-term psychotherapy. There is also a link to a discussion of general categories of treatment.

DRUG ABUSE EDUCATION

This section covers the description and evaluation of drug abuse education and prevention programs.

BOOKS

Miller, Michelle, et al. *Adolescent Relationships and Drug Use.* Mahwah, N.J.: Lawrence Earlbaum Associates, 2000. Focuses on a little-considered aspect of drug abuse prevention—the ways in which teenagers communicate with each other about drugs and drug use. The authors consider this communication in the context of relationships and consider what communication skills are most effective in helping adolescents resist drug use.

National Institute on Drug Abuse. *Preventing Drug Abuse Among Children and Adolescents: A Research-Based Guide.* Second Ed. Bethesda, Md.: National Institute on Drug Abuse, 2003. Also available online. URL: http://www.drugabuse.gov/pdf/prevention/RedBook.pdf. Intended for parents, educators, and community leaders, this booklet begins by identifying risk factors for drug abuse, then describes "prevention principles" common to successful programs. Strategies for implementation are followed by a description of proven programs for elementary, middle, and high school Life Skills Training (LST).

Ross, Houkje. *Substance Abuse Prevention: What's Working to Keep Our Youth Drug Free?* Washington, D.C.: Office of Minority Health, U.S. Dept. of Health and Human Services, June/July 2001. Also available online. URL: http://www.omhrc.gov/ctg/ctg_072001.pdf. This issue of the agency's newsletter *Closing the Gap* examines six areas or "life domains" in which the risk of substance abuses manifests itself and where it must be combated. The areas are society, community, school, family, peer, and individual. The role of mentors is particularly important. The newsletter also includes several related articles on subjects such as the role of the faith community in substance abuse prevention, provision for substance abuse treatment in managed care, and review of software for planning prevention programs.

Schwebel, Robert. *Saying No Is Not Enough: Helping Your Kids Make Wise Decisions about Alcohol, Tobacco, and Other Drugs.* 2nd revised ed. New York: Newmarket Press, 1998. As the title suggests, this book is intended to help parents help their children avoid drug use. It offers both general advice (such as about how to be clear but nonjudgmental when discussing drugs) with samples of dialogue that can be used to explain drugs to children at various age levels. Some topics to bring up with children include the difference between medical and abusive use of drugs, the effects of drugs, and the particular dangers of tobacco. Finally, parents are encouraged to listen to their children's concerns, work out agreements with them, and be consistent in holding children accountable when they break the agreement.

United Nations Office on Drugs and Crime. *Using the Internet for Drug Abuse Prevention.* Vienna: United Nations Office on Drugs and Crime, 2003. Also available online. URL: http://www.unodc.org/youthnet/pdf/handbook_internet_english.pdf. A basic guide for creating and using web sites as a tool for drug abuse education and prevention. Discusses advantages and potential problems, including lack of adequate net access in developing countries.

ARTICLES

Cohn, Jason. "Drug Education: The Triumph of Bad Science." *Rolling Stone*, May 24, 2001, pp. 41ff. The author begins his critique of drug education programs by reporting that DARE, the best known such program, is now trying to face its shortcomings and revise its curriculum. However, because most drug education programs are evaluated only by their proponents, data tends to be presented selectively, and there is little scientific rigor. Also, with money, careers, and political interests at stake, there is strong incentive to perpetuate programs even if there is little evidence of success.

Fishbein, Martin, et al. "Avoiding the Boomerang: Testing the Relative Effectiveness of Antidrug Public Service Announcements Before a National Campaign." *American Journal of Public Health*, February 2002, pp. 238–245. This study attempts to determine which antidrug PSAs (public service announcements) are perceived as effective by the audience. The results show considerable variation in effectiveness of different types of antidrug messages. Perhaps not surprisingly, PSAs that realistically portray the effects of more dangerous drugs such as heroin or methamphetamines are perceived as more effective than those that exaggerate the dangers of marijuana. It is important to determine whether a PSA is effective (and not counterproductive) before beginning a new campaign.

Ives, Nat. "The Maker of OxyContin, a Painkiller that Is Addictive, Sponsors a Campaign on Drug Abuse." *New York Times*, September 4, 2003, p. C7. Reports that Purdue Pharma, the manufacturer of the widely abused prescription drug OxyContin, is running television public service messages about the dangers of abuse of prescription drugs, although their product is not mentioned by name. While some critics believe the effort is too little, too late and is designed primarily to stave off further regulation, other observers believe that it shows corporate responsibility in dealing with the problem.

Lacayo, Richard. "Just Don't Say Anything: A Drug-Ad Deal Goes Bad." *Time*, vol. 155, January 24, 2000, p. 67. Reveals details of a controversial program where, as part of a government program to buy antidrug TV spots on the major networks, the latter agreed to match the purchased time with additional time of their own. When the networks wanted to renege on the deal in order to save money, the government allowed them to earn "credits" by including antidrug messages in the actual programs. However, the government got to decide which messages were acceptable, thus influencing the content of programming.

Lavelle, Marianne. "Teen Tobacco Wars: An Antismoking Ad Blitz vs. New Cigarette Marketing Ploys." *U.S. News & World Report*, February 7, 2000, pp. 14–16. Clever, "edgy" antismoking ads seem to be reaching teens, with Florida recording a 20 percent drop in teen smoking from 1998 to 1999. However, tobacco companies are fighting back by marketing to popular youth venues through the introduction of flavored cigarettes and partnerships with young adult organizations and other programs ostensibly aimed at legal young adult smokers. The authors believe that states must be more aggressive in their antismoking programs, including increasing cigarette taxes to fund them and strengthening antismoking ordinances.

Moilanen, Renee. "Just Say No Again: The Old Failures of New and Improved Anti-Drug Education." *Reason*, January 2004, pp. 34–41. The author looks at the highly touted new "evidence based" approach to drug education and the new emphasis on fostering "decision-making" skills in young people as a way to help them resist drug use, and decides it is mostly the same old product in a new package. The guidelines for making "healthy decisions," for example, are structured in such a way that a young person who follows them does not really have to think or weigh alternatives but is automatically prompted to say no. Recent evaluations of programs such as Life Skills Training have not shown them to be effective.

WEB DOCUMENTS

Bosworth, Kris."Drug Abuse Prevention: School-Based Strategies that Work. ERIC Digest." ERIC Clearinghouse on Teaching and Teacher Education. Available online. URL: http://www.ericfacility.net/ericdigests/ed409316.html. Posted on July 7, 1997. Summarizes research on drug use prevention programs in schools. The author concludes that a number of common approaches such as using scare tactics, providing only "objective" information about drugs and their effects, self-esteem building, and values clarification show little evidence of effectiveness. Some approaches that show more promise include showing teenagers that drug use is not the norm; improving social skills and assertiveness; helping students recognize external pressures (such as advertising or peers); giving students repeated, credible information about the risks of drug use; encouraging development of positive aspects of life such as caring and sharing; and helping students refuse to use drugs while still maintaining friendships with peers.

"Bret and Lee Ann Richardson: Interview." *Frontline*, PBS Online. Available online. URL: http://www.pbs.org/wgbh/pages/frontline/shows/dope/dare/richardsons.html. Posted in 1998. Interviews with two police officers involved with D.A.R.E. activities in the schools. They deny having any interest in having students report on their parents' drug use. They suggest their focus is on providing a good role model and resource for children who may have problems with or questions about drugs.

"A Different Look at D.A.R.E." DRCNet. Available online. URL: http://drcnet.org/DARE/. Downloaded December 10, 2003. Gives background on the D.A.R.E. (Drug Abuse Resistance Education) program and provides evidence that the program is ineffective and misleading. Suggestions are offered for parents and others to organize to convince school boards to withdraw from the program.

"A Guide to the Drug-Prevention Movement." Families in Action. Available online. URL: http://www.nationalfamilies.org/prevention/organization_index.html. Posted in 2001. A listing describing a number of drug prevention organizations, with links, contact information, and mission statements.

"How Effective is D.A.R.E.?" *Frontline*, PBS Online. Available online. URL: http://www.pbs.org/wgbh/pages/frontline/shows/dope/dare/. Downloaded December 12, 2003. This resource for the *Frontline* show "Busted: America's War on Drugs" provides an update on studies of the effectiveness of the nation's most prominent drug abuse prevention and education campaign. There is also a link to a 2001 study from the surgeon general that concludes that D.A.R.E. is a good example of a program that does *not* work.

The War on Drugs

DRUG WAR POLICIES

This section covers general descriptions of the War on Drugs and "mainstream" policies. For alternatives, see the sections on Legalization and Decriminalization of Drugs and on Harm Reduction.

BOOKS

Baum, Dan. *Smoke and Mirrors: The War on Drugs and the Politics of Failure.* Boston: Little Brown, 1996. This sharp, vividly written polemic relentlessly attacks the war on drugs. According to the author, after 30 years the only winners have been bureaucratic empire-builders and drug-trafficking kingpins. The losers have been drug users facing long prison terms, communities wracked by violence, and the citizens and taxpayers whose liberties and tax dollars have been recklessly abused.

Cavanagh, Suzanne, and David Teasley. *Community Anti-Crime Weed and Seed Program: Current Developments.* Washington, D.C.: Congressional Research Service, 1998. Describes the Weed and Seed program, an effort to reduce violent crime and drug abuse by simultaneously disrupting criminal activity and providing alternatives in the form of economic and social programs.

Gordon, Diana. *The Return of the Dangerous Classes: Drug Prohibition and Policy Politics.* New York: W.W. Norton, 1994. The theme of this exploration of drug policy and politics is on how drug abusers are characterized. In particular, groups associated with drug abuse (such as minorities, immigrants, and even youth) are treated as "dangerous classes" in much the same way the threatening "outsider" has been characterized throughout American history. Although the specific policies and programs addressed by this book are now somewhat dated, the perspective remains important.

Gray, Mike, ed. *Busted: Stoned Cowboys, Narco-Lords, and Washington's War on Drugs.* New York: Thunder's Mouth Press, 2002. An anthology of provocative writings by pundits and essayists who take issue with various aspects of the war on drugs. Contributors include conservative humorist P.J. O'Rourke, who compares the harm done by marijuana to that done by door-kicking drug raiders; Christopher Hitchens, who discusses secret U.S. military commando missions in Colombia and Peru; and others such as Gore Vidal, William F. Buckley, Jr., Milton Friedman, and Oliver Stone.

Inciardi, James A. *The War on Drugs III: The Continuing Saga of the Mysteries and Miseries of Intoxication, Addiction, Crime, and Public Policy.* Boston: Allyn & Bacon, 2002. A collection rich in information and quotes gathered from interviews with drug traffickers, users, law enforcers, scholars, and policy makers. Rather than trying to draw broad conclusions, the author offers a variety of fresh perspectives to help readers explore the nature of drug use and abuse and the contemporary debate on drug policy.

Macoun, Robert J., and Peter Reuter. *Drug War Heresies: Learning from Other Vices, Times, & Places.* New York: Cambridge University Press, 2001. The authors present an objective, historical, and data-driven analysis of many aspects of drug use and drug control policy. They compare the current punitive / prohibitionist approach in the United States to the less punitive, harm reduction–oriented policies of western European nations. Many factors and gradations of policies are explored, with detailed discussion of effects and tradeoffs.

Miller, Richard Lawrence. *Drug Warriors and Their Prey: From Police Power to Police State.* Westport, Conn.: Praeger Publishers, 1996. This rather radical critique argues that the war on drugs represents an attack on a class of people (drug users/abusers) comparable to the Nazi policy toward the Jews. The author identifies what he says are common features of the two programs: identification, ostracism, confiscation, concentration, and annhiliation. He further argues that the warped sensibilities of the drug war spread beyond their intended target to threaten the civil liberties of the entire society.

Office of National Drug Control Policy. *President's National Drug Control Strategy, The.* Washington, D.C.: Office of National Drug Control Policy, 2003. Also available online. URL: http://www.whitehousedrugpolicy. gov/publications/policy/ndcs03/index.html. This official annual statement of drug control policy reports that for the first time since the 1990s, drug use is down among junior high and high school students. The report presents data and charts on various aspects of drug abuse as well as outlining three national priorities: drug education, drug treatment, and attacking the economic bases of the drug trade.

Reinarman, Craig, and Harry G. Levine, ed. *Crack in America: Demon Drugs and Social Justice.* Berkeley: University of California Press, 1997. The contributors to this collection put the "crack epidemic" into perspective in terms of the poverty and other problems in the minority communities where it took hold, and in the way in which it was portrayed in the mainstream media and by political leaders and policy makers. What most contributors consider to be a failed U.S. drug policy is compared with the ways in which other highly addictive drugs have been handled in other developed countries.

Sharp, Elaine B. *The Dilemma of Drug Policy in the United States.* New York: HarperCollins, 1997. The author uses U.S. drug policy during the Nixon, Reagan, and George H. W. Bush administrations as an example for exploring the dynamics of policy formation and to explain how policies tend to persist through many administrations despite growing evidence of their failure.

Sullum, Jacob. *For Your Own Good: The Anti-Smoking Crusade and the Tyranny of Public Health.* New York: Simon & Schuster, 1998. The author attacks the justifications that have been made for controlling or even banning smoking in many areas of our society. Although the health risks of smoking are real, the net cost to society may actually be positive because smokers die earlier and thus do not consume as much Social Security and medical resources. Sullum also asserts that there is no conclusive evidence that exposure to secondhand smoke has any impact on life expectancy. The only justification for the antismoking crusade, then, must be that it is "for your own good." In that case, however, Sullum, a writer for the libertarian magazine *Reason*, asks why the government should have the power to decide what choices can be made by consenting adults.

Szasz, Thomas. *Ceremonial Chemistry: The Ritual Persecution of Drugs, Addicts, and Pushers.* Revised Ed. Syracuse, N.Y.: Syracuse University Press, 2003. This classic and controversial work explores the cultural and social underpinnings for attitudes toward and treatment of drug users and traffickers.

It suggests that drug policy has more to do with social control and fear of the "outsider" than about the drugs themselves and has helped spark the drug legalization movement.

Walker, Samuel. *Sense and Nonsense About Crime and Drugs: A Policy Guide.* Fifth ed. Belmont, Calif.: Thomas/Wadsworth Learning, 2001. The author uses an evidence-based approach to evaluate a variety of policies and programs that attempt to control crime and drugs. His conclusions include the following: Most proposals are "nonsense" and are not based on evidence, the "war" metaphor is wrong for dealing with crime, and attempts to beef up police or restrict rights given to criminal defendants will not significantly reduce crime. The author also views liberal nostrums such as increased social programs and gun control as being ineffective. With regard to drugs, most enforcement, education, and treatment measures are also ineffective. The author reserves judgment on whether decriminalizing drugs might reduce crime.

ARTICLES

Bender, Stephen. "American Banks and the War on Drugs." *Z Magazine,* March 2001, pp. 39–43. The author argues that the complicity of many American banks in money laundering is caused not so much by lack of regulatory oversight or the greed of individuals but rather "the triumph of market forces over government and civil society." The triumph of untrammeled "free trade" has led to capital flow without restrictions or responsibility, and the illegal economy is not that different from the legal one. Meanwhile, the war on drugs is mainly a war against the poor around the world, with powerful banks and corrupt officials reaping the benefits.

Cooper, Mary H. "Drug Policy Debate: The Issues." *CQ Researcher,* July 28, 2000, pp. 595–604. Despite 30 years and billions of dollars being spent on the war on drugs, drug use remains widespread. While defenders of the current effort point to some decline in drug use, critics argue that the priorities are all wrong—that treatment and prevention should come ahead of enforcement and incarceration. Other reformists argue for focusing not on drugs but on the associated crime and violence, taking a harm reduction approach. The debate over mandatory minimum sentences and on what to do about parolees who relapse is also covered.

Cose, Ellis. "The Casualties of War." *Newsweek,* September 6, 1999, p. 29. According to the author the focus on imprisoning drug offenders is not only doing little to solve the drug problem, it is also devastating black and Hispanic communities. Many prisoners receive no treatment for their substance abuse, virtually guaranteeing that they will re-offend after being released.

Gillespie, Nick. "The 13th Step." *Reason*, vol. 32, March 2001, p. 5. A review of the movie *Traffic*, which is criticized for its clichéd, stereotyped portrayal of drug users and degraded, helpless addicts. Although much of the screenplay criticizes the war on drugs, the author believes this message is undercut by the emphasis on the dark side of drug use (and abuse) without portraying people who can manage their social or recreational drug use.

"A Long and Winding Trip: Hollywood and Drugs." *The Economist* (U.S.), January 27, 2001, p. 1. Reviews the portrayal of drug use in Hollywood films. Traditionally drug use has been portrayed in conformance to the Hollywood Production Code as a dead-end street that leads to inevitable ruin—and Hollywood continued on this course long after it stopped portraying illicit sex that way. However, the recent movie *Traffic*, while still portraying drug use negatively, may be showing the beginning of a more nuanced attitude in its portrayal of a failed war on drugs.

Loury, Alden K. "West Side Residents Battle Drug War Realities." *The Chicago Reporter*, vol. 31, May 2002, pp. 6ff. Profiles a number of individuals struggling with drug use—their neighbors' or their own—in Chicago's West Side neighborhood. They include an elderly lady who uses moral suasion to discourage drug dealing on her street, a high school principal trying to keep promising students away from drugs, and a former drug dealer who was given a second chance.

Massing, Michael. "Home-Court Advantage: What the War on Drugs Teaches Us About the War on Terrorism." *The American Prospect*, vol. 12, December 3, 2001, pp. 24ff. Following the attacks of September 11, 2001, General Richard B. Myers, chairman of the Joint Chiefs of Staff, drew an analogy between the new war on terrorism and the ongoing war on drugs. If this is true, the author says, "Heaven help us. The war on drugs has been a miserable failure." He suggests that the proper analogy would point to the need in both cases to address the root causes of the problem, not just the symptoms. A focus on domestic enforcement rather than foreign intervention might also help, although the potential civil liberty problems are a major concern.

Tree, Sanho. "The War at Home: Our Jails Overflow with Nonviolent Drug Offenders. Have We Reached the Point Where the Drug War Causes More Harm than the Drugs Themselves?" *Sojourners*, vol. 32, May–June 2003, pp. 20ff. The chief result of the drug war and mandatory minimum sentences is that the United States has about a quarter of the world's prisoners—and about a quarter of those prisoners are there for nonviolent drug offenses. Meanwhile international efforts to eradicate drugs just seem to push the production from one area to another. The author suggests it is the fear of political repercussions that keeps the drug war going even though it is a failure. He suggests a shift to treatment and prevention and the adopting of harm reduction policies.

Voth, Eric A. "America's Longest 'War.'" *World & I*, vol. 15, p. 24. The author looks at the history of the "war" in the past 25 years. He argues that the "war" was a valid response to social turmoil and burgeoning drug use in the 1970s and that the effort has been successful—drug use peaked in the 1970s but had dropped substantially by the early 1990s. However, the author argues that this progress was reversed by a number of factors, including pro-drug imagery in the media and the emergence of a well-organized and well-financed campaign to legalize drugs. He concludes by saying that various liberal policies such as "harm reduction" have failed in the United States and abroad and the focus must be on "primary prevention" of illegal drug use, backed by treatment, drug screening/testing, and a cultural counteroffensive against drugs.

WEB DOCUMENTS

"Drug War Distortions." Common Sense for Drug Policy. Available online. URL: http://www.drugwardistortions.org/. Updated on January 22, 2003. Describes 15 "distortions" or wrong conclusions concerning drugs and the fight against them. Facts and statistics are marshaled to rebut each assumption. Examples include assertions that needle exchanges and other harm reduction strategies are ineffective, the idea of "gateway drugs," and attitudes of young people toward drug use.

Ramsey, Bob. "A History of U.S. Drug Laws – or – How Did We Get into This Mess?" Drug Policy Forum of Florida. Available online. URL: http://dpffl.org/wodhistory.htm. Downloaded on January 6, 2004. Describes the early development of U.S. drug laws and the changing emphases in the war on drugs. This is part 1, covering 1898–1933. (Part 2 was not found online.)

INTERNATIONAL DRUG TRAFFICKING

This section covers description and analysis of international drug trafficking and the programs and policies designed to combat it, including diplomatic and military efforts.

BOOKS

Bowden, Mark. *Killing Pablo: The Hunt for the World's Greatest Outlaw*. New York: Atlantic Monthly Press, 2001. The author of the bestseller *Black*

Hawk Down gives an equally compelling account of the rise and fall of Pablo Escobar, perhaps the greatest of the Colombian drug lords. The book focuses on the final phase, when the U.S. government put considerable resources into hunting down Escobar, who by the early 1990s had become a fugitive. The book hints that it may have been an American agent rather than a Colombian who finally shot Escobar in a gun battle in 1993.

Carpenter, Ted Galen. *Bad Neighbor Policy: Washington's Futile War on Drugs in Latin America.* New York: Palgrave Macmillan, 2003. The author surveys what he considers to be a rapidly deteriorating diplomatic situation in which the United States continues heavy-handed pressure on Latin American countries to reduce their drug production. In turn, governments in the region have been spurred to eradicate drug crops with herbicides that are harmful to health and the environment, and already poor communities have been further impoverished. The result has been an increase in government repression, civil unrest, and overall violence.

Chepesiuk, Ron. *The Bullet or the Bribe: Taking Down Colombia's Drug Cartel.* Westport, Conn.: Greenwood Publishing Group, 2003. Describes how perhaps the most sophisticated criminal organization in history, distributor of more than 70 percent of the world's cocaine, was finally dismantled by an unprecedented international effort spearheaded by the United States.

———. *Hard Target: The U.S. War against International Drug Trafficking.* Jefferson, N.C.: McFarland Publishing, 1999. An overview of U.S. antidrug policy and the major targets—the often highly successful international drug trafficking organizations of the 1980s and 1990s. The author concludes that while the drug warriors may have won some battles, they cannot win the war.

Cockburn, Alexander, and Jeffrey St. Clair. *Whiteout: The CIA, Drugs and the Press.* New York: Verso, 1998. Exposes the Central Intelligence Agency's relationship with drug traffickers, first admitted in a congressional hearing in 1998. The authors trace the involvement of U.S. intelligence agencies in the narcotics trade from 1944, when the OSS (the CIA's ancestor) made a deal with the Sicilian mafia to help in the war against Italy to CIA-sponsored experiments with LSD in the 1950s and the machinations of Oliver North in the Iran-Contra arms and drugs scandal of the 1980s. The authors also argue that the mainstream press has largely ignored this story or even attacked investigative reporters such as Gary Webb, who wrote a series of articles for the *San Jose Mercury-News* connecting CIA connections with drug cartels in Latin America to the crack cocaine epidemic in poor black communities.

Ehrernfeld, Rachel. *Funding Evil: How Terrorism Is Financed and How to Stop It.* Chicago: Bonus Books, 2003. The author argues that international terrorism is fueled not so much by fanaticism as by a huge flow of laundered money—mainly from illicit drug trafficking by organized crime syndicates and cartels. This network provides a conduit that supporters of terrorism can use to launder money and get it to organizations such as the PLO, Hezbollah, Hamas, and Islamic Jihad. She also argues that the powerful political interests that benefit from this money flow are the chief obstacle to getting a handle on the terror financing network.

Kirk, Robin. *More Terrible than Death: Massacres, Drugs, and America's War in Colombia.* New York: Public Affairs, 2004. A researcher with Human Rights Watch vividly chronicles the ongoing violence in Colombia between paramilitary forces, guerrillas, and drug cartels. Drawing upon extensive interviews and observations, the author focuses mainly on the situation within Colombia but also points out ways in which U.S. policy has contributed to the violence.

Lee, Rensselaer. *Afghanistan: Prospects for Opium Eradication.* Washington, D.C.: Congressional Research Service, 2003. Reports on the progress of opium eradication under the new Afghanistan government that was installed following the removal of the Taliban in 2002. Two major problems with the effort are the lack of effective government control outside the capital at Kabul and the likelihood that other U.S. priorities (such as political stability and economic development) will take precedence over drug control issues.

Leech, Garry M. *Killing Peace: Colombia's Conflict and the Failure of U.S. Intervention.* New York: Information Network of the Americas, 2002. A relatively brief yet comprehensive overview of the conflict in Colombia over the past half century and the roles of the various players—the army, leftist guerrillas, right-wing paramilitaries, drug traffickers, and U.S. antidrug agencies. The latest element covered is the merging of the international war on drugs into the new war on terrorism.

Lilley, Peter. *Dirty Dealing: The Untold Truth about Global Money Laundering.* 2nd ed. Sterling, Va.: Kogan Page, 2003. An extensive, revealing look at the sophisticated money-laundering techniques being used by criminal and terrorist groups, and their effect on national and international economies. Drugs in particular are a source of much of the funds that can be laundered and surreptitiously transferred in ways that can be very difficult to detect. The author also covers the growing importance of the Internet as a conduit for money laundering.

Livingstone, Grace. *Inside Colombia: Drugs, Democracy, and War.* London: Latin American Bureau, 2003. Provides historical background and up-to-date accounts of the Colombian insurgency (or civil war), extreme poverty, and other factors that promote the production of illicit drugs in the country. The book concludes with an account of the role and policies of the United States in trying to eradicate Colombian drug production.

Annotated Bibliography

McCoy, Alfred W. *The Politics of Heroin: CIA Complicity in the Global Drug Trade.* 2nd rev. ed. Chicago, Ill.: Lawrence Hill Books, 2003. This revised edition of a detailed but controversial study by a professor and specialist in Southeast Asian history documents the involvement of the Central Intelligence Agency in the heroin trade. The roots of this involvement can be traced back to an alliance between U.S. intelligence agencies and the Sicilian mafia during World War II. According to the author, during the Cold War the CIA's involvement in heroin trafficking was "inadvertent" at first, but then developed into a series of complex entanglements in Southeast Asia and Central America (particularly in Colombia). This updated edition also covers involvement in Afghanistan and Pakistan before and after the fall of the Taliban.

Perl, Raphael. *Drug Control: International Policy and Approaches.* Washington, D.C.: Congressional Research Service, 2003. Also available online. URL: http://www.thememoryhole.org/crs/IB88093.pdf. This brief report provides an overview of current U.S. policies toward narcotics-producing nations with regard to eradication of narcotic crops, interdiction, law enforcement, international cooperation, sanctions and economic assistance, and development of institutions. This is followed by a discussion of policy issues involving expansion of efforts in these various areas.

Scott, Peter Dale. *Drugs, Oil, and War: The United States in Afghanistan, Colombia, and Indochina.* Landham, Md.: Rowman & Littlefield, 2003. Argues that U.S. policy in these regions has largely been driven by business interests seeking control of oil, while the Central Intelligence Agency has often used illicit drug trafficking to help allies to carry out U.S. policy. The author also points with concern to the recent resurgence of drug production in Afghanistan following the fall of the Taliban regime.

Serafino, Nina M. *Colombia: Conditions and U.S. Policy Options.* Washington, D.C.: Congressional Research Service, 2001. An overview of U.S. policy issues and efforts regarding Colombia. Areas covered include trade and political stability, as well as combating narcotics production and trafficking. There is also a summary of "Plan Colombia" and other aid efforts.

Steffen, George S., and Samuel M. Candelaria. *Drug Interdiction: Partnership, Legal Principles, and Investigative Methodologies for Law Enforcement.* Boca Raton, Fla.: CRC Press, 2003. Written for law enforcement officers and with a "cop's eye" viewpoint, this text explains how to identify and interview suspected drug traffickers, how to use a wide range of investigative tools, and how to form partnerships with the business community to fight drug crime. Legal and civil liberties considerations are also thoroughly discussed, so this book would provide students and researchers with a good look at "best practices" for drug law enforcement.

Drug Abuse

Storrs, K. Larry. *Andean Regional Initiative: FY2002 Assistance for Colombia and Neighbors.* Washington, D.C.: Congressional Research Service, 2002. Also available online. URL: http://www.thememoryhole.org/crs/RL31016.pdf. Describes the current drug supply situation in Colombia, Peru, Bolivia, Venezuela, and neighboring countries, along with congressional action on appropriations for the Andean Regional Initiative. An appendix covers the controversy over spray eradication efforts in southern Colombia.

Veillette, Connie, and Jose E. Arvelo-Velze. *Colombia and Aerial Eradication of Drug Crops: U.S. Policy and Issues.* Washington, D.C.: Congressional Research Service, 2003. Discusses the effectiveness and potential risks of the policy of destroying narcotic crops by aerial spraying. This policy has been criticized for causing damage to human health and the environment, as well as economic hardships to farmers.

Webb, Gary. *Dark Alliance: The CIA, the Contras and the Crack Cocaine Explosion.* Revised Ed. New York: Seven Stories Press, 1999. This controversial exposé by a *San Jose Mercury-News* investigative reporter of CIA involvement in foreign drug trafficking and the crack explosion in America's inner cities brought, in turn, charges of shoddy, biased journalism. Meanwhile, disturbing evidence from investigation into the Iran-Contra weapons and drugs scandal, as well as later FBI and DEA reports, keeps the question of official complicity in the tragedy of drug abuse open.

ARTICLES

"The Andean Coca Wars: A Crop that Refuses to Die." *The Economist*, March 4, 2000, pp. 23–25. A coca eradication program has cut the coca crop in the area around the Apurimac River in Peru by more than 60 percent since the mid-1990s. However, crop estimates done by satellite can be inaccurate, and the progress may have been at the expense of human rights and democracy. Any loss in the supply of coca may be made up in Colombia on land controlled by the leftist FARC guerrillas.

Cochrane, Joe. "Blood in Bangkok Streets: A Spate of Killings Raises Questions about Thailand's Drug War." *Newsweek International*, March 10, 2003, p. 37. The rampant drug trafficking in Thailand led to popular outrage, and Prime Minister, Thaksin Shinawatra declared war against the drug lords in February 2003. However, the result has been a bloodbath in which more than 1,000 people were killed in the first month of the campaign. The government insists that the deaths are being caused by drug dealers fighting one another, but human rights groups believe that the police may be behind most of the killings. The government notes that many dealers have turned themselves in to avoid being arrested, new drug treatment programs are underway, and a quadrupling of the price of some drugs has occurred.

Annotated Bibliography

Coles, Clifton. "Alternatives to Growing Drugs: First World Policies that Keep Food Cheap Counteract the War on Drugs." *The Futurist*, vol. 37, May–June 2003, p. 13. Researchers at the University of Bonn, Germany, have concluded that programs to substitute legal crops for drug crops in South America are not working. One major reason is that food-importing countries in the developed world subsidize their own farming, keeping crop prices down. As a result a farmer in Central or South America can get about $2,500 a year for growing coca, but only about $300 for growing a legitimate crop. One long-term solution is to promote industrialization so farmers can seek better-paying jobs in the cities.

Davies, Frank. "Ads Linking Drugs to Terrorism Seen as Sharp, but Political Tool." *Knight Ridder/Tribune News Service*, March 15, 2002, p. K1358. Following September 11, 2001, a number of government-sponsored television ads have tried to dramatically link the war on terrorism with the war on drugs. Some ads ask viewers "Where do terrorists get their money? If you buy drugs, some of it may come from you." Critics of the drug war say the link between the domestic drug trade and international terrorism is tenuous at best and suggest that the new campaign is a political ploy to strengthen support for the faltering war on drugs by linking it to the popularly supported war on terrorism.

Gaul, Gilbert M., and Mary Pat Flaherty. "Google Just Says No to Unlicensed Pharmacy Advertising." *San Francisco Chronicle*, December 1, 2003, p. A4. Reports on the growing effort to combat the illegal sale of prescription drugs over the Internet. Google and other Internet search engines and portals are beginning to search for and filter out ads from illicit pharmacies (often outside the United States) that offer controlled drugs without requiring a prescription. Authorities are also beginning to focus on the credit card companies, banks, and shippers whose services are being used by the illicit traffickers.

Kohl, Ben, and Linda Farthing. "At the Price of Success: Bolivia's War Against Drugs and the Poor." *NACLA Report on the Americas*, vol. 35, July 2001, p. 35. Reports that the destruction of nearly three-quarters of Bolivia's coca crop has severely impacted the poor, marginalized peasants who have lost their livelihood. The Bolivian economy as a whole has suffered from a severe contraction and rampant unemployment. Meanwhile, the price of cocaine on the street remains low.

LeoGrande, William, and Kenneth Sharpe. "Two Wars or One: Drugs, Guerrillas, and Colombia's New *Violencia*." *World Policy Journal*, Fall 2000, pp. 1–11. The authors suggest that the new U.S. approach to fighting drugs in Colombia is seriously flawed. The United States will now be focusing on providing military aid and joining the Colombian military in fighting the Marxist guerrillas, who have become major sponsors of drug trafficking. However, joining two unwinnable wars—against insurgency and against drugs—does not seem likely to produce a victory. The background for the two struggles is explored, as well as recent developments. The authors conclude that the two wars needed to be separated: A negotiated peace with the insurgents is possible, but attempting to eradicate drugs in Colombia is futile because production and traffic will simply move elsewhere.

Lowry, Richard. "This Is a Bust: The Futility of Drug Interdiction." *National Review*, vol. 53, July 9, 2001, n.p. A touted victory in the drug war occurred when coca cultivation declined in both Bolivia and Peru between 1995 and 2000. However, as noted in the annual report from the Office of National Drug Control Policy, overall drug trafficking increased during the same time in Haiti, the Dominican Republic, and Puerto Rico. The author suggests that such shifts will always happen, making any success in drug interdiction or supply reduction only temporary. For one thing, the price of coca leaf is only a tiny fraction of the street cost of cocaine, so making coca a bit more expensive will have no effect on demand for the drug. It is the very illegality of drugs that keeps prices—and profits—high.

Naim, Moises. "The Five Wars of Globalization." *Foreign Policy*, January–February 2003, pp. 28ff. Places the war on drugs in the context of other "wars" that are fueled by the globalization that is pitting the unchecked power of multinational corporations against the efforts of national governments and international institutions. (The other wars are against arms smuggling, human smuggling, money laundering, and terrorism.) In response, governments must achieve more effective ways to regulate and harness market forces rather than relying on prohibition and the use of armed force.

Oborne, Peter, and Lucy Morgan Edwards. "A Victory for Drug Pushers: Opium Production in Afghanistan Is Booming." *Spectator*, vol. 292, May 31, 2003, pp. 26ff. Reports that post-Taliban Afghanistan is having a massive bumper crop of opium poppies. Besides providing huge new profits for drug traffickers (and possibly terrorist allies) and a new source of cheap heroin, this development is proving embarrassing for the United States and Britain, which promised to work with Afghanistan to drastically reduce opium production. The lack of aid and follow-through by the West after the overthrow of the Taliban is a major reason for the lack of success.

Peterson, Sarah. "People and Ecosystems in Colombia: Casualties of the Drug War." *Independent Review*, vol. 6, Winter 2002, pp. 427ff. A little-known source of opposition to the war on drugs is environmentalists, who point out the devastation to people and ecosystems being caused by drug crop eradication efforts in the Andean and Amazonian regions of South

America. The author describes some of these consequences of operations such as the ongoing Plan Colombia, including threats to the biodiversity of the Amazon, one of the world's richest ecosystems, and health threats from the herbicides used. Coca eradication efforts also threaten the survival of cultural groups and violate norms of human rights. An alternative strategy, crop substitution, has some promise but can cause economic problems when highly profitable crops are replaced by less remunerative ones.

Rosenberg, Tim. "The Great Cocaine Quagmire." *Rolling Stone*, April 12, 2001, pp. 51ff. Describes the cocaine eradication program in Colombia started by the Clinton administration and continued by the George W. Bush administration. According to the author, a foreign affairs writer for the *New York Times*, the effort is likely doomed to failure because most of the cocaine production is in territory controlled by guerrillas.

WEB DOCUMENTS

"International Narcotics Control Strategy Report, 2003." Bureau for International Narcotics and Law Enforcement Affairs, U.S. Department of State. Available online. URL: http://www.state.gov/g/inl/rls/nrcrpt/2003. Posted March 2004. This annual report details U.S. efforts to control narcotics trafficking through international aid and cooperation. The report includes policy and program developments during the preceding year as well as overviews of the narcotics situation by region and country.

ENFORCING THE DRUG LAWS

This section includes materials on domestic drug law enforcement, including prosecution and sentencing.

BOOKS

Alcohol Policies in the United States: Highlights from the 50 States. Minneapolis: Alcohol Epidemiology Program, University of Minnesota School of Public Health, 2000. Also available online. URL: http://www.epi.umn.edu/alcohol/pdf/Chrtbook.pdf. A summary of trends and specific state laws and policies with regard to the sale and distribution of alcoholic beverages, taxation, and drinking and driving. For example, the legal blood alcohol limit for driving has decreased from an average of .15 grams/deciliter in 1968 to .10 g/dL in 2000, with 19 states now having a limit of 0.08 g/dL.

Calkins, Jonathan P., et al. *Mandatory Minimum Sentences: Throwing Away the Key or the Taxpayers' Money?*, Santa Monica: RAND, 1997. The authors attempt to calculate the cost-effectiveness of mandatory minimum sentences for crimes related to cocaine distribution. This sentencing policy is compared to normal sentencing (without minimums) and to drug treatment. The conclusion is that mandatory minimum sentences are the least cost-effective policy, with drug treatment being the best investment of public expenditures.

Cavanagh, Suzanne, and David Teasley. *Drug Courts: An Overview.* Washington, D.C.: Congressional Research Service, 1998. Describes the key features of drug courts, which focus on supervised treatment and rehabilitation of offenders rather than incarceration.

Nolan, James L. *Reinventing Justice: The American Drug Court Movement.* Princeton, N.J.: Princeton University Press, 2001. A comprehensive picture of drug courts, special courts designed to deal with drug offenders with an emphasis on supervised treatment rather than incarceration. The author then draws some larger perspectives about how this approach to drug crimes might be part of a new concept of "therapeutic" justice quite at odds with classical notions of retribution or restitution.

ARTICLES

Butterfield, Fox. "As Drug Use Drops in Big Cities, Small Towns Confront Upsurge." *New York Times*, February 11, 2002, p. A1. Reports that the focus of drug dealing is shifting to small towns and rural areas, where the drugs of choice include methamphetamines and OxyContin as well as crack cocaine and marijuana. Drug use among high school students in some rural areas now exceeds that in big cities. An example is Jefferson Davis County, Mississippi, where drugs have become their "major industry."

"Drugs, Youth, and the Internet." *Information Bulletin*, National Drug Intelligence Center, October 2002, pp. 1–5. Also available online. URL: http://www.usdoj.gov/ndic/pubs2/2161/index.htm. When the large proportion of young people who use the Internet is combined with the prevalence of web sites providing information about drug use or even selling illegal drugs, it becomes clear that efforts to control drug abuse must involve the online world. Law enforcers must also develop effective and acceptable investigative techniques that are appropriate to this elusive new medium.

Georges, William P., and John C. Lawn. "Battling Hardcore Drunk Driving." *Police Chief*, July 1999, pp. 47–50. Reports on efforts to combat "hardcore" drunk driving, defined as offenders caught repeatedly with high blood alcohol levels. The authors believe that effectively deterring this behavior requires a certainty of significant punishment, then channeling offenders into effective treatment programs. A new charge of "aggravated DUI" should be applied to offenders with alcohol levels of .15 or higher. Increased patrols and checkpoints are also necessary for making would-be drunk drivers perceive greater risk of arrest.

Gould, John. "Zone Defense: Drug-Free School Zones Were Supposed to Keep Dealers Away from Kids. But What Happens When the Zones Engulf Whole Cities?" *Washington Monthly*, vol. 34, June 2002, pp. 33ff. Drug-free school zones, according to the author, "rank among the country's most specious criminal drug statutes." In many cities, the zones have been expanded so much that they now blanket most of the area. There is no evidence the laws have been responsible for the dip in drug use by schoolchildren. Their only effect seems to be to increase the sentences faced by low-level drug offenders, most of whom are minorities.

Hargreaves, Guy. "Clandestine Drug Labs: Chemical Time Bombs." *FBI Law Enforcement Bulletin*, April 2000, pp. 1–6. Also available online. URL: http://www.fbi.gov/publications/leb/2000/apr00leb.pdf. The author, an FBI special agent, reports that raiding "meth labs" has become one of the most dangerous operations in law enforcement. Meth labs contain highly explosive, flammable, and toxic chemicals—and sometimes booby traps as well. The article provides an overview of meth trafficking and production, including a list of typical chemicals and other products found in meth labs.

Hutlock, Todd. "Addressing Concerns About Drug Courts: Despite Political Popularity, This Treatment Method Still Garners Some Criticisms." *Behavioral Health Management*, vol. 23, March–April 2003, pp. 16ff. Drug courts emerged in the 1980s as an alternative to criminal punishment for drug offenders. Since then this approach has become popular among advocates and political leaders. However, the author considers the arguments of some critics who continue to question the effectiveness of drug courts. First, despite their growing use, drug courts are still handling only a small fraction of drug offenders—perhaps 4 to 8 percent. Many programs are implemented without sufficient resources to make sure entrants are properly screened and given appropriate treatment. It is also argued that the presence of a drug court encourages police to make arrests in order to get people into treatment, increasing costs. The author sides with defenders of drug courts, noting that they ultimately save money by avoiding expensive incarceration.

Mosedale, Mike. "Meth Myths, Meth Realities." *City Pages*, vol. 24, May 14, 2003, n.p. Also available online. URL: http://www.citypages.com/databank/24/1171/article11254.asp. A comprehensive and vivid account of the history and realities of methamphetamines, among the most widely abused and dangerous illicit drugs in the United States today. The article includes firsthand accounts of the dangers of dealing with illicit "meth labs," which use extremely noxious chemicals such as anhydrous ammonia. People who "cook" methamphetamines not surprisingly show little regard for their safety, that of their neighbors, or for the surrounding environment. The meth production process is described, along with ways in which the necessary ingredients are secured without tipping off authorities. The article concludes with discussion of the many ways in which the drug is used, its short- and long-term effects (including the equivalent of paranoid schizophrenia), and the seeming intractability of the meth problem.

"Ohio Voters Soundly Reject Drug Reform Ballot Initiative." *Alcohol & Drug Abuse Weekly*, vol. 14, November 11, 2002, pp. 1ff. Although there seems to have been a wave of drug-law reform efforts at the state level in recent years, there have recently been some setbacks for the movement. In November 2002, Ohio voters defeated, by a substantial margin, a ballot proposition that would have guaranteed substance abuse treatment for certain first- and second-time drug possession offenders. This issue has led to a clash between the pro-reform Drug Policy Alliance and the White House Office of National Drug Control Policy, whose director John Walters actively campaigns against reform measures. The growing strength of the opposition to reform measures in some states may be due to several factors: concern about cost and wasteful duplication of facilities, the loss of judges' ability to use their own discretion, and resentment at well-organized "outsiders" entering a state to campaign for reform.

"Raves." *Information Bulletin*, National Drug Intelligence Center, April 2001, pp. 1–6. Also available online. URL: http://www.usdoj.gov/ndic/pubs/656/index.htm. Covers the history of raves and the use of "club drugs" such as MDMA (ecstasy) and anti-rave initiatives. Although beginning as an underground movement in Europe, these high-energy all-night dance parties featuring "techno" or "house" music have now become a large commercial industry. Many cities have used curfew, liquor licensing, health and safety laws and other legal tools to curtail raves.

Resignato, Andrew J. "Violent Crime: A Function of Drug Use or Drug Enforcement?" *Applied Economics*, vol. 32, May 15, 2000, p. 681. A review of the research literature suggests there is little connection between the pharmacological effects of illegal drugs and violence. The relationship between economic compulsion (the need for addicts to get money for drugs) and violent crime seems mixed. What appears to cause most drug-related violence is the efforts of competing dealers to expand or protect their markets in a situation where the normal legal restraints and recourses are not available.

Sikes, Gini. "The $10,000 Dare." *Mademoiselle*, May 2000, pp. 153–155. Describes the harrowing experience of women who are paid to be drug "mules," smuggling potentially fatal quantities of drugs inside their bodies. A sidebar questions the variable but often harsh sentences meted out to mules while the kingpins who profit from the drugs often escape justice.

Spanberg, Erik. "Trial Puts Spotlight on Steroids: Some Analysts Say Drug-Testing Programs in Pro Sports Fall Short and Call for Radical New Measures." *Christian Science Monitor,* November 28, 2003, p. 13. Reports on the widening investigation around a San Francisco Bay Area company accused of producing steroids for use by professional athletes. A grand jury is hearing evidence from witnesses including Olympic athletes and baseball superstar Barry Bonds. Although there is a push in Congress to ban more types of performance-enhancement supplements, sports league officials insist that they can deal with the problem without government oversight.

WEB DOCUMENTS

"Case Histories: Jodie Israel and Will Foster." *Frontline,* PBS Online. Available online. URL: http://www.pbs.org/wgbh/pages/frontline/shows/dope/cases/. Posted in 1998. Interviews of a woman who was convicted of conspiracy because her husband grew marijuana, and a marijuana reform activist who was sentenced to 93 years for "marijuana cultivation and possession in the presence of a child."

"Judge Thelton Henderson: Interview." *Frontline,* PBS Online. Available online. URL: http://www.pbs.org/wgbh/pages/frontline/shows/dope/interviews/judge.html. Updated in 1998. Interview with a federal judge who is opposed to mandatory minimum sentences because "they're unduly harsh and don't allow the judge the discretion to deal with individual problems."

LEGAL AND CIVIL LIBERTIES ISSUES

This section covers legal and civil liberties issues arising from the prosecution of the war on drugs. (See also the next section for issues relating to drug testing.)

BOOKS

American Civil Liberties Union, Drug Policy Litigation Project. *Position Paper: Race and the War on Drugs.* Washington, D.C.: American Civil Liberties Union, 2003. This brochure presents facts and statistics that suggest that blacks and other minorities are being disproportionately targeted by the war on drugs, from arrest through to imprisonment. The fact that the same five-year sentence is given for 500 grams of powder cocaine (used more by whites) and five grams of crack (used more by blacks) is also cited as a form of racial discrimination. Current federal policy is attacked for its punitive emphasis and its lack of resources devoted to treatment.

Bowers, Jean M. *Asset Forfeiture and the War on Drugs: Selected References.* Washington, D.C.: Congressional Research Service, 1998. A bibliography on the use (or abuse) of asset forfeiture against drug suspects, including policy discussion and advocacy pro and con.

Grosshandler, Janet. *Drugs and the Law.* Revised ed. New York: Rosen Publishing Group, 1997. Written for junior high school students but useful for older students as well, this book describes federal and state drug laws, including different types of drug offenses and the likely penalties offenders will receive.

Hardaway, Robert M. *No Price Too High: Victimless Crimes and the Ninth Amendment.* Westport, Conn.: Praeger Publishers, 2003. The author argues that the Ninth Amendment to the U.S. Constitution, which speaks of rights reserved to the people, creates a robust protection for privacy that extends to a variety of activities (such as use of drugs) as long as they do not directly harm another person. Drug policies should thus seek to minimize harm while protecting these rights.

Irons, Peter, ed. *May It Please the Court: Courts, Kids, and the Constitution.* New York: New Press, 2000. Focusing on Supreme Court cases involving students, teachers, and schools, this set includes cassette tapes with actual oral arguments heard before the Supreme Court, with commentary to put it in context. Issues in these cases include drug testing in schools, as well as broader privacy and Fifth Amendment issues that come into play as schools attempt to detect and control drug use.

Long, Carolyn N. *Religious Freedom and Indian Rights: The Case of Oregon v. Smith.* Lawrence: University Press of Kansas, 2000. Discusses a controversial Supreme Court decision that pitted the right to use peyote in Native American religious ceremonies against the state's right to prohibit use of the drug. The Court's finding in favor of the state is only the beginning of the story—religious freedom activists got Congress to pass a law protecting religious freedom, but the Court in turn declared the law unconstitutional. A major focus of the book is on the importance of these developments for contemporary Native American history.

Miller, Gary J. *Drugs and the Law.* New York: Gould Publications, 1997. This textbook seems to be written primarily for students of law enforcement and criminal justice, but it provides a well-organized summary of drug use, individual drugs, federal and California drug laws, the process of investigating and prosecuting drug offenses, and more.

Annotated Bibliography

ARTICLES

Gagan, Bryony J. "Ferguson v. City of Charleston, South Carolina: 'Fetal Abuse,' Drug Testing, and the Fourth Amendment." *Stanford Law Review*, vol. 53, November 2000, p. 491. Reports on a case that arose from the drug testing, forced treatment, and arrest of a pregnant woman in a Charleston, South Carolina, hospital as part of a controversial program to stop drug-induced damage to children. The article discusses the historical background in the war on drugs, growing concern about fetal abuse, the movement for fetal rights and its role in the abortion debate, the Fourth Amendment privacy guarantees, and the "special needs" exemption to privacy rights. The compulsory testing and treatment program was later found to be unconstitutional by the Supreme Court.

Gross, Samuel R., and Katherine Y. Barnes. "Road Work: Racial Profiling and Drug Interdiction on the Highway." *Michigan Law Review*, vol. 101, December 2002, pp. 651ff. This detailed statistical analysis of highway stops concludes that the Michigan State Police did engage in racial profiling on the highway—no other explanation fits the data. And although racial profiling seems to increase the probability of the police finding large hauls of drugs, such hauls are rare. At any rate the cost of racial profiling to thousands of innocent persons cannot be justified by the meager amount of drugs seized.

Hollandsworth, Skip. "Snow Job: Two Aggressive Dallas Cops. One Confidential Informant. Hundreds of Pounds of Cocaine. Fifty-Three Drug Traffickers Busted. Sound Too Good to Be True? It Was." *Texas Monthly*, vol. 30, April 2002, pp. 44ff. Reports on a major scandal in which a group of Dallas narcotics agents planted "drugs" (actually ground-up sheetrock) on Hispanics who were then arrested and received long jail sentences. This scandal, together with the trumped-up arrests of black suspects in Tulia, Texas, raises serious questions about corruption and temptation to abuse power in the war on drugs.

Labi, Nadya. "Stop! And Say Cheese: Wilmington Police Are Snapping Pictures of People in High-Crime Areas and Taking Names." *Time*, vol. 160, September 23, 2002, p. 53. Reports that police in Wilmington, Delaware, are trying to discourage narcotics dealing and other crime by "jumping out" of cars and stopping individuals (particularly in a minority neighborhood) and taking their pictures "for anything you might do in the future." Although the police claim that they conduct surveillance to establish a reason for stopping individuals, civil libertarians believe many stops are not legal under rules established by the Supreme Court. Ironically, police may be free to take pictures in public places even when they do not stop anyone.

185

O'Meara, Kelly Patricia. "When Feds Say Seize and Desist." *Insight on the News,* vol. 16, August 7, 2000, p. 20. The ability of the government to seize property—even whole houses—that it says is associated with a crime has raised substantial civil liberties concerns. Even when a defendant is found innocent of criminal wrongdoing, the property seizure, which is a civil matter, must be fought in court without the resources and protections guaranteed to criminal defendants. About half of all civil forfeiture cases are drug-related, and officials argue that forfeiture is a good way to get profits from drug trafficking out of the hands of criminals and use them to support drug law enforcement. However, concern about abuses—particularly involving low-level cases and "ordinary" defendants—led to the passage of the Civil Asset Forfeiture Reform Act of 2000, which places some restrictions on the practice.

Sedeno, David. "Texas Governor Pardons 35 Convicted in Tulia Drug Sting." *Knight Ridder/Tribune News Service,* August 22, 2003, p. K6170. Reports that Texas governor Rick Perry has pardoned 35 people, most of them black, who had been convicted in a 1999 drug sting in Tulia, Texas. The undercover agent responsible for the original arrests, Tom Coleman, now stands accused of having made up his uncorroborated testimony about drug transactions.

Small, Deborah. "The War on Drugs Is a War on Racial Justice." *Social Research,* vol. 68, Fall 2001, pp. 896ff. This radical viewpoint argues that the war on drugs "has become the newest tool used to disrupt communities and generate today's slaves, aka prisoners." Just as slaves fueled the economy of early America, the millions of people imprisoned for drug offenses fuel an economy that enriches the people who build and manage the prisons. Drug laws, although neutral in language, are biased in their effect on minorities, and one in three black men in their twenties is in prison, on probation, or on parole. Although blacks make up only 13 percent of drug users, they make up 74 percent of the persons imprisoned for drug possession. The author also argues that this disproportionate imprisonment (accompanied by deprivation of voting rights) contributes greatly to political marginalization of minority communities. However, a growing number of black legislators and political leaders are now working to reform the drug laws.

DRUGS IN THE SCHOOLS, SPORTS, AND THE WORKPLACE

This section includes works dealing with drug testing and other issues relating to drugs in the schools, in athletics, and in the workplace.

Annotated Bibliography

BOOKS

Bennett, Joel B., and Wayne E. K. Lehman, eds. *Preventing Workplace Substance Abuse: Beyond Drug-Testing to Wellness.* Washington, D.C.: American Psychological Association, 2002. With the controversy about the use and justification for drug testing in the workplace continuing, the contributors to this book aim at convincing the government to go beyond testing to a comprehensive program that includes educational and prevention components as well as an approach to overall health.

National Center on Addiction and Substance Abuse. *Malignant Neglect: Substance Abuse and America's Schools.* New York: National Center on Addiction and Substance Abuse at Colombia University, September 2001. Also available online. URL: http://www.casalibrary.org/CASAPublications/malignant.pdf. Students from 12 to 17 years old have consistently reported that drugs are the number one problem they face at school. Drug abuse costs schools at least $41 billion a year. The report argues that the underlying problem is that teachers, administrators, and parents have largely looked the other way—either assuming that existing programs would take care of the problem or believing that drug experimentation for youth "was a relatively benign rite of passage."

Newton, David E. *Drug Testing: An Issue for School, Sports, and Work.* Springfield, N.J.: Enslow Publishers, 1999. Written for junior and high school students but useful for older students and adults as well, this book explains the motivation behind drug testing in schools, sports, and the workplace and the development of testing programs and policies. The author also explores important legal and ethical concerns such as privacy, the accuracy of tests, and the balancing of individual rights and public safety. Includes bibliographies and a listing of Internet resources.

ARTICLES

Hickey, John. "MLB to Test for Drugs. 5–7% of Players Failed Tests for Steroids. New Policy Begins in 2004." *Seattle Post-Intelligencer,* November 14, 2003, p. D1. Reports that Major League Baseball has admitted that between 5 and 7 percent of major league players fail tests for steroids. The leagues have announced that as a result, players will face stricter testing and stiffer penalties for being caught using steroids and other banned performance-enhancing substances.

Longman, Jere. "Test Results Demand Time for Introspection." *New York Times,* November 15, 2003, p. D1. The disparity between the very strict drug bans for Olympic athletes and the relatively minor sanctions recently enacted by Major League Baseball has provoked questions of fairness and consistency—especially when one official, Donald M. Fehr, is both the executive director of the baseball players' union and on leave as a member of the board of directors of the Olympic Committee. A number of voices have been raised calling for taking use of steroids and other enhancements in sports more seriously.

Longman, Jere, and Joe Drape. "Decoding a Steroid: Hunches, Sweat, Vindication." *New York Times*, November 2, 2003, p. A1. Profiles Dr. Donald H. Catlin, a researcher and "chemical detective" who uses science to discover designer steroids that have become popular with athletes because they cannot be detected by existing tests. The article features Catlin's discovery of a steroid called THG and his development of a test for it. As a result, a San Francisco grand jury is investigating a firm accused of producing the substance and selling it to athletes.

Springen, Karen. "Rethinking Zero Tolerance: A Few Schools Are Inching Away from One-Strike Policies." *Newsweek*, February 12, 2001, p. 46. Reports that some schools are starting to come up with alternatives where students caught with drugs receive treatment and counseling either instead of or in addition to expulsion from school. This may be a reaction to the extremes that zero tolerance has sometimes led to, such as a student being suspended for giving another student a cough drop. Some experts believe that while schools need to give a consistent, unambiguous antidrug message, expelling students so they have no contact with help does not make sense.

Yamaguchi, Ryoko, Lloyd D. Johnston, and Patrick M. O'Malley. "Relationship Between Student Illicit Drug Use and School Drug-Testing Policies." *Journal of School Health*, vol. 73, April 2003, pp. 159ff. After examining national surveys the authors found no association between drug testing of students (or student athletes) and the rate of reported illicit drug use. This lack of effectiveness may undermine a major legal justification for school drug testing often cited by the Supreme Court.

WEB DOCUMENTS

"Guidelines for a Drug-Free Workforce." U.S. Drug Enforcement Administration. 4th ed. Available online. URL: http://www.usdoj.gov/dea/demand/dfmanual/index.html. Posted Summer 2003. Provides recommendations for employers regarding drug testing and other measures for reducing drug use in the workplace and dealing with employees who test positive for drugs. The guide asserts that the legal risk of failing to be proactive is generally higher than the risk of legal action by affecting employees.

Jones, Eliot. "Drug Testing in Schools." International Debate Education Association. Available online. URL: http://www.debatabase.org/details.

asp?topicID=95. Updated November 6, 2000. Provides pro and con materials for debaters on the question: "Should school students face mandatory drug tests?" Also includes some resource links.

MEDICAL USE OF MARIJUANA

This section covers the debate over whether marijuana should be legalized for medical use.

BOOKS

Doyle, Charles. *Marijuana for Medical Purposes: The Supreme Court's Decision in United States v. Oakland Cannabis Buyers' Cooperative and Related Legal Issues.* Washington, D.C.: Congressional Research Service, 2002. Summarizes the Supreme Court's latest medical marijuana decision, which refused to recognize a medical necessity defense for cultivating or distributing marijuana. The existence of state laws sanctioning medical marijuana have no federal effect. Related constitutional issues that may still come before the Court are summarized.

Joy, Janet E., Stanley J. Watson, and John A. Benson, eds. *Marijuana and Medicine: Assessing the Science Base,* Washington, D.C.: National Academy Press, 1999. Researchers with the National Institute of Medicine summarize the conclusions of current scientific knowledge and research on marijuana in order to inform the current controversy over medical use of the drug. Considerations include efficacy for treating various conditions (such as glaucoma and multiple sclerosis), effects of different methods of administration (such as smoking vs. pills), and acute and long-term effects on health and behavior. The conclusion attempts to evaluate how well marijuana might fit into the accepted standards for medicines.

Mack, Alison, and Janet Joy. *Marijuana as Medicine? The Science Beyond the Controversy.* Washington, D.C.: National Academy Press, 2001. Recent findings from a National Institute of Medicine study are explained in lay terms, assessing the value of marijuana for treating various illnesses and types of pain. The book also discusses possible negative effects. Alternative forms of marijuana (such as Marinol) are also considered, and the current legal situation is explained.

Randall, Blanchard, IV. *Medical Use of Marijuana: Policy and Regulatory Issues.* Washington, D.C.: Congressional Research Service, 2002. Describes the development of the medical marijuana issue and summarizes and analyzes policy issues. Government regulatory decisions, congressional proposals, and state ballot initiatives are also discussed.

Rätsch, Christian. *Marijuana Medicine: A World Tour of the Healing and Visionary Powers of Cannabis.* Rochester, Vt.: Healing Arts Press, 2001. Translated from German, this work by an eminent anthropologist and specialist in ethnomedicine traces the use of the cannabis plant by many different cultures throughout history. It focuses on ceremonial and especially healing uses of the plant, including remedies for a variety of conditions.

Zimmerman, Bill, Rick Bayer, and Nancy Crumpacker. *Is Marijuana the Right Medicine for You?* New Canaan, Conn.: Keats Publishing, 1998. Given that the lead author, Zimmerman, is a neurologist who spearheaded the California medical marijuana ballot campaign, it is not surprising that the answer to the question given is an unabashed "yes." The book claims that marijuana is efficacious for a wide variety of illnesses—not just glaucoma but also multiple sclerosis, epilepsy, migraines, arthritis, and even AIDS and cancer. This perspective should be balanced against the more modest claims of other researchers.

ARTICLES

Eidelman, William S., and Eric A. Voth. "Should Physicians Support the Medical Use of Marijuana?" *The Western Journal of Medicine,* vol. 176, March 2002, pp. 76ff. Two British physicians debate the medical value of marijuana. Eidelman, the proponent, says that the drug "can be effective when all else fails" and has a long history of medical use. He cites a report by the U.S. Institute of Medicine that confirmed that marijuana was safe and beneficial in a wide range of conditions. He also cites a Johns Hopkins University study that found no long-term cognitive impairment in marijuana users. Voth, who opposes medical use of marijuana, flips the argument around and argues that marijuana contains hundreds of substances whose safety has never been shown. He says that marijuana does not meet any of the standards that are applied to new medicines today. Smoking marijuana is likely to be particularly harmful in terms of cancer risk and other effects.

Koch, Kathy. "Medical Marijuana." *CQ Researcher,* August 20, 1999, pp. 705–728. Covers the medical marijuana movement, state initiatives, and the question of legality of cannabis buyers' clubs.

McDonough, James R. "Marijuana on the Ballot." *Policy Review,* April/May 2000, pp. 51–61. The author surveys research findings that suggest that the medical benefits of marijuana are modest at best. He further argues that whatever the medical merits of marijuana, smoking is not the right way to deliver the drug. The growing movement to legalize medical marijuana by ballot initiative is threatening to derail the proper development of medical marijuana delivery systems such as inhalers.

WEB DOCUMENTS

"Drug War Facts: Medical Marijuana." Common Sense for Drug Policy. Available online. URL: http://www.drugwarfacts.org/medicalm.htm. Updated on September 12, 2003. Provides facts and statistics (with sources) on the implementation of medical marijuana programs in the United States and testimony by experts as to marijuana's effectiveness as a medicine.

"Medical Marijuana Program." State of Oregon, Department of Health and Human Services. Available online. URL: http://www.ohd.hr.state.or.us/mm/index.cfm Downloaded on January 8, 2004. Provides basic facts and answers to frequently asked questions about Oregon's medical marijuana program.

Zeese, Kevin B. "Research Findings on Medicinal Properties of Marijuana." Medical MJ Science.org. Available online. URL: http://www.medmjscience.org/Pages/history/zeese.bhtml. Downloaded January 8, 2004. An attorney and advocate involved in federal marijuana rescheduling cases summarizes the history of medicinal use of marijuana and describes major research studies that have tended to confirm the medical value of marijuana for certain conditions such as anorexia, nausea, and glaucoma.

LEGALIZATION AND DECRIMINALIZATION OF DRUGS

This section covers a major alternative to the drug policy—varying degrees of legalization or decriminalization of drugs.

BOOKS

Croft, Jennifer. *Drugs and the Legalization Debate.* Revised ed. New York: Rosen Publishing Group, 2000. Presents the controversy over drug legalization to high school students, offering various viewpoints and relevant facts and statistics.

Friedman, Milton, and Thomas Szasz. *On Liberty and Drugs.* Washington, D.C.: Drug Policy Foundation Press, 1992. Friedman, a Nobel Prize–winning free market economist, and Szasz, a radical critic of psychiatry and medicine, join forces to write a fundamental critique of the state's right to regulate drug use. In addition to the philosophical argument on libertarian principles, the economic and social consequences of such regulation are compared to those of a policy under which drugs would be available with some limited regulation.

Goode, Erich. *Between Politics and Reason: The Drug Legalization Debate.* New York: St. Martin's Press, 1997. Also available online. URL: http://www.druglibrary.org/special/goode/bpr.htm. The author describes the current situation with regard to drugs, drug abuse, and drug control, including explanation of terms and concepts. He then looks at the current "punitive" system and asserts that it is maintained by political and ideological interests despite its lack of success. Alternative ideologies and agendas (such as legalization, various degrees of decriminalization, and harm reduction) are explained and evaluated in connection with drug use and crime.

Gottfried, Ted. *Should Drugs Be Legalized?* Brookfield, Conn.: Twenty-First Century Books, 2000. Despite the focus implied in the title, this is actually a comprehensive and accessible introduction to drugs and their effects, important events in the history of drug use in the United States, and approaches to drug treatment and the war on drugs, including the alternatives of harm reduction and legalization.

Gray, James P. *Why Our Drug Laws Have Failed and What We Can Do About It: A Judicial Indictment of the War on Drugs.* Philadelphia: Temple University Press, 2001. A veteran judge and former federal prosecutor argues that the war on drugs has failed and proposes alternatives, notably allowing sale of drugs under government regulation and taxed sufficiently to provide treatment funds and to discourage access by children.

McWilliam, Peter. *Ain't Nobody's Business if You Do: The Absurdity of Consensual Crimes in a Free Society.* Los Angeles: Prelude Press, 1993. The author is a writer of popular self-help and computer books who colleagues say died prematurely because he was denied access to medical marijuana. He offers a wide-ranging libertarian polemic that draws on sources as diverse as St. Augustine and Elvis Presley to argue that consensual acts such as drug abuse should not be punished by the government.

Rosenthal, Ed, and Steve Kubby. *Why Marijuana Should Be Legal.* 2nd ed. New York: Thunder's Mouth Press, 2003. Two activists (who would both be convicted for use of medical marijuana) argue passionately for the medical value of the drug for treating glaucoma and helping cancer patients, tout the value of industrial hemp, and demand an end to marijuana prohibition, which they believe has been responsible for taking the freedom of millions of innocent people and threatening everyone's civil liberties.

Sullum, Jacob. *Saying Yes: In Defense of Drug Use.* New York: J. P. Tarcher/Putnam, 2003. The author argues not that drugs may not be harmful, but that, as with alcohol, people vary greatly in their ability to get desired benefits from their drug use without running into problems such as impairment or dependency. Because of this, he believes that it is inappropriate to vilify certain drugs or users or to have the state prohibit drug taking or any other acts by or between consenting adults. Rather, we should focus on helping people better manage drug use.

Szasz, Thomas. *Our Right to Drugs: The Case for a Free Market.* Westport, Conn.: Greenwood Publishing Group, 1992. The author, a well-known radical critic of psychiatry and medicine, provides a comprehensive argument for allowing people to buy the drugs of their choice. Among other things he says that the system of doctor-mediated prescriptions undermines the ability of individuals to make fundamental choices about their health and what should go into their body. While drugs certainly can be abused, Szasz makes the broad libertarian point that adults should have the right to make a broad range of choices, including those that might have harmful consequences. He argues that the present system is paternalistic and treats adults as though they were children, as well as persecuting minorities in the name of the public good.

ARTICLES

Casriel, Erika. "The New Coalition Against the Drug War." *Rolling Stone,* August 2001, pp. 33ff. Opposition to the drug war is becoming mainstream, with drug policy reform proponents running the gamut from right-wing Republicans to doctors to minority advocates and musicians. A variety of sample statements pro and con are included.

Cass, Connie. "Candidates' Past Pot Use No Big Deal: Dems Seeking Presidency Talk Frankly About Inhaling." *San Francisco Chronicle,* November 29, 2003, p. A2. Many of the Democratic primary candidates and other political figures no longer see their past experimentation with marijuana as a problem, and they are willing to freely admit to it without equivocation. Advocates of legalizing marijuana are taking some heart from what seems to be a cultural shift toward tolerance of the drug.

Duke, Steven. "End the Drug War." *Social Research,* vol. 68, Fall 2001, pp. 875ff. According to the author, ending the drug war by legalizing and regulating drugs would have important advantages over prohibition, a policy that with alcohol promoted crime and deadly moonshine that poisoned thousands. With legal drugs, regulations could ensure quality and lack of contamination. Scientific research into determining the objective effects and dangers of drugs would be allowed. Finally, there would be an end to drug-fueled crime, civil liberties abuses, and disparate treatment of minorities.

Grinspoon, Lester. "The Harmfulness Tax." *Social Research,* vol. 68, Fall 2001, pp. 880ff. The author proposes a realistic approach to a situation where, in a free society, people will take drugs that can be harmful. Drugs would be legalized and taxed, with the tax being used to pay for drug education and for the medical and social costs of drug abuse. The amount of tax for a given drug would be based on a particular assessment of that drug's impact on society. This can already be done for the legal drugs of tobacco and alcohol, and among illegal drugs, marijuana would be a good place to start because of its relatively modest costs and dangers.

Macoun, Robert, and Peter Reuter. "Marijuana, Heroin, and Cocaine: The War on Drugs May Be a Disaster, but Do We Really Want a Legalized Peace?" *The American Prospect*, vol. 13, June 3, 2002. n.p. Also available online. URL: http://www.prospect.org/print/v13/10/maccoun-r.html. The authors of the article, who also wrote the book *Drug War Heresies*, agree that legalizing drugs such as heroin, cocaine, and marijuana would lead to large reductions in drug-related crime and violence, but assert that it would also lead to a large increase in the number of addicts. Legalization advocates often suggest that taxation, regulation, and treatment would help control legal drug use, but experience with abuse of legalized gambling and especially with alcohol (with alcoholism rising sharply after the repeal of Prohibition) suggests otherwise. The authors suggest that neither total legalization nor the existing total prohibition are good choices and that some combination of harm reduction and decriminalized, regulated use (as with marijuana) needs to be crafted with different drugs and situations in mind.

Miron, Jeffrey. "The Economics of Drug Prohibition and Drug Legalization." *Social Research*, vol. 68, Fall 2001, pp. 835ff. This detailed economic analysis concludes that the cost of the effects of drug prohibition (such as crime and imprisonment and other legal effects on users) is high, while the reduction in drug use compared to the situation under legalization is modest and could be accomplished through a variety of harm minimization policies. The final part of the paper analyzes the specific benefits and drawbacks of policies such as "sin taxes," subsidized drug treatment, provision of drugs under medical supervision, needle exchanges, and public education campaigns.

Roosevelt, Margot. "The War Against the War on Drugs." *Time*, May 7, 2001, pp. 46–47. Although the Bush administration has taken a rather hard line in the drug war, many states are taking a more moderate course—17 have passed ballot propositions providing for alternatives to long prison sentences for drug offenders. Nine states have legalized marijuana for medical use. Meanwhile, some prominent philanthropists such as billionaire George Soros are funding initiatives for reform of drug laws.

Silbering, Robert. "The 'War on Drugs': A View from the Trenches." *Social Research*, vol. 68, Fall 2001, pp. 890ff. A former special narcotics prosecutor for the city of New York refutes arguments for drug legalization. He believes that the war on drugs has not been lost—it has not really been fought with the national commitment that would be required. Giving up by legalizing drugs would increase the number of drug users. The age restrictions that many legalization proponents would retain would just create a new black market in drugs among young people. The author also argues that horror stories about long sentences for mere possession of drugs are generally not borne out by reality, where most possession cases are plea bargained down to probation.

WEB DOCUMENTS

Endersby, Alastair. "Drugs in Sport." International Debate Education Association. Available online. URL: http://www.debatabase.org/details. asp?topicID=28. Updated September 29, 2000. This resource page for student debaters provides pro and con arguments on the question: "Should the use of performance-enhancing drugs be legalized?" Some resources links are included.

"Speaking Out Against Drug Legalization." Drug Enforcement Administration, U.S. Department of Justice. Available online. URL: http://www. usdoj.gov/dea/demand/speakout/. Posted November 2002. Provides talking points for defending current U.S. drug policy and refuting advocates of legalizing drugs. Argues that progress is being made in reducing drug abuse and that a balanced approach of prevention, enforcement, and treatment is necessary. Arguments against legalization include illegal drugs are dangerous, smoked marijuana is not a medicine, and legalization would increase drug use.

HARM REDUCTION STRATEGIES

This section covers advocacy for and implementation of various harm reduction strategies such as needle exchange programs.

BOOKS

Alexandrova, Anna, ed. *AIDS, Drugs, and Society.* New York: International Debate Education Association, 2002. Includes both background readings and policy debates concerning the relationship between the worldwide epidemic of AIDS and drug abuse. There is a particular emphasis on harm reduction strategies and initiatives, and source documents include official statements and relevant human rights treaties.

Denning, Pat, Adina Glickman, and Jeannie Little. *Over the Influence: The Harm Reduction Guide for Managing Drugs and Alcohol.* New York: Guilford Publications, 2003. The authors explain how harm reduction is an alternative approach that can help people who have tried to quit alcohol or drugs (perhaps by following a 12-step program) but have been unable to keep their commitment to abstinence. The importance of dealing with underlying problems such as depression, stress, and relationship conflicts is especially noted, and the authors also give practical tools to help people identify their problems and work on them.

Erickson, Patricia G., et al., eds. *Harm Reduction: A New Direction for Drug Policies and Programs.* Toronto: University of Toronto Press, 1997. Describing the growing effort, begun in the early 1990s, to articulate a new approach to drug policy. Harm reduction seeks to reduce serious effects of drug abuse such as HIV/AIDS infection and drunk driving through needle exchange programs, methadone maintenance, training alcohol servers, and other efforts. Contributors also offer perspectives on dealing with special populations and on evaluating the success of harm reduction programs.

Fernando, M. Daniel. *AIDS and Intravenous Drug Use: The Influence of Morality, Politics, Social Science, and Race in the Making of a Tragedy.* Westport, Conn.: Praeger Publishers, 1993. The author argues that an attitude that characterized AIDS sufferers as well as drug abusers as "sinners," together with racial and social stereotypes, has tragically held back effective treatment. The author's suggestion that providing clean needles would help control the spread of infection has been acted on to some extent in the decade since the book was written. However, another suggestion, that possession of drug paraphernalia be legalized, has found less acceptance.

Marlatt, G. Alan, David B. Abrams, and David C. Lewis. *Harm Reduction: Pragmatic Strategies for Managing High-Risk Behaviors.* New York: Guilford Publications, 2002. This comprehensive guide to the philosophy and practice of harm reduction deals not only with drug abuse but also with other high-risk behaviors such as unsafe sex and preventing AIDS. The book begins by explaining how the harm reduction strategy came about as a response to the ineffectiveness of punitive and simplistic approaches. The authors give examples of effective strategies and assess how much progress has been made in implementing policies based on the harm reduction approach.

ARTICLES

Broadhead, Robert S., Yael van Hulst, and Douglas D. Heckathorn. "The Impact of a Needle Exchange's Closure." *Public Health Reports,* September/October 1999, pp. 446–447. This study evaluates the impact of closing a needle exchange program in Windham, Connecticut, in 1997 after it was blamed for spreading drug use and causing neighborhood blight.

After the closure, a higher proportion of injection drug users reported they were getting their needles from an unsafe source, and more users were sharing needles. Meanwhile, closing the needle exchange did not improve the conditions that critics had complained about.

Ho, Vanessa. "'Harm Reduction' for Drug Users." *Seattle Post-Intelligencer,* December 3, 2002, p. B2. Reports on a national conference on harm reduction held in Seattle and describes some strategies being used to make drug abusers safer. For example, the mayor of Vancouver, B.C., wants to create a safe place off the streets where addicts can inject drugs. In Chicago and Albuquerque, New Mexico, addicts are allowed to carry a supply of naloxone, a drug that helps prevent narcotics overdoses. Addicts are also being trained in how to administer CPR, and needle-exchange programs are being increasingly used.

Kleiman, Mark A. R. "Science and Drug Abuse Control Policy." *Society,* May/June 2001, pp. 7–12. The author describes the importance of good science for informing drug policy but also cautions that science has limited value in answering policy questions.

Levine, Daniel. "This Is No Way to Fight the Drug War." *Reader's Digest,* February 2000, pp. 70–76. The author quotes former drug czar General Barry McCaffrey as saying that the risk of increased drug usage outweighs any potential benefit for needle exchange programs. Although the author's extensive interviews with drug users, drug treatment specialists, police, and others did not conclusively prove McCaffrey was correct, much of the anecdotal evidence suggested that the needle exchanges were not working as intended. Users were frequently obtaining clean needles and then sharing them with others or selling them to buy drugs.

Loconte, Joe. "Killing Them Softly." *Policy Review* (Heritage Foundation), July–August 1998, pp. 14–22. The author argues that while there is some public health justification for providing clean needles in order to reduce infection, needle exchange programs are part of a larger movement to abandon the attempt to confront drug-taking behavior as a moral problem. The result is that the drug use, which eventually kills more addicts than does AIDS or other infections, is allowed to continue.

Whiteacre, Kevin W., and Hal Pepinsky. "Controlling Drug Use." *Criminal Justice Policy Review,* March 2002, pp. 21–31. The authors take an unconventional approach to the problem of drug abuse. According to the "peacemaking" theory, the goal should not be attaining an impossible victory in the war on drugs, but instead to focus on better communication and providing information about responsible drug use. This includes conveying the risks of drug use realistically and trying to ensure that drug use takes places in an environment free of violence. Role models for responsible drug use are also needed.

WEB DOCUMENTS

"Mark Kleiman: Interview." *Frontline*, PBS Online. Available online. URL: http://www.pbs.org/wgbh/pages/frontline/shows/dope/interviews/ kleiman.html. Updated in 1998. A long and thoughtful interview with a professor of Public Policy and Social Research at the University of California, Los Angeles. He joins with a growing movement seeking a "middle of the road" between total legalization of drugs on the one hand and the current punitive policy on the other. He suggests that removing marijuana from the realm of illegal drugs would simplify matters somewhat but would not address the core of the problem, which focuses on cocaine and other hard drugs. He also believes legalization of hard drugs would either create a new industry that profits from addiction (as with tobacco today) or, if the government distributed drugs, a bureaucracy that would also have an incentive to maintain addicts. Kleiman seems to have some sympathy for decriminalization of marijuana but notes that the biggest drug problem is neither marijuana nor cocaine but alcohol.

CHAPTER 8

ORGANIZATIONS AND AGENCIES

Following are listings for selected organizations and agencies involved with drug abuse enforcement, research, treatment, education, and prevention as well as policy advocacy. The listing is divided into two parts: government agencies and private organizations.

GOVERNMENT AGENCIES

This section lists federal government agencies (as well as one United Nations organization). State and local drug abuse treatment and education organizations are far too numerous to list here. For help in finding local resources, see the web site for the Regional Alcohol and Drug Awareness Resource (RADAR) network at http://ncadi.samhsa.gov/radar/, which includes a directory of resources by state. Individuals with substance abuse concerns can also obtain referrals through Drughelp.org (http://www.drughelp.org), a nonprofit service operated by the American Council for Drug Education.

Bureau for International Narcotics and Law Enforcement Affairs
URL: http://www.state.gov/g/inl/narc
Phone: (202) 647-4000
U.S. Department of State
2201 C Street, NW
Washington, DC 20520
This agency, part of the U.S. State Department, helps develop policies and programs to combat international narcotics and crime. It imple-ments the International Narcotics Control element in U.S. foreign assistance programs. International efforts focus on law enforcement and interdiction, criminal justice system reform, eradication of drug crops, alternative development, and demand reduction.

Center for Substance Abuse Prevention (CSAP)
URL: http://www.samhsa.gov/centers/csap/csap.html

E-mail: info@samhsa.org
Phone: (301) 443-8956
Rm. 12-105 Parklawn Building
5600 Fishers Lane
Rockville, MD 20857
The mission of this program of the U.S. Substance Abuse and Mental Health Services Administration (SAMHSA) is "to decrease substance use and abuse by bringing effective prevention to every community." The organization does this by developing programs and services, particularly to prevent youth from beginning to use illegal drugs, alcohol, or tobacco.

Department of Homeland Security (DHS)
URL: http://www.dhs.gov
E-mail: Web form
U.S. Dept. of Homeland Security
Washington, DC 20528
The U.S. Department of Homeland Security (DHS) was established in 2002 as a single, coordinated effort for protecting the territory of the United States from terrorists. The new department has incorporated a number of existing agencies (such as the Coast Guard, U.S. Immigration, and the Secret Service) and new agencies (such as the Transportation Security Administration), as well as coordinating efforts with intelligence agencies such as the FBI and CIA. Many U.S. antidrug efforts are likely to be impacted by this reorganization, changes in priorities, and linkages being made between the war on drugs and the war on terrorism.

Drug Enforcement Administration (DEA)
URL: http://www.usdoj.gov/dea
Phone: (202) 307-1000
2401 Jefferson Davis Highway
Alexandria, VA 22301
The DEA, which is part of the U.S. Department of Justice, is the principal federal enforcement agency for controlled substances. Its investigative and enforcement activities target manufacture and distribution of illegal drugs in cooperation with state, local, and foreign governments.

Federal Bureau of Investigation (FBI)
URL: http://www.fbi.gov
E-mail: Field offices contact page
Phone: (202) 324-5520
935 Pennsylvania Avenue, NW
Washington, DC 20535
Although the Drug Enforcement Administration is the primary federal agency charged with fighting drug trafficking, the FBI also becomes involved in the war on drugs, particularly through its efforts to fight organized crime and money laundering.

National Clearinghouse for Alcohol and Drug Information (NCADI)
URL: http://www.health.org
E-mail: Web form
Phone: (800) 729-6686
11420 Rockville Pike
Rockville, MD 20852
Sponsored by the Substance Abuse and Mental Health Services Administration (SAMHSA) of the

U.S. Department of Health and Human Services, the National Clearinghouse for Alcohol and Drug Information provides information about substance abuse prevention and addiction treatment to both professionals and the public.

National Institute on Drug Abuse (NIDA)
URL: http://www.nida.nih.gov
E-mail: Information@lists.nida.nih.gov
Phone: (301) 443-1124
Neuroscience Center Building
6001 Executive Blvd.
Rockville, MD 20852
The National Institute on Drug Abuse is a division of the National Institutes of Health. Its mission is to "lead the nation in bringing the power of science to bear on drug abuse and addiction." NIDA has sponsored more than 85 percent of the world's research on the health aspects of drug abuse and addiction.

National Prevention Information Network (NPIN)
URL: http://www.cdcnpin.org
E-mail: info@cdcnpin.org
Phone: (800) 458-5231
P.O. Box 6003
Rockville, MD 20849-6003
A program of the Centers for Disease Control and Prevention (CDC), the National Prevention Information Network provides information and referrals for communicable diseases such as tuberculosis, HIV/AIDS, and other sexually transmit-

ted diseases. Because drug abuse adds to the spread of these infections, there is a close relationship between drug abuse prevention and treatment and disease control.

Office of National Drug Control Policy (ONDCP)
URL: http://www.whitehousedrugpolicy.gov
E-mail: Web form
Phone: (800) 666-3332
P.O. Box 6000
Rockville, MD 20849-6000
The ONDCP is an office in the White House whose primary mission is "to establish policies, priorities, and objectives for the nation's drug control program. The goals of the program are to reduce illicit drug use, manufacturing, drug-related crime and violence, and drug-related health consequences." The office produces an annual report called the National Drug Control Strategy.

Substance Abuse and Mental Health Services Administration (SAMHSA)
URL: http://www.samhsa.gov
E-mail: info@samhsa.gov
Phone: (301) 443-4795
Rm. 12-105 Parklawn Building
5600 Fishers Lane
Rockville, MD 20857
This federal agency conducts research and other programs aimed at improving the quality and availability of prevention, treatment, and rehabilitative services for drug abusers. It provides a variety of

resources, including distributing information through the National Clearinghouse on Alcohol and Drug Information.

United Nations Office on Drugs and Crime (UNODC)
URL: http://www.unodc.org
E-mail: unodc@unodc.org
Phone: +43 1 26060 0
Vienna International Centre
P.O. Box 500
A-1400 Vienna
Austria

Founded in 1997, the UNODC conducts "an integrated approach to counter drugs, crimes, and terrorism." Its headquarters is in Vienna, Austria, and there are 22 field offices worldwide. The organization is divided into a Crime Programme, involved with law enforcement, and a Drug Programme, involved with substance abuse research and education, as well as reducing drug production by providing alternative means of development for drug-producing countries.

PRIVATE ORGANIZATIONS

The following are some major private organizations involved in drug abuse research, education, prevention, and treatment, as well as drug policy advocacy.

Al-Anon/Alateen
URL: http://www.al-anon.org
E-mail: WSO@al-anon.org
Phone: (757) 563-1600
1600 Corporate Landing
Parkway
Virginia Beach, VA 23454-5617
Al-Anon is a national support organization for family members of alcoholics, and Alateen performs the same function for children of alcoholics. The organization is derived from Alcoholic Anonymous and adapts the 12 steps and other AA traditions to help persons intimately affected by others' abuse of alcohol. There are more than 24,000 Al-Anon and 2,300 Alateen groups in 115 countries worldwide.

Alcoholics Anonymous (AA)
URL: http://www.aa.org
E-mail: See contact
information for local offices
on web site
Phone: (212) 870-3400
Grand Central Station
P.O. Box 459
New York, NY 10163
AA is perhaps the most influential organization in the history of substance abuse treatment. Its 12 steps, although controversial, have been credited with helping thousands of people overcome alcoholism and drug abuse. The national organization provides education and resources to thousands of local groups worldwide.

Organizations and Agencies

American Civil Liberties Union
URL: http://www.aclu.org/
E-mail: Web form
Phone: (888) 567-ACLU
125 Broad Street
18th Floor
New York, NY 10004
The ACLU is one of the nation's oldest and most formidable advocates for civil liberties. With regard to drug law enforcement, the ACLU is particularly concerned about issues such as disparities in sentencing that affect minorities, racial profiling, asset forfeiture, and drug testing.

American Council for Drug Education (ACDE)
URL: http://www.acde.org
E-mail: ACDE@phoenixhouse.org
Phone: (800) 488-DRUG
164 West 74th Street
New York, NY 10023
The ACDE prepares programs and materials for substance abuse education and prevention, based on the most current scientific research. Its web site is tailored to provide information for different groups of users, including health professionals, educators, parents, and youth. The group also provides a free referral service.

Association for Medical Education and Research in Substance Abuse (AMERSA)
URL: http://www.amersa.org
Phone: (401) 349-0000
125 Whipple St.

Third Floor, Suite 300
Providence, RI 02908
AMERSA is a multidisciplinary organization dedicated to improving the education of medical professionals in the care of individuals with substance abuse problems. It holds conferences and distributes information to medical educators.

CATO Institute
URL: http://www.cato.org
E-mail: Web form
Phone: (202) 842-0200
1000 Massachusetts Ave., NW
Washington, DC 20001-5403
The CATO Institute is a libertarian policy "think tank" that generally advocates individual liberty and strict limitations on government power. CATO has been critical of many current drug regulations, including the growing restrictions on smoking and what one Cato researcher calls "the new war on social drinking."

Center for Substance Abuse Research (CESAR)
URL: http://www.cesar.umd.edu/
E-mail: Web form
Phone: (301) 405-9770
4321 Hartwick Road
Suite 501
College Park, MD 20740
CESAR is located at the University of Maryland at College Park. Its twofold mission is to conduct research relevant to drug abuse policy issues and to inform policymakers, practitioners, and the general public

about the latest statistics and research findings.

**Community Anti-Drug
  Coalitions of America
  (CADCA)**
URL: http://www.cadca.org
E-mail: Web form
Phone: (800) 54-CADCA
901 North Pitt Street
Suite 300
Alexandria, VA 22314
The mission of this organization is to create and strengthen community antidrug coalitions, by providing technical assistance, training, and assistance with media outreach and marketing. The organization also conducts conferences and special events.

**Drug Abuse Resistance
  Education (D.A.R.E.) America**
URL: http://www.dare.com
E-mail: Web form
9800 LaCienega Boulevard
Suite 400
Inglewood, CA 90301
D.A.R.E. is the nation's largest and best-known drug abuse prevention program. The national organization provides materials and support to educators, parents, and children via its web site, plus training for volunteers who bring the D.A.R.E. curriculum into thousands of schools each year.

**Drug-Free America Foundation
  (DFAF)**
URL: http://www.dfaf.org
E-mail: questions@dfag.org
Phone: (727) 828-0211
P.O. Box 11298
St. Petersburg, FL 33733
The Drug-Free America Foundation publicizes the dangers and negative impacts of drug abuse on many aspects of society and campaigns against drug-legalization initiatives. The group's web site is organized around the theme of a "community," with different buildings representing aspects of the drug problem.

Drug Policy Alliance
URL: http://www.dpf.org
E-mail: dc@drugpolicy.org
Phone: (202) 216-0035
925 15th Street, NW
2nd Floor
Washington, DC 20005
The Drug Policy Alliance (formerly the Drug Policy Foundation of the Lindesmith Center) is an advocacy organization that "envisions a just society in which the use and regulation of drugs are grounded in science, compassion, health and human rights . . . " It provides information for advocates and the general public and helps coordinate reform groups throughout the United States and around the world. Its practical focus is on promoting adoption of harm reduction techniques.

**Drug Reform Coordination
  Network (DRCNet)**
URL: http://www.drcnet.org
E-mail: drcnet@drcnet.org
Phone: (202) 293-8340

1623 Connecticut Avenue, NW
3rd Floor
Washington, DC 20009
DRCNet is a major educational and advocacy organization working for reform of U.S. drug laws with an ultimate goal of an end to drug prohibition and the war on drugs, both in the United States and worldwide. The organization provides reports on issues such as the effectiveness of D.A.R.E. and other education efforts and the impact and costs of current U.S. drug policies. The DRCNet Drug Library web site provides extensive resources for students and researchers.

Institute for a Drug-Free
Workplace
URL: http://www.
drugfreeworkplace.org
E-mail: Web forms
Phone: (202) 842-7400
1225 I Street, NW
Suite 1000
Washington, DC 20005-3914
This coalition of businesses, business groups, and individuals promotes efforts to reduce drug and alcohol abuse in the workplace in order to protect the health and safety of workers as well as business productivity. It also supports drug-testing programs when done under proper guidelines to protect employees' rights.

Mothers Against Drunk Driving
(MADD)
URL: http://www.madd.org
E-mail: Web form

Phone: (800) 438-6233
518 East John Carpenter Flewyn
Suite 700
Irving, TX 75062
MADD is one of the largest and most effective crime victims' organizations in the world. Its mission is "to stop drunk driving, support the victims of this violent crime, and prevent underage drinking." The organization has been quite effective in lobbying to lower legal blood-alcohol limits for drivers and to increase the resources devoted to identifying and prosecuting drunk drivers. MADD also promotes the distribution of safety and anti-drunk driving messages to employers as well as servers and customers in alcohol-related businesses.

Narcotics Anonymous
URL: http://www.na.org
E-mail: fsmail@na.org
Phone: (818) 773-9999
P.O. Box 9999
Van Nuys, CA 94109
Narcotics Anonymous started in the late 1940s as an attempt to apply the successful 12-step program of Alcoholics Anonymous to narcotics abusers. Today the organization holds more than 31,000 weekly meetings in more than 100 countries worldwide.

National Center on Addiction
and Substance Abuse at
Columbia University (CASA)
URL: http://www.
casa.columbia.org
E-mail: Web form

Phone: (212) 841-5200
633 Third Avenue
19th Floor
New York, NY 10017-6706
CASA is a major research and education organization that focuses on publicizing the economic and social costs of substance abuse and on developing and providing effective tools for prevention, treatment, and law enforcement. The organization conducts annual conferences and produces annual reports as well as surveys and research studies.

National Council on Alcoholism and Drug Dependence (NCADD)
URL: http://www.ncadd.org
E-mail: national@ncadd.org
Phone: (212) 269-7797
20 Exchange Place
Suite 2902
New York, NY 10005
The purpose of NCADD is to provide objective information (including statistics, expert opinion, and recommendations) to students, parents, the general public, and the media. It seeks to dispel the stigma attached to alcoholics and drug abusers and replace it with understanding. A variety of fact sheets are available relating to substance abuse, addiction, and effects—the focus is on alcohol but there is also information on other drugs.

National Organization for the Reform of Marijuana Laws (NORML)
URL: http://www.norml.org
E-mail: norml@norml.org
Phone: (202) 483-5500
1600 K Street, NW
Suite 501
Washington, DC 20036
NORML is one of the nation's oldest drug policy reform organizations. Its focus is to change public opinion so as to achieve the repeal of laws against marijuana use. It believes that responsible use rather than prohibition is the proper way to deal with the drug. NORML has played an important role in decriminalizing minor marijuana offenses in 11 states and in lowering penalties elsewhere.

Partnership for a Drug Free America (PDFA)
URL: http://www.drugfreeamerica.org
E-mail: Web form
Phone: (212) 922-1570
405 Lexington Avenue
Suite 1601
New York, NY 10174
This organization's thrust is to try to reduce demand for illegal drugs by using the media and other forms of outreach to portray the dangers of drug use and to change societal attitudes that condone drug use. The PDFA web site offers a variety of resources, including descriptions of drugs of abuse.

RAND Corporation
URL: http://www.rand.org
E-mail: correspondence@rand.org
Phone: (310) 393-0411

P.O. Box 2138
1700 Main Street
Santa Monica, CA 90407-2138
The RAND Corporation is one of the world's oldest and best known "think tanks." Over the years RAND has produced numerous studies and reports on various aspects of substance abuse. There is a page devoted to this topic on the organization's web site at http://www.rand.org/research_areas/substance_abuse/.

Secular Organization for Sobriety (SOS)
URL: http://www.secularhumanism.org/sos/index.htm#whatis

E-mail: sos@cfiwest.org
Phone: (323) 666-4295
SOS National Clearinghouse
The Center for Inquiry—West
4773 Hollywood Boulevard
Hollywood, CA 90026
This organization provides a non-religious alternative to Alcoholics Anonymous and other 12-step groups. It was formed by secular humanists who understood the need to confront their substance abuse problems, wanted to create a supportive environment, but found that entrusting themselves to a "higher power" was not compatible with their beliefs. Today the organization has groups meeting in every state.

PART III

APPENDICES

APPENDIX A

ACRONYMS

The following acronyms for organizations, drugs, and other terms are commonly encountered in discussions of drug abuse.

AA	Alcoholics Anonymous
ACDE	American Council for Drug Education
ACLU	American Civil Liberties Union
AIDS	Acquired Immunodeficiency Syndrome
AMERSA	Association for Medical Education and Research in Substance Abuse
AOD	alcohol and other drugs
BJS	Bureau of Justice Statistics
CADCA	Community Anti-Drug Coalitions of America (CADCA)
CASA	National Center on Addiction and Substance Abuse
CDC	Centers for Disease Control and Prevention
CESAR	Center for Substance Abuse Research
CSA	Controlled Substances Act
CSAP	Center for Substance Abuse Prevention
DARE	Drug Abuse Resistance Education
DAWN	Drug Abuse Warning Network
DEA	Drug Enforcement Administration
DHS	Department of Homeland Security
DOJ	Department of Justice
DRCNet	Drug Reform Coordination Network
DUI	driving under the influence
DWI	driving while intoxicated
FBI	Federal Bureau of Investigation
GHB	gamma-hydroxybutyrate
HGH	human growth hormone
HIV	human immunodeficiency virus
INSCR	International Narcotics Control Strategy Report

LSD	lysergic acid diethylamide
MADD	Mothers Against Drunk Driving
MDMA	ecstasy (3-4, methylenedioxymethamphetamine)
MM	methadone maintenance
MTF	Monitoring the Future Study
NA	Narcotics Anonymous
NDCS	National Drug Control Strategy
NIDA	National Institute on Drug Abuse
NIH	National Institutes of Health
NIJ	National Institute of Justice
NORML	National Organization for the Reform of Marijuana Laws
ONDCP	Office of National Drug Control Policy
PCP	phencyclidine
PDFA	Partnership for a Drug Free America
RADAR	Regional Alcohol and Drug Abuse Resources
SAMHSA	Substance Abuse and Mental Health Services Administration
SOS	Secular Organization for Sobriety
STD	sexually transmitted disease
TB	tuberculosis
UCR	Uniform Crime Reports
UNODC	United Nations Office on Drugs and Crime

APPENDIX B

STREET NAMES FOR DRUGS

There are literally thousands of street or slang names for drugs of abuse, and they often change over time. The following list includes some of the more commonly used terms and the drugs to which they refer. The Indiana Prevention Resource Center at Indiana University maintains a searchable database of more than 3,800 street drug names at http://www.drugs.indiana.edu/slang/home.html.

Street Name	Drug	
acid	LSD (lysergic acid diethylamide)	
Adam	MDMA (methylenedioxymethamphetamine)	
angel dust	PCP (phencyclidine)	
Apache	fentanyl	
barbs	barbiturates	
bennies	amphetamine	
blotter	LSD (lysergic acid diethylamide)	
blow	cocaine	
blunt	marijuana (cigarette)	
boom	hashish	
brown sugar	heroin	
buttons	mescaline	
cactus	mescaline	
candy	cocaine	
Captain Cody	codeine	
China girl	fentanyl	
China white	fentanyl	
chronic	hashish	
Cody	codeine	
coke	cocaine	
crack	cocaine (rocks)	*(continues)*

Drug Abuse

(continued)

Street Name	Drug
crank	methamphetamine
crystal meth	methamphetamine
date rape drug	Rohypnol (flunitrazepam)
dope	heroin, marijuana, narcotics
downers	tranquilizers (benzodiazepines)
ecstasy	MDMA (methylenedioxymethamphetamine)
forget-me pill	Rohypnol (flunitrazepam)
gangster	hashish
ganja	marijuana
Georgia home boy	GHB (gammahydroxybutyrate)
grass	marijuana
grievous bodily harm	GHB (gammahydroxybutyrate)
hash	hashish
herb	marijuana
horse	heroin
ice	methamphetamine
joint	marijuana (cigarette)
junk	heroin
liquid ecstasy	GHB (gammahycroxybutyrate)
ludes	Quaalude (methaqualone)
magic mushroom	psilocybin
Mary Jane	marijuana
microdot	LSD (lysergic acid diethylamide)
nose candy	cocaine
Oxy	Oxycodone, OxyContin
peyote	mescaline
phennies	barbiturates
poppers	inhalants
pot	marijuana
purple passion	psilocybin
reds	barbiturates
reefer	marijuana
rock	cocaine
roids	anabolic steroids
roofies, rophies	Rohypnol (flunitrazepam)
shrooms	psilocybin
sinsemilla	marijuana
skag	heroin

Appendix B

Street Name	Drug
smack	heroin
snow	cocaine
Special K	Ketamine
speed	amphetamine, methamphetamine
TNT	fentanyl
tooies	barbiturates
toot	cocaine
uppers	amphetamine
vitamin K	Ketamine
vitamin R	Ritalin
weed	marijuana
white horse	heroin
XTC	MDMA (methylenedioxymethamphetamine)
yellow jackets	barbiturates
yellow sunshines	LSD (lysergic acid diethylamide)
yellows	barbiturates

APPENDIX C

———————■———————

STATISTICS ON DRUG ABUSE AND ENFORCEMENT

The following graphics provide some indication of the extent of abuse of both legal and illicit drugs in the United States, as well as of enforcement efforts and the worldwide struggle against narcotics trafficking.

PREVALENCE OF DRUG ABUSE

The *National Survey on Drug Use and Health* (formerly the *National Household Survey on Drug Abuse*) of the federal Substance Abuse and Mental Health Services Administration (SAMHSA) provides a detailed annual "snapshot" of the prevalence of drug abuse in our society. The charts in this and the following section are based on the findings of this survey for 2002.

USE OF SELECTED ILLICIT DRUGS

The graph "Incidence of Use of Illicit Drugs" measures the percentage of persons in the population aged 12 years or older who have used various illicit drugs at least once in the month surveyed. Of the individual drugs listed, marijuana is, as might be expected, the most commonly used. The category "psychotherapeutic" refers to prescription-type drugs, including antidepressants and painkillers. The growing use of the painkiller OxyContin is contributing to the increase in this total.

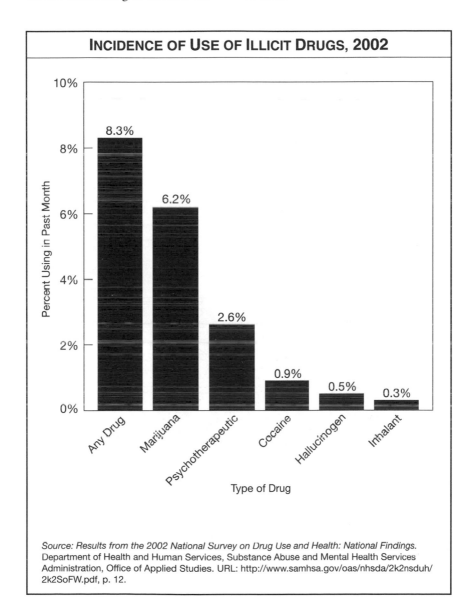

INCIDENCE OF USE OF ILLICIT DRUGS, 2002

Source: Results from the 2002 National Survey on Drug Use and Health: National Findings. Department of Health and Human Services, Substance Abuse and Mental Health Services Administration, Office of Applied Studies. URL: http://www.samhsa.gov/oas/nhsda/2k2nsduh/ 2k2SoFW.pdf, p. 12.

Illicit Drug Use by Age Group

The graph "Illicit Drug Use by Age Group" shows that the percentage of respondents reporting that they used some illicit drug at least once in the month surveyed peaks with the 18–20 age group, falls somewhat but remains high to the mid-20s, falls further in the late 20s, and is on a more or less even plateau through age 49 before falling again.

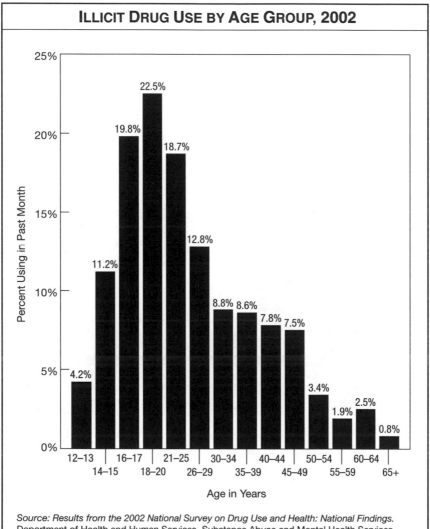

Source: Results from the 2002 National Survey on Drug Use and Health: National Findings. Department of Health and Human Services, Substance Abuse and Mental Health Services Administration, Office of Applied Studies. URL: http://www.samhsa.gov/oas/nhsda/2k2nsduh/ 2k2SoFW.pdf, p. 14.

ALCOHOL USE BY AGE GROUP

With the graph "Alcohol Use by Age," we turn to the most popular legal drug. Although the curve for overall alcohol use is somewhat smoother than for illicit drugs, the overall shape is similar, peaking at ages 21–25, then falling to a plateau and remaining there through age 49. Another, lower plateau is found between ages 50 and 64. This consistency probably reflects the fact that most alcohol users continue to use the drug throughout much of their lives.

The shaded portion that represents "binge drinking" does decline steadily after age 25. Binge drinking does exact a toll on health, as well as bring legal and other risks, and it seems clear that many young binge drinkers exhibit this behavior less frequently as they get older.

The darkest portion of the graph indicates heavy alcohol use—what one could roughly call alcoholic or borderline alcoholic. This level of usage tends not to decline much with age, reflecting the difficulty of overcoming addiction or dependency.

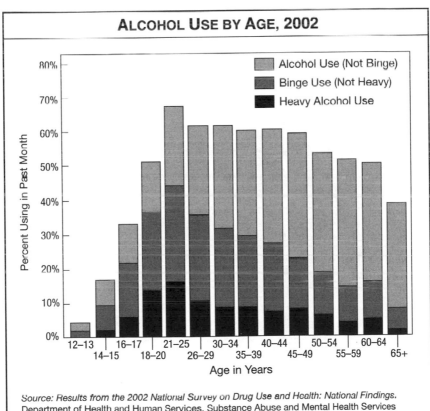

Source: Results from the 2002 National Survey on Drug Use and Health: National Findings. Department of Health and Human Services, Substance Abuse and Mental Health Services Administration, Office of Applied Studies. URL: http://www.samhsa.gov/oas/nhsda/2k2nsduh/2k2SoFW.pdf, p. 24.

Drug Abuse

Tobacco Use by Type and Age Group

The graph "Tobacco Use by Age" indicates that tobacco use in general is highest in the 18–25 age group, perhaps reflecting the heavy marketing by tobacco companies to the young adult group, plus the fact that tobacco products become legal for users starting at age 18. Note the considerable drop in tobacco use in the 26 and older group.

Cigarettes are, of course, the most popular way to use tobacco, but cigars have been embraced as a fashionable alternative by a minority of smokers. The effort to educate people about the dangers of smokeless tobacco (snuff or chewing tobacco) and its banning from professional baseball has reduced usage of that form of tobacco in recent years. Other data indicates that the prevalence of smoking declines with education, with college graduates much less likely to smoke than persons with only a high school education or no diploma.

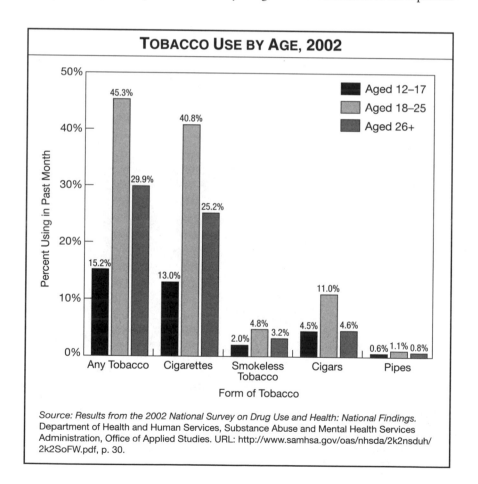

Source: Results from the 2002 National Survey on Drug Use and Health: National Findings. Department of Health and Human Services, Substance Abuse and Mental Health Services Administration, Office of Applied Studies. URL: http://www.samhsa.gov/oas/nhsda/2k2nsduh/2k2SoFW.pdf, p. 30.

TRENDS IN DRUG ABUSE

Another part of the drug abuse picture is the change in incidence over time. The *National Survey* provides some useful data about these trends. The sample data shown here focus on the use of marijuana and tobacco and the abuse of prescription drugs.

MARIJUANA USE AMONG YOUNG PERSONS, 1965–2002

The graph "Marijuana Use among Young People" records the percentage of persons aged 12 to 25 who have used marijuana at least once. The data is broken into two subgroups: ages 12–17 and ages 18–25. Although the rate of use by the older subgroup is much higher, the shape of the two curves is similar.

In general, marijuana use (and indeed overall illicit drug use) peaked a bit after 1980, declined in the 1980s, and then increased during the 1990s to about its former peak. (It is too early to discern much of a trend in the current decade, although there may be a slight decline underway.)

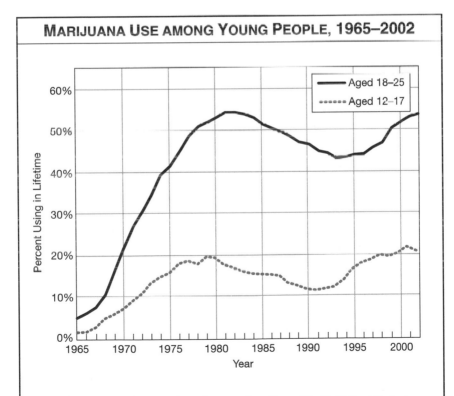

MARIJUANA USE AMONG YOUNG PEOPLE, 1965–2002

Source: Results from the 2002 National Survey on Drug Use and Health: National Findings. Department of Health and Human Services, Substance Abuse and Mental Health Services Administration, Office of Applied Studies. URL: http://www.samhsa.gov/oas/nhsda/2k2nsduh/2k2SoFW.pdf, p. 38.

Drug Abuse

NEW USERS OF MARIJUANA AMONG YOUNG PERSONS, 1965–2001

The number of persons who use a drug for the first time in a given year is an important measurement because it presumably relates to the effectiveness of drug abuse education and prevention programs (although there are many other potential variables, of course). The chart "New Users of Marijuana, 1965–2001" measures first-time users in thousands per year. The data is broken into three groups: under age 18, age 18 and older, and all ages.

As one might expect from cultural history, first-time marijuana use rose sharply from the mid-1960s to mid-1970s. There was then a significant overall decline until 1990, when the rate began rising again. A new decline may have begun in the late 1990s, but there is not much data yet.

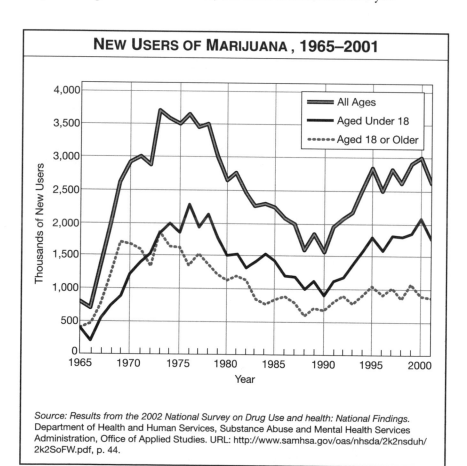

Source: Results from the 2002 National Survey on Drug Use and health: National Findings. Department of Health and Human Services, Substance Abuse and Mental Health Services Administration, Office of Applied Studies. URL: http://www.samhsa.gov/oas/nhsda/2k2nsduh/2k2SoFW.pdf, p. 44.

Appendix C

CIGARETTE USE AMONG YOUNG PEOPLE, 1965–2002

The graph "Cigarette Use among Young People, 1965–2002" measures the percentage of persons aged 12–17 who have tried cigarettes at least once. The data is broken down by gender.

In the mid-1960s about twice as many young males smoked as did young females. The rates for the two genders converged around 1985. Both rates then declined (but the rate for females declined more steeply). In the early 1990s both rates began to increase again: Recent data suggests a small decline after 2001.

Other *National Survey* data paints a somewhat more hopeful picture, however. Indeed between 1997 and 2001 the number of youth who took up smoking for the first time declined by about a third, suggesting that the regulatory and educational effort to reduce tobacco use is meeting with some success.

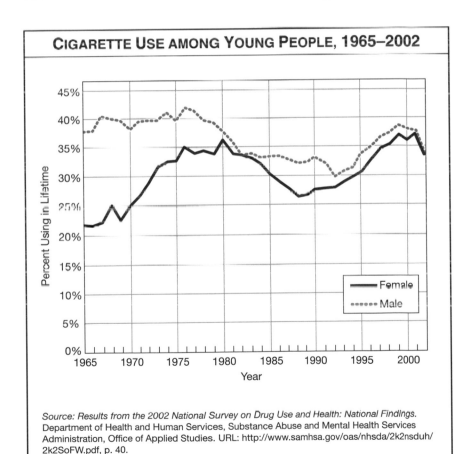

Source: Results from the 2002 National Survey on Drug Use and Health: National Findings. Department of Health and Human Services, Substance Abuse and Mental Health Services Administration, Office of Applied Studies. URL: http://www.samhsa.gov/oas/nhsda/2k2nsduh/2k2SoFW.pdf, p. 40.

Drug Abuse

TRENDS IN OTHER ILLICIT DRUG USE

The overall trends in substance abuse in recent years are mixed. The following is quoted from the summary of findings for the *National Survey:*

Cocaine

- Incidence of cocaine use generally rose throughout the 1970s to a peak in 1980 (1.7 million new users) and subsequently declined until 1991 (0.7 million new users). Cocaine initiation steadily increased during the 1990s, reaching 1.2 million in 2001.

- Age-specific incidence rates generally have mirrored the overall incidence trends, with greater initiation among adults than among youths under 18. Approximately 70 percent of cocaine initiates in 2001 were age 18 or older.

- Since 1975 males have generally comprised the majority of cocaine initiates. In 2001 there were 0.7 million new male users and 0.5 million new female users.

- The average age of cocaine initiates rose from 18.6 years in 1968 to 23.8 years in 1990 and subsequently declined to approximately 21 years from 1995 to 2001.

Heroin

- During the latter half of the 1990s, the annual number of heroin initiates rose to a level not reached since the late 1970s. In 1974 there were an estimated 246,000 heroin initiates. Between 1988 and 1994 the annual number of new users ranged from 28,000 to 80,000. Between 1995 and 2001 the number of new heroin users was consistently greater than 100,000.

Hallucinogens

- The incidence of hallucinogen use has exhibited two notable periods of increase. Between 1966 and 1970 the annual number of initiates rose almost sixfold, from 168,000 to 956,000. This increase was driven primarily by use of LSD. The second period of increase in first-time hallucinogen use began in 1992, when there were approximately 706,000 new users. By 2000 the number of initiates rose to 1.7 million, which is similar to the number for 2001 (1.6 million). The hallucinogen increase in the 1990s appears to have been driven by increases in use of ecstasy (i.e., MDMA).

- Initiation of ecstasy use has been rising since 1993, when there were 168,000 new users. There were 1.9 million initiates in 2000 and 1.8 million in 2001 (not a statistically significant decline).

Appendix C

ABUSE OF PRESCRIPTION DRUGS, 1965–2001

One of the biggest substance abuse problems in recent years has involved prescription drugs that have legitimate medical applications but are being used for nonmedical reasons (that is, are being abused).

The graph "Nonmedical Use of Prescription Drugs, 1965–2001" shows the thousands of persons per year abusing each of four types of prescription drugs: sedatives, stimulants, tranquilizers, and pain relievers. The last category has shown the greatest and sharpest increase, reflecting a burgeoning abuse problem with OxyContin and similar drugs.

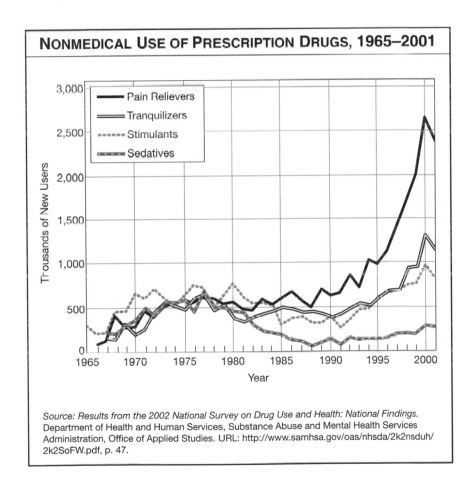

NONMEDICAL USE OF PRESCRIPTION DRUGS, 1965–2001

Source: Results from the 2002 National Survey on Drug Use and Health: National Findings. Department of Health and Human Services, Substance Abuse and Mental Health Services Administration, Office of Applied Studies. URL: http://www.samhsa.gov/oas/nhsda/2k2nsduh/2k2SoFW.pdf, p. 47.

THE WAR ON DRUGS

This section discusses drug law enforcement and the effort to reduce international drug production and trafficking.

DRUG ARRESTS BY DRUG, 1982–2002

The graph "Drug Arrests by Drug, 1982–2002" gives an overall picture of drug abuse from the enforcement point of view. Generally, since the mid-1990s, arrests for heroin and cocaine have been declining, while marijuana arrests have increased. There has also been a gradual increase in the relatively small number of arrests for "synthetic" or designer drugs.

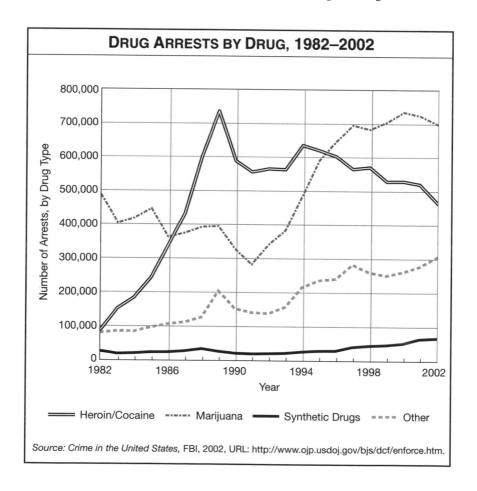

DRUG ARRESTS BY DRUG, 1982–2002

Source: Crime in the United States, FBI, 2002, URL: http://www.ojp.usdoj.gov/bjs/dcf/enforce.htm.

Appendix C

THE WAR ON DRUGS AROUND THE WORLD

Following the overthrow of the Taliban regime by the United States and its local allies in 2002, **Afghanistan** has again become the world's largest producer of illicit opium (the raw material for heroin production), with an estimated 61,000 hectares in production by 2003. This could yield as much as 2,865 metric tons of opium.

Bolivia has experienced a decline in cocaine production, from 240 metric tons in 1995 to 60 metric tons in 2001, a reduction of 75 percent. However, Bolivia's poorly controlled border regions make it a major route for transit for a Peruvian cocaine base, mainly destined for Brazil.

Burma is second only to Afghanistan as an opium / heroin producer, but production of the illicit drug has been declining substantially, having fallen about 75 percent between 1996 and 2000. Burma remains the principal source of amphetamines and related substances to neighboring areas in Asia.

The border between **Canada** and the United States has seen an increase in marijuana seizures. Production of marijuana in Canada for export to the United States is a problem, as is diversion of pharmaceuticals such as pseudoephedrine tables.

The **Caribbean** region is a major route for large shipments of cocaine from Colombia to the United States. The banking secrecy laws in many Caribbean nations help facilitate money laundering operations by drug traffickers.

Colombia is the producer of the coca "base" used to produce nearly 80 percent of the world's cocaine. Colombia also produces a small but growing amount of high-grade heroin. Aided by the United States, the Colombian government is stepping up aerial coca eradication efforts, and production has declined modestly. However, the struggle against drugs in Colombia is greatly complicated by the ongoing conflict between the government and the leftist FARC guerrillas, who control much of the cocaine production. (A right-wing paramilitary group called the United Self Defense Forces of Colombia is also a major player.)

Many countries in **Europe,** including the United Kingdom, the Netherlands, and Switzerland, have significant drug abuse problems. However, European countries have long been innovative on the drug policy front. Countries such as Switzerland and the Netherlands have tried increasingly to manage domestic drug abuse by decriminalization and harm reduction strategies, plus emphasis on treatment rather than law enforcement.

Laos is the world's third largest opium producer (behind Afghanistan and Burma), with about 23,000 hectares of poppy production. There is also a growing amphetamine problem. Laos is a transit route for drug shipments from Myammar (Burma) to China.

227

Drug Abuse

Mexico produces an estimated 6,700–8,600 metric tons of marijuana annually. Stricter border controls following the September 11, 2001, terrorist attacks have had at least a temporary impact on the flow of marijuana from Mexico into the United States.

Pakistan functions as a transit route for opiates and hashish produced in Afghanistan, and Pakistanis play an important role in this trafficking. Pakistan's importance to the United States as an ally against Islamic terrorism has complicated efforts to increase Pakistani cooperation on the drug front.

Peru is the world's second largest producer of cocaine (after Colombia). As part of an "Andean Initiative," the United States has encouraged Peruvian farmers to grow alternative, legal crops.

Thailand is often cited as a success story in the international war against drugs. Once a major opium producer, eradication efforts have greatly re-

THE WAR ON DRUGS AROUND THE WORLD, 2002

Source: White House Office of National Drug Control Policy.
URL: http://www.whitehousedrugpolicy.gov/international/index.html.

228

duced poppy production. "Yaba," a locally produced amphetamine-like substance, remains a serious problem in Thailand.

The **United States** is the world's largest consumer of illicit drugs, which makes reducing demand through education and prevention efforts crucial. But the United States is also a significant drug producer (mostly for local consumption), particularly with regard to "crystal meth" (methamphetamines), marijuana, and "designer drugs."

The following map shows major countries and areas involved with the production or transit of illicit drugs. The summaries given below are based on data provided by the White House Office of National Drug Control Policy.

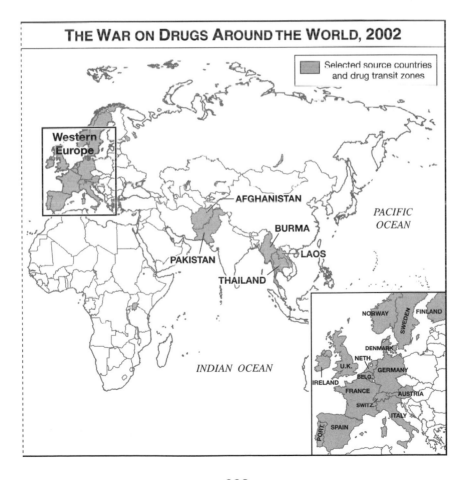

APPENDIX D

SCHEDULING OF DRUGS UNDER THE CONTROLLED SUBSTANCES ACT OF 1970

The following text is excerpted from the U.S. Code sections for the Controlled Substances Act of 1970. These portions describe the rationale for classifying controlled substances, the criteria used for placing substances in particular schedules (categories), and the lists of drugs or chemicals in each category.

Sec. 801. Congressional findings and declarations: controlled substances

The Congress makes the following findings and declarations:

(1) Many of the drugs included within this subchapter have a useful and legitimate medical purpose and are necessary to maintain the health and general welfare of the American people.

(2) The illegal importation, manufacture, distribution, and possession and improper use of controlled substances have a substantial and detrimental effect on the health and general welfare of the American people.

(3) A major portion of the traffic in controlled substances flows through interstate and foreign commerce. Incidents of the traffic which are not an integral part of the interstate or foreign flow, such as manufacture, local distribution, and possession, nonetheless have a substantial and direct effect upon interstate commerce because —

   (A) after manufacture, many controlled substances are transported in interstate commerce,

   (B) controlled substances distributed locally usually have been transported in interstate commerce immediately before their distribution, and

230

(C) controlled substances possessed commonly flow through interstate commerce immediately prior to such possession.
(4) Local distribution and possession of controlled substances contribute to swelling the interstate traffic in such substances.
(5) Controlled substances manufactured and distributed intrastate cannot be differentiated from controlled substances manufactured and distributed interstate. Thus, it is not feasible to distinguish, in terms of controls, between controlled substances manufactured and distributed interstate and controlled substances manufactured and distributed intrastate.
(6) Federal control of the intrastate incidents of the traffic in controlled substances is essential to the effective control of the interstate incidents of such traffic.
(7) The United States is a party to the Single Convention on Narcotic Drugs, 1961, and other international conventions designed to establish effective control over international and domestic traffic in controlled substances.

Sec. 801(a). Congressional findings and declarations: psychotropic substances

The Congress makes the following findings and declarations:

(1) The Congress has long recognized the danger involved in the manufacture, distribution, and use of certain psychotropic substances for nonscientific and nonmedical purposes, and has provided strong and effective legislation to control illicit trafficking and to regulate legitimate uses of psychotropic substances in this country. Abuse of psychotropic substances has become a phenomenon common to many countries, however, and is not confined to national borders. It is, therefore, essential that the United States cooperate with other nations in establishing effective controls over international traffic in such substances.
(2) The United States has joined with other countries in executing an international treaty, entitled the Convention on Psychotropic Substances and signed at Vienna, Austria, on February 21, 1971, which is designed to establish suitable controls over the manufacture, distribution, transfer, and use of certain psychotropic substances. The Convention is not self-executing, and the obligations of the United States thereunder may only be performed pursuant to appropriate legislation. It is the intent of the Congress that the amendments made by this Act, together with existing law, will enable the United States to meet all its obligations under the Convention and that no further legislation will be necessary for that purpose.

231

(3) In implementing the Convention on Psychotropic Substances, the Congress intends that, consistent with the obligations of the United States under the Convention, control of psychotropic substances in the United States should be accomplished within the framework of the procedures and criteria for classification of substances provided in the Comprehensive Drug Abuse Prevention and Control Act of 1970 (21 U.S.C. 801 et seq.). This will insure that (A) the availability of psychotropic substances to manufacturers, distributors, dispensers, and researchers for useful and legitimate medical and scientific purposes will not be unduly restricted; (B) nothing in the Convention will interfere with bona fide research activities; and (C) nothing in the Convention will interfere with ethical medical practice in this country as determined by the Secretary of Health and Human Services on the basis of a consensus of the views of the American medical and scientific community.

Sec. 811. Authority and criteria for classification of substances

(a) Rules and regulations of Attorney General; hearing
The Attorney General shall apply the provisions of this subchapter to the controlled substances listed in the schedules established by section 812 of this title and to any other drug or other substance added to such schedules under this subchapter. Except as provided in subsections (d) and (e) of this section, the Attorney General may by rule —
(1) add to such a schedule or transfer between such schedules any drug or other substance if he —
(A) finds that such drug or other substance has a potential for abuse, and
(B) makes with respect to such drug or other substance the findings prescribed by subsection (b) of section 812 of this title for the schedule in which such drug is to be placed; or (2) remove any drug or other substance from the schedules if he finds that the drug or other substance does not meet the requirements for inclusion in any schedule. Rules of the Attorney General under this subsection shall be made on the record after opportunity for a hearing pursuant to the rulemaking procedures prescribed by subchapter II of chapter 5 of title 5. Proceedings for the issuance, amendment, or repeal of such rules may be initiated by the Attorney General (1) on his own motion, (2) at the request of the Secretary, or (3) on the petition of any interested party.

(b) Evaluation of drugs and other substances

The Attorney General shall, before initiating proceedings under subsection (a) of this section to control a drug or other substance or to remove a drug or other substance entirely from the schedules, and after gathering the necessary data, request from the Secretary a scientific and medical evaluation, and his recommendations, as to whether such drug or other substance should be so controlled or removed as a controlled substance. In making such evaluation and recommendations, the Secretary shall consider the factors listed in paragraphs (2), (3), (6), (7), and (8) of subsection (c) of this section and any scientific or medical considerations involved in paragraphs (1), (4), and (5) of such subsection. The recommendations of the Secretary shall include recommendations with respect to the appropriate schedule, if any, under which such drug or other substance should be listed. The evaluation and the recommendations of the Secretary shall be made in writing and submitted to the Attorney General within a reasonable time. The recommendations of the Secretary to the Attorney General shall be binding on the Attorney General as to such scientific and medical matters, and if the Secretary recommends that a drug or other substance not be controlled, the Attorney General shall not control the drug or other substance. If the Attorney General determines that these facts and all other relevant data constitute substantial evidence of potential for abuse such as to warrant control or substantial evidence that the drug or other substance should be removed entirely from the schedules, he shall initiate proceedings for control or removal, as the case may be, under subsection (a) of this section.

(c) Factors determinative of control or removal from schedules

In making any finding under subsection (a) of this section or under subsection (b) of section 812 of this title, the Attorney General shall consider the following factors with respect to each drug or other substance proposed to be controlled or removed from the schedules:

(1) Its actual or relative potential for abuse.

(2) Scientific evidence of its pharmacological effect, if known.

(3) The state of current scientific knowledge regarding the drug or other substance.

(4) Its history and current pattern of abuse.

(5) The scope, duration, and significance of abuse.

(6) What, if any, risk there is to the public health.

(7) Its psychic or physiological dependence liability.

(8) Whether the substance is an immediate precursor of a substance already controlled under this subchapter.

(d) International treaties, conventions, and protocols requiring control; procedures respecting changes in drug schedules of Convention on Psychotropic Substances

    (1) If control is required by United States obligations under international treaties, conventions, or protocols in effect on October 27, 1970, the Attorney General shall issue an order controlling such drug under the schedule he deems most appropriate to carry out such obligations, without regard to the findings required by subsection (a) of this section or section 812(b) of this title and without regard to the procedures prescribed by subsections (a) and (b) of this section.

[Remainder of subsection omitted]

(e) Immediate precursors

The Attorney General may, without regard to the findings required by subsection (a) of this section or section 812(b) of this title and without regard to the procedures prescribed by subsections (a) and (b) of this section, place an immediate precursor in the same schedule in which the controlled substance of which it is an immediate precursor is placed or in any other schedule with a higher numerical designation. If the Attorney General designates a substance as an immediate precursor and places it in a schedule, other substances shall not be placed in a schedule solely because they are its precursors.

(f) Abuse potential

If, at the time a new-drug application is submitted to the Secretary for any drug having a stimulant, depressant, or hallucinogenic effect on the central nervous system, it appears that such drug has an abuse potential, such information shall be forwarded by the Secretary to the Attorney General.

(g) Exclusion of non-narcotic substances sold over the counter without a prescription; dextromethorphan; exemption of substances lacking abuse potential

    (1) The Attorney General shall by regulation exclude any non-narcotic substance from a schedule if such substance may, under the Federal Food, Drug, and Cosmetic Act (21 U.S.C. 301 et seq.), be lawfully sold over the counter without a prescription.

    (2) Dextromethorphan shall not be deemed to be included in any schedule by reason of enactment of this subchapter unless controlled after October 27, 1970 pursuant to the foregoing provisions of this section.

(3) The Attorney General may, by regulation, exempt any compound, mixture, or preparation containing a controlled substance from the application of all or any part of this subchapter if he finds such compound, mixture, or preparation meets the requirements of one of the following categories:

(A) A mixture, or preparation containing a nonnarcotic controlled substance, which mixture or preparation is approved for prescription use, and which contains one or more other active ingredients which are not listed in any schedule and which are included therein in such combinations, quantity, proportion, or concentration as to vitiate the potential for abuse.

(B) A compound, mixture, or preparation which contains any controlled substance, which is not for administration to a human being or animal, and which is packaged in such form or concentration, or with adulterants or denaturants, so that as packaged it does not present any significant potential for abuse.

(h) Temporary scheduling to avoid imminent hazards to public safety

(1) If the Attorney General finds that the scheduling of a substance in schedule I on a temporary basis is necessary to avoid an imminent hazard to the public safety, he may, by order and without regard to the requirements of subsection (b) of this section relating to the Secretary of Health and Human Services, schedule such substance in schedule I if the substance is not listed in any other schedule in section 812 of this title or if no exemption or approval is in effect for the substance under section 505 of the Federal Food, Drug, and Cosmetic Act (21 U.S.C. 355). Such an order may not be issued before the expiration of thirty days from

(A) the date of the publication by the Attorney General of a notice in the Federal Register of the intention to issue such order and the grounds upon which such order is to be issued, and

(B) the date the Attorney General has transmitted the notice required by paragraph (4).

(2) The scheduling of a substance under this subsection shall expire at the end of one year from the date of the issuance of the order scheduling such substance, except that the Attorney General may, during the pendency of proceedings under subsection (a)(1) of this section with respect to the substance, extend the temporary scheduling for up to six months.

(3) When issuing an order under paragraph (1), the Attorney General shall be required to consider, with respect to the finding of an imminent hazard to the public safety, only those factors set forth in paragraphs (4), (5), and (6) of subsection (c) of this section,

including actual abuse, diversion from legitimate channels, and clandestine importation, manufacture, or distribution.

(4) The Attorney General shall transmit notice of an order proposed to be issued under paragraph (1) to the Secretary of Health and Human Services. In issuing an order under paragraph (1), the Attorney General shall take into consideration any comments submitted by the Secretary in response to a notice transmitted pursuant to this paragraph.

(5) An order issued under paragraph (1) with respect to a substance shall be vacated upon the conclusion of a subsequent rulemaking proceeding initiated under subsection (a) of this section with respect to such substance.

(6) An order issued under paragraph (1) is not subject to judicial review.

[The following portions of the Controlled Substances Act of 1970 (21 USC Sec. 812) define the five schedules for controlled substances and specify the substances included in each schedule. Note that in order to comply with the Convention on Psychotropic Substances, signed at Vienna, Austria, on February 21, 1971, pipradol and SPA (also known as (-)-1-dimethylamino-1,2-diphenylethane) were added to Schedule 4. By amendment in 2000 GHB (gamma hydroxybutyric acid) was added to Schedule 1.]

Sec. 812. Schedules of controlled substances

(a) Establishment
There are established five schedules of controlled substances, to be known as schedules I, II, III, IV, and V. Such schedules shall initially consist of the substances listed in this section. The schedules established by this section shall be updated and republished on a semiannual basis during the two-year period beginning one year after October 27, 1970, and shall be updated and republished on an annual basis thereafter.

(b) Placement on schedules; findings required
Except where control is required by United States obligations under an international treaty, convention, or protocol, in effect on October 27, 1970, and except in the case of an immediate precursor, a drug or other substance may not be placed in any schedule unless the findings required for such schedule are made with respect to such drug or other substance. The findings required for each of the schedules are as follows:

(1) Schedule I. —
(A) The drug or other substance has a high potential for abuse.

(B) The drug or other substance has no currently accepted medical use in treatment in the United States.

(C) There is a lack of accepted safety for use of the drug or other substance under medical supervision.

(2) Schedule II. —

(A) The drug or other substance has a high potential for abuse.

(B) The drug or other substance has a currently accepted medical use in treatment in the United States or a currently accepted medical use with severe restrictions.

(C) Abuse of the drug or other substances may lead to severe psychological or physical dependence.

(3) Schedule III —

(A) The drug or other substance has a potential for abuse less than the drugs or other substances in schedules I and II.

(B) The drug or other substance has a currently accepted medical use in treatment in the United States.

(C) Abuse of the drug or other substance may lead to moderate or low physical dependence or high psychological dependence.

(4) Schedule IV.

(A) The drug or other substance has a low potential for abuse relative to the drugs or other substances in schedule III.

(B) The drug or other substance has a currently accepted medical use in treatment in the United States.

(C) Abuse of the drug or other substance may lead to limited physical dependence or psychological dependence relative to the drugs or other substances in schedule III.

(5) Schedule V. —

(A) The drug or other substance has a low potential for abuse relative to the drugs or other substances in schedule IV.

(B) The drug or other substance has a currently accepted medical use in treatment in the United States.

(C) Abuse of the drug or other substance may lead to limited physical dependence or psychological dependence relative to the drugs or other substances in schedule IV.

(c) Initial schedules of controlled substances

Schedules I, II, III, IV, and V shall, unless and until amended[1] pursuant to section 811 of this title, consist of the following drugs or

---

[1] Revised schedules are published in the Code of Federal Regulations, Part 1308 of Title 21, Food and Drugs.

other substances, by whatever official name, common or usual name, chemical name, or brand name designated:

SCHEDULE I

(a) Unless specifically excepted or unless listed in another schedule, any of the following opiates, including their isomers, esters, ethers, salts, and salts of isomers, esters, and ethers, whenever the existence of such isomers, esters, ethers, and salts is possible within the specific chemical designation:

  (1) Acetylmethadol.
  (2) Allylprodine.
  (3) Alphacetylmathadol.[2]
  (4) Alphameprodine.
  (5) Alphamethadol.
  (6) Benzethidine.
  (7) Betacetylmethadol.
  (8) Betameprodine.
  (9) Betamethadol.
  (10) Betaprodine.
  (11) Clonitazene.
  (12) Dextromoramide.
  (13) Dextrorphan.
  (14) Diampromide.
  (15) Diethylthiambutene.
  (16) Dimenoxadol.
  (17) Dimepheptanol.
  (18) Dimethylthiambutene.
  (19) Dioxaphetyl butyrate.
  (20) Dipipanone.
  (21) Ethylmethylthiambutene.
  (22) Etonitazene.
  (23) Etoxeridine.
  (24) Furethidine.
  (25) Hydroxypethidine.
  (26) Ketobemidone.
  (27) Levomoramide.
  (28) Levophenacylmorphan.
  (29) Morpheridine.

---

[2] So in original. Probably should be "Alphacetylmethadol."

(30) Noracymethadol.

(31) Norlevorphanol.

(32) Normethadone.

(33) Norpipanone.

(34) Phenadoxone.

(35) Phenampromide.

(36) Phenomorphan.

(37) Phenoperidine.

(38) Piritramide.

(39) Propheptazine.

(40) Properidine.

(41) Racemoramide.

(42) Trimeperidine.

(b) Unless specifically excepted or unless listed in another schedule, any of the following opium derivatives, their salts, isomers, and salts of isomers whenever the existence of such salts, isomers, and salts of isomers is possible within the specific chemical designation:

(1) Acetorphine.

(2) Acetyldihydrocodeine.

(3) Benzylmorphine.

(4) Codeine methylbromide.

(5) Codeine-N-Oxide.

(6) Cyprenorphine.

(7) Desomorphine.

(8) Dihydromorphine.

(9) Etorphine.

(10) Heroin.

(11) Hydromorphinol.

(12) Methyldesorphine.

(13) Methylhydromorphine.

(14) Morphine methylbromide.

(15) Morphine methylsulfonate.

(16) Morphine-N-Oxide.

(17) Myrophine.

(18) Nicocodeine.

(19) Nicomorphine.

(20) Normorphine.

(21) Pholcodine.

(22) Thebacon.

(c) Unless specifically excepted or unless listed in another schedule, any material, compound, mixture, or preparation, which contains any quantity of the following hallucinogenic substances, or which contains any of their salts, isomers, and salts of isomers, whenever the existence of such salts, isomers, and salts of isomers is possible within the specific chemical designation:

(1) 3,4-methylenedioxy amphetamine.
(2) 5-methoxy-3,4-methylenedioxy amphetamine.
(3) 3,4,5-trimethoxy amphetamine.
(4) Bufotenine.
(5) Diethyltryptamine.
(6) Dimethyltryptamine.
(7) 4-methyl-2,5-diamethoxyamphetamine.
(8) Ibogaine.
(9) Lysergic acid diethylamide.
(10) Marihuana.
(11) Mescaline.
(12) Peyote.
(13) N-ethyl-3-piperidyl benzilate.
(14) N-methyl-3-piperidyl benzilate.
(15) Psilocybin.
(16) Psilocyn.
(17) Tetrahydrocannabinols.

SCHEDULE II

(a) Unless specifically excepted or unless listed in another schedule, any of the following substances whether produced directly or indirectly by extraction from substances of vegetable origin, or independently by means of chemical synthesis, or by a combination of extraction and chemical synthesis:

(1) Opium and opiate, and any salt, compound, derivative, or preparation of opium or opiate.
(2) Any salt, compound, derivative, or preparation thereof which is chemically equivalent or identical with any of the substances referred to in clause (1), except that these substances shall not include the isoquinoline alkaloids of opium.
(3) Opium poppy and poppy straw.
(4) coca[3] leaves, except coca leaves and extracts of coca leaves from which cocaine, ecgonine, and derivatives of ecgonine or their salts have been removed; cocaine, its salts, optical and geometric isomers, and salts of isomers; ecgonine, its derivatives, their salts,

---

[3] So in original. Probably should be capitalized.

isomers, and salts of isomers; or any compound, mixture, or preparation which contains any quantity of any of the substances referred to in this paragraph.

(b) Unless specifically excepted or unless listed in another schedule, any of the following opiates, including their isomers, esters, ethers, salts, and salts of isomers, esters and ethers, whenever the existence of such isomers, esters, ethers, and salts is possible within the specific chemical designation:

(1) Alphaprodine.
(2) Anileridine.
(3) Bezitramide.
(4) Dihydrocodeine
(5) Diphenoxylate.
(6) Fentanyl.
(7) Isomethadone.
(8) Levomethorphan.
(9) Levorphanol.
(10) Metazocine.
(11) Methadone.
(12) Methadone-Intermediate, 4-cyano-2-dimethylamino-4,4-diphenyl butane.
(13) Moramide-Intermediate, 2-methyl-3-morpholino-1, 1-diphenyl-propane-carboxylic acid.
(14) Pethidine.
(15) Pethidine-Intermediate-A, 4-cyano-1-methyl-4-phenylpiperidine.
(16) Pethidine-Intermediate-B, ethyl-4-phenylpiperidine-4-carboxylate.
(17) Pethidine-Intermediate-C, 1-methyl-4-phenylpiperidine-4-carboxylic acid.
(18) Phenazocine.
(19) Piminodine.
(20) Racemethorphan.
(21) Racemorphan.

(c) Unless specifically excepted or unless listed in another schedule, any injectable liquid which contains any quantity of methamphetamine, including its salts, isomers, and salts of isomers.

SCHEDULE III

(a) Unless specifically excepted or unless listed in another schedule, any material, compound, mixture, or preparation which contains any quantity of the following substances having a stimulant effect on the central nervous system:

(1) Amphetamine, its salts, optical isomers, and salts of its optical isomers.

(2) Phenmetrazine and its salts.

(3) Any substance (except an injectable liquid) which contains any quantity of methamphetamine, including its salts, isomers, and salts of isomers.

(4) Methylphenidate.

(b) Unless specifically excepted or unless listed in another schedule, any material, compound, mixture, or preparation which contains any quantity of the following substances having a depressant effect on the central nervous system:

(1) Any substance which contains any quantity of a derivative of barbituric acid, or any salt of a derivative of barbituric acid.

(2) Chorhexadol.

(3) Glutethimide.

(4) Lysergic acid.

(5) Lysergic acid amide.

(6) Methyprylon.

(7) Phencyclidine.

(8) Sulfondiethylmethane.

(9) Sulfonethylmethane.

(10) Sulfonmethane.

(c) Nalorphine.

(d) Unless specifically excepted or unless listed in another schedule, any material, compound, mixture, or preparation containing limited quantities of any of the following narcotic drugs, or any salts thereof:

(1) Not more than 1.8 grams of codeine per 100 milliliters or not more than 90 milligrams per dosage unit, with an equal or greater quantity of an isoquinoline alkaloid of opium.

(2) Not more than 1.8 grams of codeine per 100 milliliters or not more than 90 milligrams per dosage unit, with one or more active, non-narcotic ingredients in recognized therapeutic amounts.

(3) Not more than 300 milligrams of dihydrocodeinone per 100 milliliters or not more than 15 milligrams per dosage unit, with a fourfold or greater quantity of an isoquinoline alkaloid of opium.

(4) Not more than 300 milligrams of dihydrocodeinone per 100 milliliters or not more than 15 milligrams per dosage unit, with one or more active, non-narcotic ingredients in recognized therapeutic amounts.

(5) Not more than 1.8 grams of dihydrocodeine per 100 milliliters or not more than 90 milligrams per dosage unit, with one or more active, non-narcotic ingredients in recognized therapeutic amounts.

(6) Not more than 300 milligrams of ethylmorphine per 100 milliliters or not more than 15 milligrams per dosage unit, with one or more active, non-narcotic ingredients in recognized therapeutic amounts.

(7) Not more than 500 milligrams of opium per 100 milliliters or per 100 grams, or not more than 25 milligrams per dosage unit, with one or more active, non-narcotic ingredients in recognized therapeutic amounts.

(8) Not more than 50 milligrams of morphine per 100 milliliters or per 100 grams with one or more active, non-narcotic ingredients in recognized therapeutic amounts.

(e) Anabolic steroids.

SCHEDULE IV

(1) Barbital.
(2) Chloral betaine.
(3) Chloral hydrate.
(4) Ethchlorvynol.
(5) Ethinamate.
(6) Methohexital.
(7) Meprobamate.
(8) Methylphenobarbital.
(9) Paraldehyde.
(10) Petrichloral.
(11) Phenobarbital.

SCHEDULE V

Any compound, mixture, or preparation containing any of the following limited quantities of narcotic drugs, which shall include one or more non-narcotic active medicinal ingredients in sufficient proportion to confer upon the compound, mixture, or preparation valuable medicinal qualities other than those possessed by the narcotic drug alone:

(1) Not more than 200 milligrams of codeine per 100 milliliters or per 100 grams.

(2) Not more than 100 milligrams of dihydrocodeine per 100 milliliters or per 100 grams.
(3) Not more than 100 milligrams of ethylmorphine per 100 milliliters or per 100 grams.
(4) Not more than 2.5 milligrams of diphenoxylate and not less than 25 micrograms of atropine sulfate per dosage unit.
(5) Not more than 100 milligrams of opium per 100 milliliters or per 100 grams.

APPENDIX E

UNITED STATES V. OAKLAND CANNABIS BUYERS' COOPERATIVE, 2001

Following is the text (without footnotes) of the Supreme Court's decision in *United States v. Oakland Cannabis Buyers' Cooperative* (2001). The decision was unanimous (8-0, with Justice Steven Breyer not participating). Justice Clarence Thomas wrote the opinion.

UNITED STATES, PETITIONER V. OAKLAND CANNABIS BUYERS' COOPERATIVE AND JEFFREY JONES, ON WRIT OF CERTIORARI TO THE UNITED STATES COURT OF APPEALS FOR THE NINTH CIRCUIT [MAY 14, 2001]

Justice Thomas delivered the opinion of the Court.

The Controlled Substances Act, 84 Stat. 1242, 21 U.S.C. § 801 *et seq.*, prohibits the manufacture and distribution of various drugs, including marijuana. In this case, we must decide whether there is a medical necessity exception to these prohibitions. We hold that there is not.

I

In November 1996, California voters enacted an initiative measure entitled the Compassionate Use Act of 1996. Attempting "[t]o ensure that seriously ill Californians have the right to obtain and use marijuana for medical purposes," Cal. Health & Safety Code Ann. §11362.5 (West Supp. 2001), the statute creates an exception to California laws prohibiting the possession and cultivation of marijuana. These prohibitions no longer apply to a patient or his primary caregiver who possesses or cultivates marijuana for the patient's medical purposes upon the recommendation or approval of a physician. *Ibid.* In the wake of this voter initiative, several groups organized "medical cannabis dispensaries" to meet the needs of qualified patients. *United States v. Cannabis Cultivators Club*, 5 F. Supp. 2d 1086, 1092 (ND Cal. 1998). Respondent Oakland Cannabis Buyers' Cooperative is one of these groups.

The Cooperative is a not-for-profit organization that operates in downtown Oakland. A physician serves as medical director, and registered nurses staff the Cooperative during business hours. To become a member, a patient must provide a written statement from a treating physician assenting to marijuana therapy and must submit to a screening interview. If accepted as a member, the patient receives an identification card entitling him to obtain marijuana from the Cooperative.

In January 1998, the United States sued the Cooperative and its executive director, respondent Jeffrey Jones (together, the Cooperative), in the United States District Court for the Northern District of California. Seeking to enjoin the Cooperative from distributing and manufacturing marijuana, the United States argued that, whether or not the Cooperative's activities are legal under California law, they violate federal law. Specifically, the Government argued that the Cooperative violated the Controlled Substances Act's prohibitions on distributing, manufacturing, and possessing with the intent to distribute or manufacture a controlled substance. 21 U.S.C. § 841(a). Concluding that the Government had established a probability of success on the merits, the District Court granted a preliminary injunction. App. to Pet. for Cert. 39a–40a, 5 F. Supp. 2d, at 1105.

The Cooperative did not appeal the injunction but instead openly violated it by distributing marijuana to numerous persons, App. to Pet. for Cert. at 21a–23a. To terminate these violations, the Government initiated contempt proceedings. In defense, the Cooperative contended that any distributions were medically necessary. Marijuana is the only drug, according to the Cooperative, that can alleviate the severe pain and other debilitating symptoms of the Cooperative's patients. *Id.*, at 29a. The District Court rejected this defense, however, after determining there was insufficient evidence that each recipient of marijuana was in actual danger of imminent harm without the drug. *Id.*, at 29a–32a. The District Court found the Cooperative in contempt and, at the Government's request, modified the preliminary injunction to empower the United States Marshal to seize the Cooperative's premises. *Id.*, at 37a. Although recognizing that "human suffering" could result, the District Court reasoned that a court's "equitable powers [do] not permit it to ignore federal law." *Ibid.* Three days later, the District Court summarily rejected a motion by the Cooperative to modify the injunction to permit distributions that are medically necessary.

The Cooperative appealed both the contempt order and the denial of the Cooperative's motion to modify. Before the Court of Appeals for the Ninth Circuit decided the case, however, the Cooperative voluntarily purged its contempt by promising the District Court that it would comply with the initial preliminary injunction. Consequently, the Court of Appeals determined that the appeal of the contempt order was moot. 190 F.3d 1109, 1112–1113 (1999).

The denial of the Cooperative's motion to modify the injunction, however, presented a live controversy that was appealable under 28 U.S.C. § 1292(a)(1). Reaching the merits of this issue, the Court of Appeals reversed and remanded. According to the Court of Appeals, the medical necessity defense was a "legally cognizable defense" that likely would apply in the circumstances. 190 F.3d, at 1114. Moreover, the Court of Appeals reasoned, the District Court erroneously "believed that it had no discretion to issue an injunction that was more limited in scope than the Controlled Substances Act itself." *Id.*, at 1114–1115. Because, according to the Court of Appeals, district courts retain "broad equitable discretion" to fashion injunctive relief, the District Court could have, and should have, weighed the "public interest" and considered factors such as the serious harm in depriving patients of marijuana. *Ibid.* Remanding the case, the Court of Appeals instructed the District Court to consider "the criteria for a medical necessity exemption, and, should it modify the injunction, to set forth those criteria in the modification order." *Id.*, at 1115. Following these instructions, the District Court granted the Cooperative's motion to modify the injunction to incorporate a medical necessity defense.

The United States petitioned for certiorari to review the Court of Appeals' decision that medical necessity is a legally cognizable defense to violations of the Controlled Substances Act. Because the decision raises significant questions as to the ability of the United States to enforce the Nation's drug laws, we granted certiorari. 531 U.S. 1010 (2000).

II

The Controlled Substances Act provides that, "[e]xcept as authorized by this subchapter, it shall be unlawful for any person knowingly or intentionally ... to manufacture, distribute, or dispense, or possess with intent to manufacture, distribute, or dispense, a controlled substance." 21 U.S.C. § 841(a)(1). The subchapter, in turn, establishes exceptions. For marijuana (and other drugs that have been classified as "schedule I" controlled substances), there is but one express exception, and it is available only for Government-approved research projects, §823(f). Not conducting such a project, the Cooperative cannot, and indeed does not, claim this statutory exemption.

The Cooperative contends, however, that notwithstanding the apparently absolute language of §841(a), the statute is subject to additional, implied exceptions, one of which is medical necessity. According to the Cooperative, because necessity was a defense at common law, medical necessity should be read into the Controlled Substances Act. We disagree.

As an initial matter, we note that it is an open question whether federal courts ever have authority to recognize a necessity defense not provided by statute. A necessity defense "traditionally covered the situation where physical forces beyond the actor's control rendered illegal conduct the lesser of two evils." *United States* v. *Bailey*, 444 U.S. 394, 410 (1980). Even at common law, the defense of necessity was somewhat controversial. See, *e.g.*, *Queen* v. *Dudley & Stephens*, 14 Q. B. 273 (1884). And under our constitutional system, in which federal crimes are defined by statute rather than by common law, see *United States* v. *Hudson*, 7 Cranch 32, 34 (1812), it is especially so. As we have stated: "Whether, as a policy matter, an exemption should be created is a question for legislative judgment, not judicial inference." *United States* v. *Rutherford*, 442 U.S. 544, 559 (1979). Nonetheless, we recognize that this Court has discussed the possibility of a necessity defense without altogether rejecting it. See, *e.g.*, *Bailey, supra*, at 415.

We need not decide, however, whether necessity can ever be a defense when the federal statute does not expressly provide for it. In this case, to resolve the question presented, we need only recognize that a medical necessity exception for marijuana is at odds with the terms of the Controlled Substances Act. The statute, to be sure, does not explicitly abrogate the defense. But its provisions leave no doubt that the defense is unavailable.

Under any conception of legal necessity, one principle is clear: The defense cannot succeed when the legislature itself has made a "determination of values." 1 W. LaFave & A. Scott, Substantive Criminal Law §5.4, p. 629 (1986). In the case of the Controlled Substances Act, the statute reflects a determination that marijuana has no medical benefits worthy of an exception (outside the confines of a Government-approved research project). Whereas some other drugs can be dispensed and prescribed for medical use, see 21 U.S.C. § 829 the same is not true for marijuana. Indeed, for purposes of the Controlled Substances Act, marijuana has "no currently accepted medical use" at all. §811.

The structure of the Act supports this conclusion. The statute divides drugs into five schedules, depending in part on whether the particular drug has a currently accepted medical use. The Act then imposes restrictions on the manufacture and distribution of the substance according to the schedule in which it has been placed. Schedule I is the most restrictive schedule. The Attorney General can include a drug in schedule I only if the drug "has no currently accepted medical use in treatment in the United States," "has a high potential for abuse," and has "a lack of accepted safety for use ... under medical supervision." §§812(b)(1)(A)–(C). Under the statute, the Attorney General could not put marijuana into schedule I if marijuana had any accepted medical use.

The Cooperative points out, however, that the Attorney General did not place marijuana into schedule I. Congress put it there, and Congress was not required to find that a drug lacks an accepted medical use before including the drug in schedule I. We are not persuaded that this distinction has any significance to our inquiry. Under the Cooperative's logic, drugs that Congress places in schedule I could be distributed when medically necessary whereas drugs that the Attorney General places in schedule I could not. Nothing in the statute, however, suggests that there are two tiers of schedule I narcotics, with drugs in one tier more readily available than drugs in the other. On the contrary, the statute consistently treats all schedule I drugs alike. See, *e.g.*, §823(a) (providing criteria for the Attorney General to consider when determining whether to register an applicant to manufacture schedule I controlled substances), §823(b) (providing criteria for the Attorney General to consider when determining whether to register an applicant to distribute schedule I controlled substances), §823(f) (providing procedures for becoming a government-approved research project), §826 (establishing production quotas for schedule I drugs). Moreover, the Cooperative offers no convincing explanation for why drugs that Congress placed on schedule I should be subject to fewer controls than the drugs that the Attorney General placed on the schedule. Indeed, the Cooperative argues that, in placing marijuana and other drugs on schedule I, Congress "wishe[d] to assert the most restrictive level of controls created by the [Controlled Substances Act]." Brief for Respondents 24. If marijuana should be subject to the most restrictive level of controls, it should not be treated any less restrictively than other schedule I drugs.

The Cooperative further argues that use of schedule I drugs generally—whether placed in schedule I by Congress or the Attorney General—can be medically necessary, notwithstanding that they have "no currently accepted medical use." According to the Cooperative, a drug may not yet have achieved general acceptance as a medical treatment but may nonetheless have medical benefits to a particular patient or class of patients. We decline to parse the statute in this manner. It is clear from the text of the Act that Congress has made a determination that marijuana has no medical benefits worthy of an exception. The statute expressly contemplates that many drugs "have a useful and legitimate medical purpose and are necessary to maintain the health and general welfare of the American people," §801(1), but it includes no exception at all for any medical use of marijuana. Unwilling to view this omission as an accident, and unable in any event to override a legislative determination manifest in a statute, we reject the Cooperative's argument.

Finally, the Cooperative contends that we should construe the Controlled Substances Act to include a medical necessity defense in order to avoid what it considers to be difficult constitutional questions. In particular, the Cooperative asserts that, shorn of a medical necessity defense, the statute exceeds Congress' Commerce Clause powers, violates the substantive due process rights of patients, and offends the fundamental liberties of the people under the Fifth, Ninth, and Tenth Amendments. As the Cooperative acknowledges, however, the canon of constitutional avoidance has no application in the absence of statutory ambiguity. Because we have no doubt that the Controlled Substances Act cannot bear a medical necessity defense to distributions of marijuana, we do not find guidance in this avoidance principle. Nor do we consider the underlying constitutional issues today. Because the Court of Appeals did not address these claims, we decline to do so in the first instance.

For these reasons, we hold that medical necessity is not a defense to manufacturing and distributing marijuana. The Court of Appeals erred when it held that medical necessity is a "legally cognizable defense." 190 F.3d, at 1114. It further erred when it instructed the District Court on remand to consider "the criteria for a medical necessity exemption, and, should it modify the injunction, to set forth those criteria in the modification order." *Id.*, at 1115.

III

The Cooperative contends that, even if the Controlled Substances Act forecloses the medical necessity defense, there is an alternative ground for affirming the Court of Appeals. This case, the Cooperative reminds us, arises from a motion to modify an injunction to permit distributions that are medically necessary. According to the Cooperative, the Court of Appeals was correct that the District Court had "broad equitable discretion" to tailor the injunctive relief to account for medical necessity, irrespective of whether there is a legal defense of necessity in the statute. *Id.*, at 1114. To sustain the judgment below, the argument goes, we need only reaffirm that federal courts, in the exercise of their equity jurisdiction, have discretion to modify an injunction based upon a weighing of the public interest.

We disagree. Although district courts whose equity powers have been properly invoked indeed have discretion in fashioning injunctive relief (in the absence of a statutory restriction), the Court of Appeals erred concerning the factors that the district courts may consider in exercising such discretion.

A

As an initial matter, the Cooperative is correct that, when district courts are properly acting as courts of equity, they have discretion unless a statute clearly provides otherwise. For "several hundred years," courts of equity have enjoyed "sound discretion" to consider the "necessities of the public interest" when fashioning injunctive relief. *Hecht Co.* v. *Bowles,* 321 U.S. 321, 329–330 (1944). See also *id.,* at 329 ("The essence of equity jurisdiction has been the power of the Chancellor to do equity and to mould each decree to the necessities of the particular case. Flexibility rather than rigidity has distinguished it"); *Weinberger* v. *Romero-Barcelo,* 456 U.S. 305, 312 (1982) ("In exercising their sound discretion, courts of equity should pay particular regard for the public consequences in employing the extraordinary remedy of injunction"). Such discretion is displaced only by a "clear and valid legislative command." *Porter* v. *Warner Holding Co.,* 328 U.S. 395, 398 (1946). See also *Romero-Barcelo, supra,* at 313 ("Of course, Congress may intervene and guide or control the exercise of the courts' discretion, but we do not lightly assume that Congress has intended to depart from established principles").

The Cooperative is also correct that the District Court in this case had discretion. The Controlled Substances Act vests district courts with jurisdiction to enjoin violations of the Act, 21 U.S.C. § 882(a). But a "grant of jurisdiction to issue [equitable relief] hardly suggests an absolute duty to do so under any and all circumstances," *Hecht, supra,* at 329 (emphasis omitted). Because the District Court's use of equitable power is not textually required by any "clear and valid legislative command," the court did not have to issue an injunction.

TVA v. *Hill,* 437 U.S. 153 (1978), does not support the Government's contention that the District Court lacked discretion in fashioning injunctive relief. In *Hill,* the Court held that the Endangered Species Act of 1973 required the District Court to enjoin completion of a dam, whose operation would either eradicate the known population of the snail darter or destroy its critical habitat. *Id.,* at 193–195. The District Court lacked discretion because an injunction was the "only means of ensuring compliance." *Romero-Barcelo, supra,* at 314 (explaining why the District Court in *Hill* lacked discretion). Congress' "order of priorities," as expressed in the statute, would be deprived of effect if the District Court could choose to deny injunctive relief. *Hill, supra,* at 194. In effect, the District Court had only a Hobson's choice. By contrast, with respect to the Controlled Substances

Act, criminal enforcement is an alternative, and indeed the customary, means of ensuring compliance with the statute. Congress' resolution of the policy issues can be (and usually is) upheld without an injunction.

B

But the mere fact that the District Court had discretion does not suggest that the District Court, when evaluating the motion to modify the injunction, could consider any and all factors that might relate to the public interest or the conveniences of the parties, including the medical needs of the Cooperative's patients. On the contrary, a court sitting in equity cannot "ignore the judgment of Congress, deliberately expressed in legislation." *Virginian R. Co. v. Railway Employees*, 300 U.S. 515, 551 (1937). A district court cannot, for example, override Congress' policy choice, articulated in a statute, as to what behavior should be prohibited. "Once Congress, exercising its delegated powers, has decided the order of priorities in a given area, it is ... for the courts to enforce them when enforcement is sought." *Hill*, 437 U.S., at 194. Courts of equity cannot, in their discretion, reject the balance that Congress has struck in a statute. *Id.*, at 194–195. Their choice (unless there is statutory language to the contrary) is simply whether a particular means of enforcing the statute should be chosen over another permissible means; their choice is not whether enforcement is preferable to no enforcement at all. Consequently, when a court of equity exercises its discretion, it may not consider the advantages and disadvantages of nonenforcement of the statute, but only the advantages and disadvantages of "employing the extraordinary remedy of injunction," *Romero-Barcelo*, 456 U.S., at 311, over the other available methods of enforcement. Cf. *id.*, at 316 (referring to "discretion to rely on remedies other than an immediate prohibitory injunction"). To the extent the district court considers the public interest and the conveniences of the parties, the court is limited to evaluating how such interest and conveniences are affected by the selection of an injunction over other enforcement mechanisms.

C

In this case, the Court of Appeals erred by considering relevant the evidence that some people have "serious medical conditions for whom the use of cannabis is necessary in order to treat or alleviate those conditions or their symptoms," that these people "will suffer serious harm if they are denied cannabis," and that "there is no legal alternative to cannabis for the effective treatment of their medical conditions." 190 F.3d, at 1115. As explained above, in the Controlled Substances Act, the balance already has been struck against a medical necessity exception. Because the statutory prohibitions cover even those who have what could be termed a medical necessity, the Act precludes consideration of this evidence. It was thus error for the Court of Appeals to instruct the District Court on remand to consider "the criteria for a medical necessity exemption, and, should it modify the injunction, to set forth those criteria in the modification order." *Ibid.*

***

The judgment of the Court of Appeals is reversed, and the case is remanded for further proceedings consistent with this opinion.
It is so ordered.

Justice Breyer took no part in the consideration or decision of this case.

INDEX

Locators in **boldface** indicate main topics. Locators followed by *g* indicate glossary entries. Locators followed by *b* indicate biographical entries. Locators followed by *c* indicate chronology entries.

Index

Index

Index

Index

261

Index

Drug Abuse

Index

265